CW01237885

COLOMAN, KING OF GALICIA AND DUKE OF SLAVONIA (1208–1241)

BEYOND MEDIEVAL EUROPE

Beyond Medieval Europe publishes monographs and edited volumes that evoke medieval Europe's geographic, cultural, and religious diversity, while highlighting the interconnectivity of the entire region, understood in the broadest sense—from Dublin to Constantinople, Novgorod to Toledo. The individuals who inhabited this expansive territory built cities, cultures, kingdoms, and religions that impacted their locality and the world around them in manifold ways.

Series Editor

Christian Raffensperger, *Wittenberg University, Ohio*

Editorial Board

Kurt Villads Jensen, *Stockholms Universitet, Stockholm*
Balázs Nagy, *Central European University, Budapest*
Leonora Neville, *University of Wisconsin, Madison*

COLOMAN, KING OF GALICIA AND DUKE OF SLAVONIA (1208–1241)

MEDIEVAL CENTRAL EUROPE AND HUNGARIAN POWER

by
Márta Font and Gábor Barabás

British Library Cataloguing in Publication Data
A catalogue record for this book is available from the British Library.

This publication has been financially supported by the Faculty of Humanities, University of Pécs.

© 2019, Arc Humanities Press, Leeds

The authors assert their moral right to be identified as the authors of their part of this work.

Permission to use brief excerpts from this work in scholarly and educational works is hereby granted provided that the source is acknowledged. Any use of material in this work that is an exception or limitation covered by Article 5 of the European Union's Copyright Directive (2001/29/EC) or would be determined to be "fair use" under Section 107 of the U.S. Copyright Act September 2010 Page 2 or that satisfies the conditions specified in Section 108 of the U.S. Copyright Act (17 USC §108, as revised by P.L. 94-553) does not require the Publisher's permission.

ISBN: 9781641890243
e-ISBN: 9781641890250

www.arc-humanities.org
Printed and bound by CPI Group (UK) Ltd, Croydon, CR0 4YY

CONTENTS

List of Illustrations vii

Foreword ix

Introduction 1

PART ONE:
COLOMAN AS CHILD RULER OF GALICIA

Chapter 1. The Galician Context in 1205 11

Chapter 2. The Agreement of Scepus 21

Chapter 3. Coloman's Coronation as King of Galicia: Date and Place 31

Chapter 4. The Hungarian Elite and Coloman's Court 43

Chapter 5. Coloman's Position in Halych, 1215–22: Campaigns and Opponents 51

Chapter 6. Upholding the Galician Claim: Coloman's Place in Hungary 57

PART TWO:
COLOMAN, DUKE OF WHOLE SLAVONIA (1226-1241)

Chapter 7. Coloman and Scepus, before 1226 63

Chapter 8. Coloman as Duke of Whole Slavonia from 1226 69

Chapter 9. Coloman's Status and the Inner Workings of the Duchy 79

Chapter 10. Coloman's Ecclesiastical and Secular Actitivities in Slavonia 91

Chapter 11. Coloman's Rule in Slavonia... 99

Chapter 12. Politics and Dynastic Affairs 105

Chapter 13. Challenges in the Balkans... 115

Chapter 14. The Mongol Attack and Coloman's Death 121

Conclusion: Coloman in the Eyes of Posterity 127

Bibliography.. 133

Index 141

LIST OF ILLUSTRATIONS

Figures

Figure 1. The Castle of Scepus in 2016.. 25

Figure 2. The Church of Pantheleimon.. 40

Figure 3. The Western Gate of the Church of Pantheleimon. 41

Figure 4. The Southern or "Princely" Gate of the Cathedral of
 Gyulafehérvár (Alba Iulia) 41

Figure 5. The Medieval Tower on the Hill Today 54

Figure 6. Spiš Castle in 2016 65

Figure 7. Coloman's Plaque on his Statue in Gödöllő 67

Figure 8. The Castle of Medvedgrad 94

Figure 9. The Church of Čazma. 95

Figure 10. Coloman's Equestrian Statue in Gödöllő 128

Maps

Map 1. The Kingdom of Hungary and its Neighbouring Territories
 in the 1230s. 7

Map 2. The Principality of Galicia–Volhynia and its Vicinity in the
 Twelfth to Thirteenth Centuries 15

Map 3. The Galician Campaigns of Andrew II in 1205–1227. 17

Map 4. Scepus (Szepesség, Spiš) in the Thirteenth Century. 24

Map 5. Halych, the Centre of the Galician Principality. 37

Map 6. The Church of the Assumption and its Surroundings 39

Map 7. The Hill of the Church of Panthaleimon.. 40

Map 8. The Hill of Halych in the Twelfth to Thirteenth Centuries.................. 53

Map 9. Slavonia, Croatia, and Neighbouring Territories in the 1230s.............. 73

Map 10. Polish Principalities in the First Half of the Thirteenth Century. 110

Map 11. The Mongol Invasion of Central Europe in 1241–42. 122

FOREWORD

THE PRESENT BOOK is a revised and expanded version of a Hungarian monograph on the life of Prince Coloman's published in 2017. The core arguments of the authors have not been changed, but the explanation and development of certain problems have of necessity been altered to cater for a wider readership, whose members may not be familiar with the intricacies of Hungarian and, in a broader sense, Eastern European medieval history. The bibliography has been changed, to include studies both in Eastern-European languages and in world languages. This shows how Hungarian and other Eastern European historians are increasingly publishing the results of their research in foreign languages, although these papers may not always be known to the Western scientific community. In addition, the number of citations has been reduced in order to make the text easier to read.

Coloman, the main character of the book, it is important to recognize, is a significant figure in the historiography of several contemporary countries, which means that we as historians need to be aware of sensitivities around his heritage. His role in Galicia makes him interesting for Ukrainian and Russian historical researchers; his Polish wife has the same importance for Polish scholars, while his years in Scepus are of note for Slovak historians and his role as the duke of Slavonia engages Croatian and Bosnian historians. But as a member of the Árpádian dynasty, Coloman's life was organized and led by the rules of the medieval Kingdom of Hungary, and so we need to examine him carefully in the context of the kingdom of the Árpáds. So, while the authors utilized information found in the historiography of various countries, a secondary aim of this book has been to make available the results of recent Hungarian research, especially as this has previously been somewhat neglected internationally due to the language barrier.

> The fact that Coloman is a key historical figure in Russia and the Ukraine, Croatia and Bosnia, Poland and Slovakia, as well as Hungary today justifies this first monograph on Coloman in English. We hope that this work will resonate among scholars in our neighbouring countries as well as among medievalists worldwide, and we hope that this publication draws more scholars into the fascinating world of medieval east-central Europe.

It is quite a challenge in the case of a study on Eastern European history written in English to handle the diverse spellings of toponyms and personal names in different versions in both historical sources and modern languages. The personal names and toponyms of Slavic languages using Cyrillic letters complicate this picture even further, especially because the rules are not the same regarding the English transcription of each language (Russian, Ukrainian, Serbian, Bulgarian, and so on). One cannot rely exclusively on spelling in sources either, because the name of a single person can appear in different versions, not to speak of the difference between the languages of the sources (especially the medieval Eastern Slavic chronicles) and those used in today's countries. Even when a set of rules exists for the transcription of Cyrillic in scientific publications, in practice one can find more than one version in historical works written in English. It seems clear to us that there is no single solution, which would not be open to criticism, which is why we have produced below a pragmatic table of alternatives and our preferred forms.

We have had to face other challenges beyond transcription and transliteration, particularly the usage of geographical and personal names in general. For toponyms for places which lay within the borders of the Medieval Kingdom of Hungary, generally Hungarian versions have been adopted, although their current names in other languages, if outside present-day Hungary, are also supplied at the first mention. Rivers are referred to in their English form (for instance, Danube, Vistula).

Furthermore, the medieval practice regarding the names of certain territories is often inconsistent, and the size of some of the territories has changed over the course of time. In certain cases, the medieval term has been used (for instance, Scepus), but in other places a different approach has proved necessary. For instance, to distinguish between the medieval principality and the settlement, the term "Galicia" is used exclusively for the principality, while "Halych" is used for the settlement, even though Eastern Slavic Chronicles did not make any distinction. The term "Poland" is also used, although the authors are aware of the fragmentation of the territory in the twelfth to thirteenth centuries. So, Poland refers in this study to a particular territory, not a single political entity. We have also added nicknames for certain persons, to help identify people with the same forenames, even if in several cases they are not historically adequate, for instance Iaroslav "the Wise," Mstislav "the Mute," and so on.

The book is in two parts. Part One focuses on Coloman's life in the Principality of Galicia and on the circumstances and events leading up to his coronation and on his reign as a Hungarian royal prince in this Rus'ian principality. Part Two concentrates on his life and actions as duke of Slavonia, when he ruled the southern territories of the Realm of St. Stephen (medieval Hungary) at the grace of his father, Andrew II, and later his older brother, King Béla IV.

The rationale for this division is that Coloman's life falls into two separate phases. He became ruler of the Rus'ian principality of Galicia as a child as a result of his father's political achievements and Hungarian expansion in the region, but after a few years he was forced to leave Galicia and move back to the Kingdom of Hungary. At this point a new phase of his life began. He became the duke of Slavonia in 1226 and consequently the second mightiest person in the kingdom, with power over several territories (Slavonia, Croatia, Dalmatia) as well as Hungarian counties. The first part of the book has been written by Márta Font, the leading expert of Hungarian-Rus'ian relations in the early and central Middle Ages, who dicusses this period of Coloman's life in its broader political context. The second part has been written by Gábor Barabás, whose research on Coloman has focused on papal-Hungarian contacts in the early thirteenth century, due to the duke having an especially good relationship with Pope Gregory IX. This book combines the fruit of their separate researches, providing new insights into both phases of Coloman's life.

The bibliography consists of a full list of primary sources and selected secondary literature. Where necessary, titles have been provided in English in square brackets. Short forms are provided in the footnotes where the full reference is in the bibliography. All other secondary material is cited in full in the footnotes.

The authors would like to express their gratitude to Dániel Bagi, Tamás Fedeles, Gergely Kiss, Endre Sashalmi and their other colleagues in Pécs, as well as colleagues at other universities and institutes in Hungary. Finally, the authors are grateful to Béla Nagy for the maps, and to Ernő Marosi, Myroslav Voloshchuk, and Péter Terejánszky for the photos, likewise to the publishers, especially to Anna Henderson, Ruth Kennedy, and the Hungarian and English peer reviewers of the book for their valuable suggestions and remarks.

The authors

Transliteration and Forms of Placenames

Form used in this book	Current names	Common English form	Hungarian form	Versions used in sources
Bács	Bač		Bács	ecclesia Bachyensis / Bachiensis
Belz	Bełz	Belz		Бельз
Berestie	Brest	Berestie		Берестье
Čazma	Čazma		Császma	Chazma
Chernigov	Чернігів	Chernigov	Csernyigov	Чернигов, Щернигов
Cherven'	Czermno	Cherven'		Червен, Чернен
Đakovo	Đakovo		Diakóvár	Dyacou
Dniester	Дністр	Dniester	Dnyeszter	Днестръ
Esztergom	Esztergom		Esztergom	Strigonium
Galicia (principality)	Галичина		Galicia	Галичь, Galicia
Gorodok	Horodok	Gorodok		Городок
Gömör County	Gemer		Gömör megye	Gemer, Gumur
Halych (city)	Галич		Halics	Галичь
Holm	Chełm	Kholm		Хольм
Iaroslavl	Jarosław	Iaroslavl		Ярославль
Jasov	Jasov		Jászó	Jazow
Kalocsa	Kalocsa		Kalocsa	ecclesia Colocenensis
Kecerlipóc	Kecerovský Lipovec		Kecerlipóc	Lipov
Kraków	Kraków	Cracow	Krakkó	Cracovia, Korokau
Limnica	Лімниця	Limnitsa		

Form used in this book	Current names	Common English form	Hungarian form	Versions used in sources
Liubachev	Lubaczów	Liubachev		Любачевь
Liubech	Любеч	Liubech		Любск, Любець, Любы
Lutsk	Луцк	Lutsk	Luck	Лоугцьк, Луческ, Лючьск
Lukva	Луква	Lukva		Луква
Lvov	Льв	Lvov	Lemberg	Львов, Lwów, Lemberg
Macsó	Mačva		Macsó	Macho
Mazovia	Mazowsze	Mazovia	Mazóvia	Masovia
Našice	Našice		Nekcse	Neccha
Nyitra	Nitra		Nyitra	Nitra
Omiš	Omiš	Almissa	Almissa	Almissa
Ozora	Usora		Ozora	Usora
Pereiaslavl	Переяславль	Pereiaslavl		Переяславль Южный
Petrinja	Petrinja		Petrinya	Petrina
Ponizhie	Поніззя	Ponizhie		Понижье
Poprád	Poprad		Poprád	Poprad
Peremyshl	Przemyśl	Peremyshl		Перемышль
Požega	Požega		Pozsega	Posega, Posaga
Rogozhino	Рогожно, Рогізно	Rogozhino		Рогожина, Погожино
Rovišće	Rovišće		Rojcsa	Riucha
Samobor	Samobor		Szamobor	Zumbur
Sanok	Сянік, Sianik	Sanok		Санок
Sáros, County	Šariš		Sáros	comitatus Sarossiensis
Scepus (district)	Spiš	Szepes	Szepesség	Scepus, Scepusium
Senj	Senj		Zengg	Senia
Slavonia	Slavonija	Slavonia	Szlavónia	Slavonia
Só	Tuzla		Só	Soli
Spiš castle	Spišský hrad	Szepes	Szepesi vár	

Form used in this book	Current names	Common English form	Hungarian form	Versions used in sources
Spišský Štiavnik	Spišský Štiavnik		Savnik	monasterium B. V. de Scepus, de ordine Cisterciensi
Split	Split		Spalato	Spalato
Suzdal'	Суздаль	Suzdal'	Szuzdal	Суздаль, Суждаль
Szepeshely	Spišská Kapitula		Szepeshely	Capitulum Scepusiense
Szepesolaszi	Spišské Vlachy		Szepesolaszi	Latina villa
Szepestamásfalva	Spišské Tomášovce		Szepestamásfalva	villa Thome
Szepesváralja	Spišské Podhradie		Szepesváralja	suburbium Scepus
Trepol'	Тернопіль	Trepol'		Трыполь
Topusko	Topusko		Toplica	Toplica
Torchesk	Торческ	Torchesk		Торчьскъ, Торочьский град
Trogir	Trogir	Trogir	Trau	Trau
Terebovl'	Теребовлія	Terebovl'		Теребовль, Trembovlia
Transylvania		Transsylvania	Erdély	Transylvania, Ultrasilvania
Várad	Oradea		Nagyvárad	Warad, Varadinum
Varaždin	Varaždin		Varasd	Worosd
Virovitica	Virovitica		Verőce	Wereuche, Vereuce
Vistula	Wisła	Vistula		Visla, Висла
Vladimir Volynsky	Владимир	Vladimir Volynsky	Vlagyimir	Владимир, Володимир
Vladimir	Владимир на Клязьме	Vladimir	Vlagyimir	Владимир, Володимир
Volhynia	Волинь	Volyn'	Volhínia	Волынь, Lodomeria, Ladomeria
Vukovar	Vukovar		Valkóvár	Walkow, Wolcou

Form used in this book	Current names	Common English form	Hungarian form	Versions used in sources
Wieprz	Wieprz			Вепрь
Wrocław	Wrocław	Breslau	Boroszló	Wratislav
Zadar	Zadar		Zára	Zara
Zagreb	Zagreb		Zágráb	Zagrab
Zvenigorod	Звенигород	Zvenigorod		Звенигород, Звинигород

Recurrent Individuals

Form used in this book	Common or alternative English form	Alternative form(s)	Dates, Title or description
Andrew II	Andrew of Jerusalem		King of Hungary (1205–35) and father of Coloman
Prince Andrew	Andrew of Hungary		Prince of Peremyshl (1224–34), Prince of Galicia (1227–34), third son of Andrew II and younger brother of Coloman
Béla IV	Béla the Great		King of Hungary (1235–1370) and older brother of Coloman
Coloman the Learned	Coloman the Learned		King of Hungary (1095–1116)
Daniil	Daniel Romanovich of Galicia	Daniil or Danylo Rurikovich	Prince of Vladimir Volynsky (1218–38), Prince of Galicia (1230–53), King of Galicia (1253–64)
Domald	Domald of Sidraga		ca. 1160–1243, Count of Split, Zadar, and Šibenik
File		Füle, Filja	military leader in Galicia, master of stewards in the court of Hungarian queen (wife of King of Béla IV) (1231–32)
Duke Friedrich	Frederick II the Quarrelsome	Friedrich II der Streitbare	Duke of Austria and Styria (1230–46)
Emperor Friedrich II	Frederick II of Sicily	Friedrich II	Holy Roman emperor (1220–50)
Grzymisława of Sandomierz	Grzymisława of Luck		ca. 1185/95–1258, duchess of Sandomierz, wife of Leszek the White, mother of Salomea, and mother-in-law of Coloman

Form used in this book	Common or alternative English form	Alternative form(s)	Dates, Title or description
Henry the Bearded	Henry I the Bearded	Henryk Brodaty, Heinrich der Bärtige	Duke of Silesia (1202–38), Prince of Kraków (1231–38)
Henry II	Henry II the Pious	Henryk Pobożny	Duke of Silesia and Kraków (1238–41)
Leszek the White	Leszek the White	Leszek Biały	Duke of Kraków and Sandomierz (1202–27)
Mstislav Udaloy, Mstislav Mstislavich	Mstislav Mstislavich the Daring		Prince of Novgorod (1210–18), Prince of Galicia (1221–27)
Roman Mstislavich	Roman II Mstislavich, the Great		Prince of Volhynia (1170–99), Prince of Galicia-Volhynia (1199–1205)
Salomea	Salomea of Kraków		1211/12–69, Wife of Coloman
Bishop Stephen	Bishop Stephen II of Zagreb		Bishop of Zagreb (1225–47)
St. Stephen	Stephen I of Hungary		King of Hungary (1000–38)
Stephen V	Stephen V of Hungary		King of Hungary (1270–72)
Thomas of Split	Archdeacon Thomas of Split, Thomas the Archdeacon	Thomas Archidiaconus	ca. 1200–68, author of the *Historia Salonitanorum atque Spalateninorum pontificum*
Vasilko	Vasilko Romanovich		Prince of Volhynia (1238–69), younger brother of Daniil Romanovich
Volodislav	Volodislav Kormilichich	Vladislav or Ladislaus Ruthenus	Leader of the *boyars* in Galicia from 1206 to the 1220s

Timeline of Coloman's Life in Galicia

1213 (September)	Andrew II's interrupted campaign; Boyar Volodislav's government
1214 (fall)	The meeting or Council of Scepus
1214 (end)	Coloman and Benedict in Galicia
1214 (end) to 1215 (early)	Coloman's coronation in Hungary
1215	Coloman in the besieged Halych; Leszek fails to send help; Andrew II asks for the mediation of the Pope
1215/16	King Andrew takes Peremyshl from Leszek
1216 (early)	Coloman's coronation in Galicia
1219 (early)	Coloman's expulsion; Mstislav's first campaign
1219 (summer)	Renewal of the Polish–Hungarian alliance
1219 (October)	Mstislav expelled by the Polish–Hungarian army
1220/21	Mstislav's second campaign
1221	File's campaign from Galicia to Volhynia
1221 (August)	Mstislav's third campaign; Coloman and his wife Salomea's captivity in Halych
1221 (end) to 1222 (early)	Mstislav's pact with King Andrew; captives are released; Prince Andrew is engaged in marriage

Timeline of Coloman's Life in the Kingdom of Hungary

1221/22 to 1226	Coloman and Salomea living in the Scepus region
1226	Coloman becomes duke of Slavonia and visits the Dalmatian cities
1233	Coloman is entrusted by Pope Gregory IX to become lay guardian of two widowed Polish duchesses
1235	Coloman participates in his older brother's coronation as sword-bearer
1236/37	Coloman's assumed campaign in Bosnia
1241 (early)	Coloman joins forces with King Béla IV against the Mongol invaders; takes part in the battle of Muhi
1241 (April)	Coloman's death in Slavonia

INTRODUCTION

MÁRTA FONT and GÁBOR BARABÁS

PRINCE COLOMAN, SECOND son of King Andrew II (1205–35) and younger brother of King Béla IV (1235–70), is perhaps not the best-known member of the Árpádian dynasty (1000–1301), nor of medieval Hungarian rulers, yet his life was quite extraordinary. He was the second member in his dynasty with this name, the first being King Coloman the Learned (1095–1116). The man who would later become King of Galicia and Duke of Slavonia was born in 1208, the fourth child of Andrew II and Queen Gertrud of Andechs, making him a prince of the ruling Árpád dynasty.[1]

Coloman was barely six years old when he was engaged for marriage to Salomea, the daughter of Leszek the White (Biały), Duke of Kraków, as a result of an agreement in 1214 between their fathers over the Scepus region (Szepes, Spiš). Not long afterwards (it is disputed exactly when, as we shall see later) he was crowned king of a principality of the Kievan Rus', Galicia (Halych), receiving the royal title with crucial papal approval and crown coming from Pope Innocent III (1198–1216).

A few years later, probably in 1221, Coloman and his wife were forced to leave Galicia, in today's western Ukraine, and moved to Hungary, and settled down in the Scepus. Another few years passed by and he became the duke (*dux*) of the southern part of the medieval Hungarian Kingdom, Slavonia, in 1226, and retained his royal title, derived from his coronation in the Rus'ian principality of Galicia. As the ruling leader of a part of the Kingdom of Hungary, he was authorized to govern Slavonia, Croatia, Dalmatia, and the attached Hungarian counties (*comitatus*). Nevertheless, he was also active in other Hungarian affairs that have not been considered strictly as his remit; for instance, he mediated between his father and older brother, Béla, or supported the new king even after his enthronement.

Coloman probably led a successful military campaign to Bosnia around 1236 against the local Bogomil heresy, the so-called Bosnian Church, and also took part in the battle of Muhi against the Mongol invaders in 1241. He was able to escape from the battlefield but was seriously wounded and died from his injuries a few weeks later near Zagreb, in Čazma (Csázma).[2]

---

1 Wertner, *Az Árpádok családi története*, 436–38, 448; Kristó, *A feudális széttagolódás Magyarországon*, 32–33; *Korai magyar történeti*, 316 (entry by Tibor Almási); Attila Zsoldos, *Az Árpádok és alattvalóik. Magyarország története 1301-ig [Árpáds and Their Subjects. History of Hungary Before 1301]* (Debrecen: Csokonai, 1997), 74–87.

2 Font, "II. András orosz politikája és hadjáratai," 125; Font, *Árpád-házi királyok*, 204–14, 217; Procházková, "Koloman Haličský na Spiši," 244–45; Procházková, "Some Notes on the Titles of Coloman," 105–6; Hollý, "Princess Salomea and Hungarian–Polish Relations," 12; Zsoldos, "Szepes megye kialakulása," 25; Györffy, "Szlavónia kialakulásának oklevélkritikai," 229; Zsoldos, "Az ifjabb király országa országa," 243–44; Zsoldos, *Családi ügy*, 24–25; Weisz and Zsoldos, "A báni joghatóság Szlavóniában," 477; Kádár, "Az Árpád-házi uralkodók," 94; Barabás, "The Titles of the Hungarian Royal Family," 37–43.

The Origin of Coloman's Name

The name Coloman was rather uncommon in the *family of the holy kings*, the so-called Árpádian dynasty. The first member who bore this name was King Coloman the Learned, and the prince was probably given this name by his mother, Sophia. The queen would have been familiar with the cult of the Irish pilgrim, Coloman, who died as a martyr at the Bavarian–Moravian border in 1012.[3] The figure of King Coloman the Learned was not very popular among later members of the dynasty, since he blinded both his brother, Prince Álmos, and his son, King Béla II (1131–1142). Therefore, it is no wonder that the name Coloman was given only to the child of Prince Boris, a son of Coloman who had been expelled to Byzantium,[4] and it must have served merely to emphasize dubious ties to the Árpáds.

It is quite surprising that Roger of Apulia, archdeacon of Nagyvárad (Oradea), in the early thirteenth century counted King Coloman among the holy kings of Hungary (i.e., the Árpáds) while describing the Mongol invasion of 1241–42 in his work *Carmen miserabile*.[5] His mistake can be possibly traced back to information in the *Hungarian Illuminated Chronicle* (*Chronicon Pictum*, a variant of the chronicle-family known in historical research as the *Chronicle-Composition of the Fourteenth Century*) that Coloman was bishop of Várad before he became ruler. Roger may have heard these favourable recollections in local oral history while he was in Várad.

Nevertheless, the memory of Coloman the Learned was not cherished in the ruling dynasty and that is why we assume that Andrew II's second son was not named after Coloman the Learned, but it just have been his mother's choice. Gertrude, being a member of the Andechs family, must have been familiar with the cult of St. Coloman, who was especially popular in the territory of the Babenbergs, in Austria. The earliest source, the *Annales Mellicenses* of Melk, mentioned the tomb of the martyr around 1012–14, and is confirmed by several later monastic annals. A *Passio* of Coloman was written in the mid-twelfth century, while a century later Friedrich of Babenberg intended to establish a new bishopric under the patronage of Coloman.[6] This testifies to the continuing popularity of the saint. In our opinion, the cult must have been known across the Austrian duchy among the members of the Andechs dynasty, even though there is no evidence of Coloman being used elsewhere as a family name. Let us also not forget Andrew II's

---

3 Font, *Koloman the Learned*, 13.

4 *Scriptores rerum Hungaricarum*, 1:429; In Byzantium Boris was called Kalamanos. see Gyula Moravcsik, *Az Árpád-kori magyar történet bizánci forrásai [Byzantine Sources for Árpádian Hungary]* (Budapest: Akadémiai Kiadó, 1988), 271 and 303.

5 *Master Roger; Korai magyar történeti*, 576–77 (entry by Tibor Almási); Kornél Szovák, "A váradi írásbeliség hagyománya," in *Nagyvárad és Bihar a korai középkorban. Tanulmányok Biharország történetéről 1*, ed. Attila Zsoldos (Nagyvárad: Varadinum Kulturális Alapítvány, 2014), 129–46 at 135–38. The section about Ladislaus might have described Coloman as the first bishop as well (see *ibid*., p. 138); Gábor Thoroczkay, "A magyarországi legendairodalom és történetírás a 14. század közepéig," in Gábor Thoroczkay, *Az ismeretlen Árpád-kor. Püspökök, legendák, krónikák* (Budapest: L'Harmattan, 2016), 184–208 at 204.

6 *Scriptores rerum Hungaricarum*, 2:552, *Scriptores rerum Hungaricarum*, 1:432.

daughter, Maria, since her son from Tsar Ivan Asen II also received the name Coloman,[7] so the name appeared again one generation later close to the Árpádian dynasty.

The Narrative Sources for Coloman's Life

Narrative sources written in Hungary are extremely laconic concerning Coloman. Just three points of interest are mentioned with regard to his life and all of them very concisely; firstly, he is listed among the children of Andrew II; secondly, his presence is noted at his elder brother's coronation; and, lastly, his death is mentioned as caused from his fight against the Mongols.[8]

The role of the young Coloman in Galicia is reflected in several *Old-Russian Chronicles*. Significant information can be found in the thirteenth-century *Codex Ipatiev*, the so-called *Galician–Volhynian Chronicle* (hereinafter *GVC*), and other texts that used this source. Several codices from the Moscowian and Novgorodian codex-family also contain relevant information, primarily related to key figures from the history of Galicia. The *First Novgorodian Chronicle* reports the deeds of Mstislav Udaloy (Удалой / Удатный / *udaloy* (the "Reckless", or "Brave") or *udatnyj* (the "Successful") who defeated and captured Coloman. The *Voskresensk Chronicle* describes the Galician interest on the part of the princes of Smolensk, especially Mstislav Romanovich Staryj ("the Old", Старый 1212–23), the grand prince of Kiev at the time of Coloman's stay in Galicia. The early-thirteenth-century events of Galicia–Volhynia also found their way, although significantly shortened, via various redactions, into the compilations constructed in Moscow in the late fifteenth century.[9]

The content from the *Galician–Volhynian Chronicle* prevailed in several traditions; the most complete form of the text can be found in the *Codex Ipatiev*, which is straight narrative with no chronological division. The separation of the text into sections by dates is solely the work of a later copyist or redactor, not the chronicler, and so the dating is not reliable. The Ukrainian historian, Hrushevsky, made the necessary corrections, clearing up the chronological mess, and historical research uses information based on his corrections. Despite the problematic chronology, the *GVC* is a very valuable source also for literary, linguistic, historical, and art-historical aspects.[10] It has impor-

---

7 Cf. Gábor Szeberényi, "A Balkán. 800–1389 [The Balkans, 800–1389]," in *Kelet-Európa és a Balkán 1000–1800 közt: intellektuális történeti konstrukciók vagy valós történeti régiók?*, ed. Endre Sashalmi (Pécs: Kelet-Európa és a Balkán Története és Kultúrája Kutatási Központ, 2007), 279–330 at 326.

8 *Scriptores rerum Hungaricarum*, 1:212, 1:464, 2:41, 2:45, 2:82, 2:205, 2:206, 2:210, 2:281, 2:339 (1); *Scriptores rerum Hungaricarum*, 1:467, 2:42, 2:206–7 (2); *Scriptores rerum Hungaricarum*, 2:42–43, 2:282, 2:570–71 (3)

9 Font, *Árpád-házi királyok*, 53–72; Márta Font, "Die Chronistik der Ostslawen," in *Handbuch Chroniken des Mittelalters*, ed. Gerhard Wolf and Norbert H. Ott (Berlin: De Gruyter, 2016), 805–35 at 826–33; PSRL, 15, 25.

10 The latest edition of the *GVC* is listed in the bibliography below under *Kronika halicko–wołyńska*. The editors argue that the original text survived in the so-called Hlebnikov Codex, in previous literature used the text of Ipatiev Codex, see: Hrushevsky, "Khronologia podij," 2; Hodinka, *Az orosz évkönyvek*, 285; Антон І. Генсьорський, Значення форм минулого часу в Галицко-Волынському

tant information also on Hungary. The text of the *GVC* contains several parts—*svod* (*свод*)—written by different authors in different places. The chapters about Coloman are in the *svod* which contains the *gesta*-style biography of Prince Daniil (1201-1264).[11] Accordingly, the Hungarian prince and his supporters as enemies of Prince Daniil are depicted negatively.

Polish narrative sources emphasize the relationships of the Polish princes in Rus', and Coloman is only touched upon because of his role in the dynastical relations and his involvement in the fight against the Mongols in 1241. The chronicle of Wincenty Kadłubek, bishop of Kraków, was written in the early thirteenth century and describes events only till 1206, so Coloman's years in Galicia are not included. Kadłubek's chronicle is useful for showing the relation of Lesser Poland to Rus' in the previous period, since it illustrates the relationship of Duke Leszek of Kraków, Coloman's father-in-law, with his eastern neighbours. Another part of the chronicle about the Kingdom of Galicia written by Bishop Boguchwał of Poznań and his continuator Godysław Pasko, also has to be considered. The value of the source is disputed, since it contains important mistakes (e.g., it calls King Coloman the Learned's descendant Boris (Colomanidis), king of Galicia, and believes him to be the son-in-law of Bolesław III (1107–38)). But the legends surrounding Salomea, Coloman's wife, is an essential part of the traditional legends in Polish literature. The princess got engaged to Coloman as a young child and after her husband's death she returned to Poland and established the Order of the Poor Clares. The princess was later beatified and her title as queen, thanks to her marriage to Coloman, has been emphasized. This seems to be the sole reason why the Hungarian prince is mentioned in the legend at all. The text reveals no details on Salomea's childhood in Galicia or her life in Hungary.[12]

The chronicle of Jan Długosz from the late fifteenth century seems to offer the most information. The author used earlier Polish chronicles, and he must have been familiar

---

літопису [Significance of the Perfect Forms of Verbs in the Galician–Volhynian Chronicle] (Київ: Видавництво Академії наук Української РСР, 1957); Антон І. Генсьорский, *Галицко-Волинский літопис (Процесс складання, релакції и редакторы) [The Galician–Volhynian Chronicle: Its Creation, Compilations, and Compilators]* (Київ: Видавництво Академії наук Української РСР, 1958); Jitka Komendová et al., *Письменность Галицко–Волинского княжества: историко-филологические исследования [Literature of the Galician–Volhynian Principality: Historical and Philological Analyses]* (Olomouc: Univerzita Palackiého, 2016). For an English translation and commentary see: *The Galician–Volhynian Chronicle*.

[11] See Font, "II. András orosz politikája és hadjáratai," 114–15; Font, *Árpád-házi királyok*, 78–79; Font, *Geschichtsschreibung des 13. Jahrhunderts an der Grenze zweier Kulturen*, 28–43; Lammich, *Fürstenbiographien des 13. Jahrhunderts in den Russischen Chroniken*; Jitka Komendová, *Středověká Rus a vnější svět [The Central Rus' and the Outside World]* (Olomouc: Monse, 2005); Dąbrowski, *Rodowód Romanowiczów*, 60–77; Dąbrowski, *Daniel Romanowicz Król Rusi. O ruskiej rodzine książęcej*.

[12] *Magistri Vincentii Chronica Polonorum* in *Monumenta Poloniae Historica*, 2:249–447; For recent dating see *ibid*.; Godysław Pasko, *Monumenta Poloniae Historica*, 2:467–598 at 515–16; For an assessment see Font, *Árpád-házi királyok*, 158. The text of the legend is at *Monumenta Poloniae Historica*, 4:776–96.

with some version of the *Old Rus'ian Chronicles*.¹³ Długosz was a great compiler from earlier works.¹⁴ For instance, his work combines the *Chronicle of Greater Poland* with Kadłubek's concerning Coloman's Galician activity, even though the merging of the two texts caused several inaccuracies and logical contradictions. Długosz recites the events of 1205–21 combined, there are repetitions concerning 1211, 1220, and 1224, and summaries for 1217 and 1220. In Labuda's view, Długosz had relatively rich source-material, and at the same time he had no information of his own. The value of Długosz as a source is hard to determine, since he got events the wrong way round sometimes and also made mistakes concerning the years, supposedly, on account of his use of the thirteenth-century *Old Rus'ian Chronicles*.¹⁵

Concluding this survey of the narrative sources, we should note a peculiar work, the so-called *Hungarian–Polish Chronicle* (*Chronicon mixtum, Chronicon Hungarico-Polonicum*).¹⁶ It is a quite extraordinary literary work, yet as a historical source it requires especially careful treatment. It contains elements from the legend of St. Ursula and from the legend of St. Stephen by Bishop Hartvik at the start of the twelfth century, yet all other stories in the chronicle regarding the conquest and early history of Hungary contradict more authentic records, so belong to the realm of imagination.¹⁷ Despite its low value as historical evidence, it has played a disproportionate role in modern histories and what it might say about Coloman. According to certain scholars, it was written in Coloman's environment, in his court in Slavonia (Ryszard Grzesik), or in the Scepus (Martin Homza), as the narrative indeed suggests. It is likewise assumed that the chronicle reflects the disagreement of Coloman and his younger brother, Andrew, which might link the chronicle to Coloman as duke of Slavonia. In terms of the survival of the text, we should mention the theory that Salomea was the one who brought the manuscript with

---

13 *Ioannis Dlugossii Annales seu Cronicae*, 6:168–286. One could have been a *svod* constructed in the first half of the thirteenth century in the southern part of the Rus', the second is the *svod* of Smolensk from the mid-fifteenth century, which contains information from Vladimir-Suzdal, Novgorod, and the southern Rus'. See Наталия Щабелева, Древняя Русь в «Польской истории» Яна Длугоша *[Old Rus' in the* History of Poland *of Jan Długosz]* (Москва: Памятники исторической мысли, 2004), 34–52.

14 Gerard Labuda, *Zaginiora kronika z pierwszej połowy XIII wieku w Rocznikach Królestwa Polskiego Jana Długosza [A Missing Chronicle from the First Half of the Thirteenth Century in Jan Długosz's* Annals of the Polish Kingdom*]* (Warszawa: Wydawnictwo Naukowe Uniwersytetu im. Adama Mickiewicza, 1983), 47–58, 160–200.

15 See Aleksander Semkowicz, *Krytyczny rozbiór Dziejów Polskich Jana Długosza (do roku 1384) [A Critical Analysis of the* Polish History *of Jan Długosz (to 1384)]* (Kraków: Akademia Umiejętności, 1887), 195–96; Labuda, *Zaginiora kronika*, 18–200 (cited in footnote above); Labuda's statement has not been accepted by every Polish researcher (e.g., Józef Matuszewski, *Relacja Długosza o najazdzie tatarskim w 1241 r [The Relation beween Długosz and the Mongol Invasion of 1241]* (Łódź: Zakład Narodowy im. Ossolińskich, 1980). See further: Font, *Árpád-házi királyok*, 115–18.

16 Critical editions exist in the *Chronica hungaro–polonica*; *Scriptores rerum Hungaricarum*, 2:289–320.

17 Péter Tóth, "A lengyel–magyar vegyes krónika [The Hungarian-Polish Chronicle]," in *Publicationes Universitatis Miskolciensis, Sectio philosophica*, 9 (2004): 223–42 at 223; Csákó, "A Magyar–lengyel Krónika," 291–92. And see further below, p. xx.

herself to Poland after her husband's death; whether that is true or false, the four extant copies are from Poland. With these caveats, we can still make use of the *Hungarian–Polish Chronicle* as historical source.

Charters as Sources of Coloman's Life

The reconstruction of Coloman's life would not be possible based solely on narrative sources; so we have to examine relevant charters. The diplomas issued in the name of the prince form most important group. Fortunately, a modern edition contains all of the necessary information regarding the known charters. Unfortunately, not every text is nowadays available in its entirety; some are only available as later transcriptions or even just mentions. The first of Coloman's charters was issued in 1226 and the last in the year of the prince's death in 1241, so all of them belong to his Slavonian era, even if some reveal information concerning his earlier years. These charters represent the corpus on which the actions of Coloman as the duke of "whole Slavonia" has been reconstructed here. However, beyond the ducal charters we can avail ourselves of the documents of his father, Andrew II, his older brother, Béla IV, and their descendants, most of all King Stephen V (1270–72). Lastly, we can make use of Hungarian ecclesiastical charters, secular ones, as well as the papal charters.[18]

Material Remains as Sources of Coloman's Life

Only a handful of material artefacts exist that could be linked to Coloman. He was likely the initiator of the construction of a part of the castle of Scepus, but separating it from other parts of the stronghold has proven almost impossible. The same can be said for several other buildings in Galicia or Slavonia. No contemporary illustration of Coloman has survived, and his tombstone with his figure carved in stone is unfortunately lost for good. The only likeness is an image of him as Salomea's husband in the church of the Poor Clares in Kraków and that dates from the seventeenth century.[19]

---

[18] See *Regesta ducum, ducissarum*, and *Regesta regum stirpis Arpadianae*. Use of the online database of the Hungarian National Archive is also essential (see DL – DF. http://archives.hungaricana.hu/hu/charters/search/); for papal charters see *Regesta Pontificum Romanorum*; *Regesti del Pontefice Onorii papae III*; and the *Registres de Grégoire IX*.

[19] Maja Cepetić, "Granice srednjovjekovnih biskupskih posjeda Dubrave, Ivanića i Čazme [The Borders of the Medieval Diocesan Estates of Dubrava, Ivanić, and Čazma]," *Starohrvatska prosvjeta* ser. 3, 40 (2013): 217–33; Goss, "Slovak and Croatian Art in the Thirteenth Century," 260–68; Janovská, "Building Activities in Spiš in the Thirteenth Century"; Михайло Фіголь, *Мистецтво стародавнього Галича. [The Art of Old Halych]* (Київ: Мистецтво, 1997); Федунків, Зеновій, "Галицький замок [Castle of Halych]," *Пам'ятки України* 189, no. 6 (2013): 44–53; Cecylian Niezgoda, *Błogosławiona Salomea Piastówna [Blessed Salomea from the Piast Family]* (Kraków: Wydawnictwo Franciszkanów Bratni Zew, 1996); Vladimir P. Goss, *Four Centuries of European Art 800–1200. A View from Southeast* (Zagreb: Golden Marketing, 2010), 212, 214.

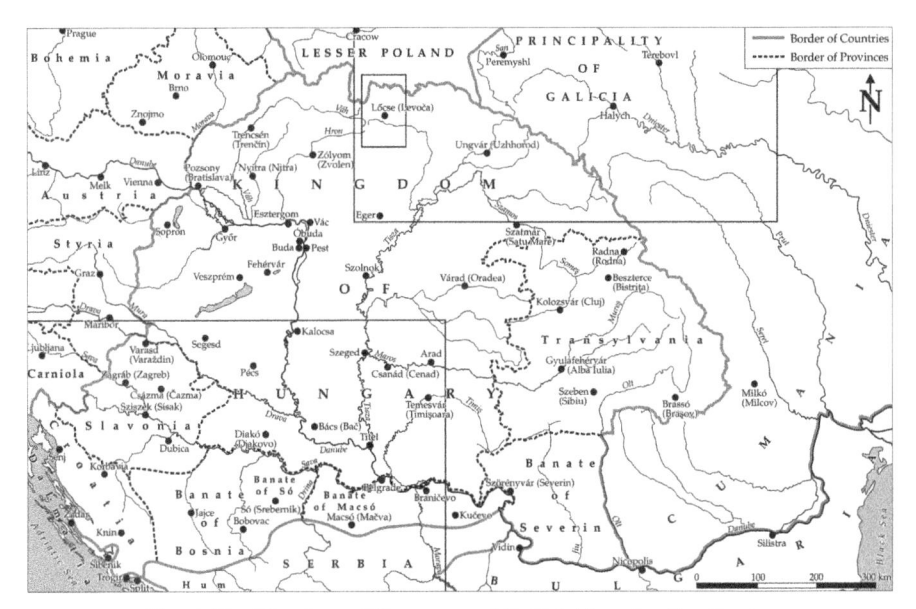

Map 1. The Kingdom of Hungary and its Neighbouring Territories in the 1230s—The Stages in Coloman's Life.

PART ONE

COLOMAN AS CHILD RULER OF GALICIA

MÁRTA FONT

This part begins with a discussion of the state of affairs in Galicia in the early thirteenth century before going on to discuss the details of Hungarian and Polish expansion in the Galician region and the chain of events that led to the coronation of Prince Coloman, second son of the Hungarian monarch, Andrew II (1205–35), as king of Galicia. We will in turn discuss this new royal title, which had not previously been used in the territory, as well as the relative brevity of Coloman's stay in Galicia, and the circumstances of his forced departure around 1221/22.

Chapter 1

THE GALICIAN CONTEXT IN 1205

TAKING OVER THE territory of Galicia was one of the aims of Andrew II's reign in Hungary (1205–35). The principality of Halych (a form of the Latinized name, Galicia) had formed during the twelfth century under the rule of Volodymerko (1124–53) and merged at the end of that century with Volhynia to create the principality of Galicia-Volhynia under Roman Mstislavich (1199–1205). The principality existed until 1340 when it was split: Galicia then fell under the control of the Polish crown, with Volhynia under the grand duchy of Lithuania. Today the territory of Galicia belongs partly to Poland (Przemyśl) and partially to Ukraine (Lviv, Halych).

Andrew's first campaign in Galicia started straight after his enthronement in 1205, and he abandoned these attempts only after the death of his youngest son, Andrew, in 1234. Whether the prince's sudden death or other circumstances forced the Hungarian king to stop, we cannot be sure, since he died the following year.

Andrew II's interest in Galicia reflects that of his father, King Béla III (1172–96), who intended to strengthen the Hungarian rule in the principality of Galicia by placing his offspring there.[1] Andrew was born around 1177, so he must have been about eleven or twelve years old at the time of the Hungarian campaign of 1188–89. He may have been aware of the nature of the Hungarian claim on Galicia, and his father's military and diplomatic plans might have made an impact on him.

Andrew II's grandmother, Euphrosyne Mstislavna, came from the Rurikid dynasty, whilst his grandfather, King Géza II (1141–62), had led several campaigns into the territory of the Kievan Rus', even if their goals diverged in several aspects from those under Béla III. Experiences from Géza II's time long predated Andrew but a memory of the campaigns probably lingered. Andrew II, in fact, did refer to his grandfather, father, and the events of their time, however different in nature.[2]

The short reign of Béla III in Galicia shows different kind of political actions. He incarcerated Vladimir Iaroslavich, the Galician prince, and started negotiations with the Galician elite and the grand prince of Kiev. Vladimir fled from the Hungarian court, and returned to Galicia, and stabilized his rule with the help of the duke of Kraków, Casimir II the Just (1177–94), and the sovereign of Vladimir-Suzdal. This episode foreshadows Polish–Hungarian struggles for Galicia.

---

1 PSRL, 2:659–67; Font, *Magyarok a Kijevi Évkönyvben*, 293–311; Font, *Árpád-házi királyok*, 179–87.

2 See the charter of King Andrew II, the so-called *Andreanum*: "our pious grandfather of blessed memory" and "our father of blessed memory" (*Anjou-kori Oklevéltár. Documenta Res Hungaricastempore Regum Andegavensium Illustrantia 1301–1387*, ed. Julius Kristó, vol. 4, *1315–1317* (Budapest and Szeged: Szegedi Középkorász Műhely, 1990–), 178–80).

The "Lordless" Territory of Galicia and Volhynia

Andrew II started his first campaign in 1205, and the reason for the attack was likely a request from a widowed princess of Galicia. To understand how this happened, we have to explore the life of Roman Mstislavich, a member of the Rurik dynasty who was previously prince of Novgorod (1168–70), and subsequently of Vladimir Volynsky in Volhynia (from 1170), and then of Halych in Galicia (from 1199). This made him leader of the western Rus' region, but in so doing brought Galicia and Volhynia into the spotlight for both Poland and Hungary.

Roman had ruled, between 1199 and 1205, not only Galicia and Volhynia, but he also controlled the river route along the Dniester down to the Black Sea, whilst his expansion towards the east had caused tension with the grand prince of Kiev, Rurik Rostislavich. Roman locked Rurik's daughter, his first wife, into a nunnery and married a new bride from the Byzantine Empire. Not satisfied with disputes in the east, the Galician prince intervened on several occasions in the quarrels of his western neighbours, with the princes of Kraków and Mazovia, which led to princes Leszek the White and Conrad respectively to unite in 1205 and turn against Roman and his expansionism. The prince of Galicia lost his life on the battlefield of Zawichost as the result of this new conflict.[3] The new situation was now ripe for eastern expansion by Kraków and Mazovia.

Roman's death did not mean that his family became extinct; he had three children from his second marriage. The oldest child, his daughter, became at some point the wife of Prince Mikhail of Chernigov. She appears in documents only when his adult son, Rostislav, made a claim to Galicia in the 1230s basing his claim on his maternal descent.[4] Roman's first-born son, Daniil, was four and his second son, Vasilko, two years old in 1205. The prince's widow attempted to hold the territory together for the benefit of their young offspring.

The Widow of Roman of Galicia-Volhynia and her Kinship with Hungary

Who Roman Mstislavich's widow was and what her ties were to the Hungarian king are long disputed. She is called a "ятровь / jatrov," a term that refers generally to the "wife of the brother," but here the word "brother" certainly does not mean sibling, or kin for that matter. It can indicate a distant relative, even a fictional one, or an ally. The name "Anna" does not appear in early documents and can only be traced backwards from later sources. Szaraniewicz asserted that Gertrude, queen of Hungary, and "Anna" were kin, but we disagree. Given that the widow's name is unknown, she could have had relatives from the Byzantine Empire too. Recent genealogical works argue for Byzantium and new archaeological research also implies this. Previous research ignored Andrew II having contact with the Byzantine world both through her mother and sister, so the

---

[3] Medieval Polish texts provide a detailed narrative of this event. See *Ioannis Dlugossii Annales seu Cronicae*, 6:192–97. For the relationships among the Polish princes see Chrzanowski, *Leszek Biały*, 64–65.

[4] PSRL, 2:776; Font, "Prince Rostislav," 64–65.

widowed Galician princess may indeed have been kin to the Hungarian king. Andrew's own mother, Anna of Antioch, was the daughter of Constance of Antioch and Reginald de Châtillon, and her sister became the wife of Emperor Manuel.[5]

The older sister of Andrew II, Margaret, married Byzantine Emperor Isaac Angelos (1185–1204).[6] Voytovych thinks that Roman's second wife might have been born from this marriage. According to him, this daughter had been born by 1187, married Roman around 1200, and may have given birth to Daniil as early as 1201. Nevertheless, Voytovych disregarded two pieces of evidence: on one hand, Margaret was born in 1175, so she could not have been older than ten by the time of her marriage; on the other hand, Prince Roman's first child was not Daniil but a daughter, born around 1199–1200 who became the future wife of Mikhail of Chernigov. In turn Alexander Maiorov built on Voytovych, and also believes that Roman's wife was the child of Isaac's elder daughter from a previous marriage, not with Margaret. Maiorov developed his argument based on a statement from Niketas Choniates. According to Choniates, the eldest daughter of Isaac became a nun and it is widely known that Roman's widow also entered a nunnery after her sons reached adulthood. Maiorov linked these two statements and corrected Voytovych's theory, yet he left the question unanswered why the Byzantine historian, Choniates, did not mention that the daughter at issue was previously the wife of Roman and had given birth to several children. Maiorov also offered a new proposition for the name of the widow, who previously was thought to be "Maria" or "Anna": her name might have been "Ephrosinia" and she adopted the name "Anna" upon entering the convent.[7]

---

5 For Prince Roman's widow see PSRL, 2:717; Izidor Szaraniewicz, *Die Hypathios Chronik als Quellen-Beitrag zur österreichischen Geschichte* (Lemberg: Dobrzańki & Groman, 1872), 42; Władysław Abraham, *Powstanie organizacji kościoła łacinskiego na Rusi. I [The Establishment of Latin Church Organization in Rus']* (Lwów: Towarzystwo popierania dla nauki polskiej, 1904), 100; Hrushevsky, *Istorija Ukrainy–Rusi*, 3:10; Włodarski, *Polska i Rus*, 33; *The Galician–Volhynian Chronicle*, 128, 130; Dąbrowski, *Rodowód Romanowiczów*, 34–44; Леонтій Войтович, *Княжа доба на Русі: портрети еліти [The Period of Princes. Portrets out of the Elite]* (Біла Церква: Пшонківський, 2006), 481–87; and Kotliar's arguments are found in *Галицько-Волинський літопис. Дослідження. Текст. Комментар [The Galician-Volhynian Chronicle. Text and Commentary]*, ed. Микола Ф. Котляр (Київ: Наукова думка, 2002), 184–89.

For Byzantine influence (Kholm, Stolp) see Andrzej Buko, "Pomiędzy Polską a Rusią: Z nowych badań archeologicznych nad wczesnym średniowieczem w ziemi chełmskiej [Between Poland and Russia: New Archaeological Research on the Early Middle Ages in Chełm]," in *Świat średniowiecza: Studia ofiarowane Profesorowi Henrykowi Samsonowiczowi*, ed. Agnieszka Bartoszewicz et al. (Kraków: Wydawnictwo Uniwerstytetu Warszawskiego, 2010), 107–28.

For Andrew II's mother see *Korai magyar történeti*, 47 (entry by Ferenc Makk); and Attila Zsoldos, *Az Árpádok és asszonyaik. A királynéi intézmény az Árpádok korában [Árpáds and Their Wives. Queenship in the Árpádian Era]* (Budapest: MTA TTI, 2005), 189.

6 See *Korai magyar történeti*, 443 (by Ferenc Makk).

7 For Roman's widow see PSRL, 2:717, 2:733–34; *Kronika halicko-wołyńska*, 7–8; Dąbrowski, *Genealogia Mścisławowiczów*, 265–66, Table 5b; Леонтій Войтович, "Мати короля Даниила (зауваження на полях монографії Д. Домбровского) [The Mother of King Daniil (Reflections on the Monograph of D. Dąbrowski], *Княжа доба* 1 (2007): 45–58 at 51. This hypothesis should be rejected, as Voytovych tried to synchronize diverse opinions without comparing them with the sources, and based himself on outdated research (J. Mailath, *Geschichte der Magyaren* (Wien, 1828));

In our opinion, Maiorov's view also needs further work, even though most research now looks for a solution in Byzantium. The name, Daniil, would also support this focus since while not unknown previously in Rus' it was only used in church circles.[8]

Customary Law and Roman Mstislavich's Widow in 1205

In Kievan Rus' and in the newly established principalities of the twelfth century, which includes Galicia, customary law prevailed, drawing on existing, traditional practice. Power within the dynasty (clan) belonged to the oldest male by order of seniority (in Slavic: *starshinstvo*). Naturally, the first condition was the belonging to the dynasty. Local chronicles report that among the princes of the Rus' conflicts were partially caused because *de iure* every member of the dynasty had the right to claim his share in power (in terms of territory and income). Distribution of power depended on who was the oldest, yet within a populous family it was often not easy to decide the ranking of seniority and this led to a great deal of conflict. On several occasions in the twelfth century actual birth order was ignored, either with the help of a fictitious father–son relation or by supporting a younger son against the first-born. Examples from Galicia during the twelfth century show that the *boyars* (or high-borns), resisted those decisions.

Roman Mstislavich's widow, in 1205, attempted to keep her late husband's territories together for her small children, whilst intending to wield power in the name of the sons. This notion completely contradicted customary law in the Kievan Rus'. The underage orphans were in no position to hold their fathers' lands, since the custom of seniority ranked them behind every adult member of the dynasty. A woman exercising power was almost unprecedented, and maternal ancestry gave no legitimacy on a candidate for gaining a territory; even an attempt based on support from outsiders would have offered better chances. A statement in a later source that Daniil and Vasilko "had a right" to the territories of their father is no more than the opinion of a later, sympathetic chronicler (Daniil's *Gesta* being written by an author with ties to the prince's court). This comment has instead been taken by modern historians at face value.[9]

Military Conflict in Galicia from 1205 to 1214

The events of 1205 made it obvious that a key part of the local elite, the so-called *boyars*, was not willing to accept the rule of the underage princes and their mother; they preferred the Hungarian or Polish claims. Both options had their supporters in Galicia, and this contradiction was apparently solved with the first Polish–Hungarian agreement in

---

Олександр Майоров, *Єфросинія Галицька дочка візантійського імператора в Галицько-Волинській Русі: княгиня і черниця* [*Ephrosinia of Galicia, Daughter of a Byzantine Emperor in Galician-Volhynian Rus': Princess and Nun*] (Біла Церква: Пшонківський, 2013), 23, 198–204.

8 For instance, Monk Daniel, who went on a pilgrimage to the Holy Land, or Daniel "the Exile" (Zatochnik, Заточник), the author of a petition to a prince (see Gerhard Podskalsky, *Christentum und theologische Literatur in der Kiever Rus' (988–1237)* (München: Beck, 1982), 195).

9 PSRL, 2:430, 2:657. For more recent analysis see Font, *Geschichtsschreibung des 13. Jahrhunderts an der Grenze zweier Kulturen*, 28–40; Font, "Daniil Romanovych of Galicia," 92.

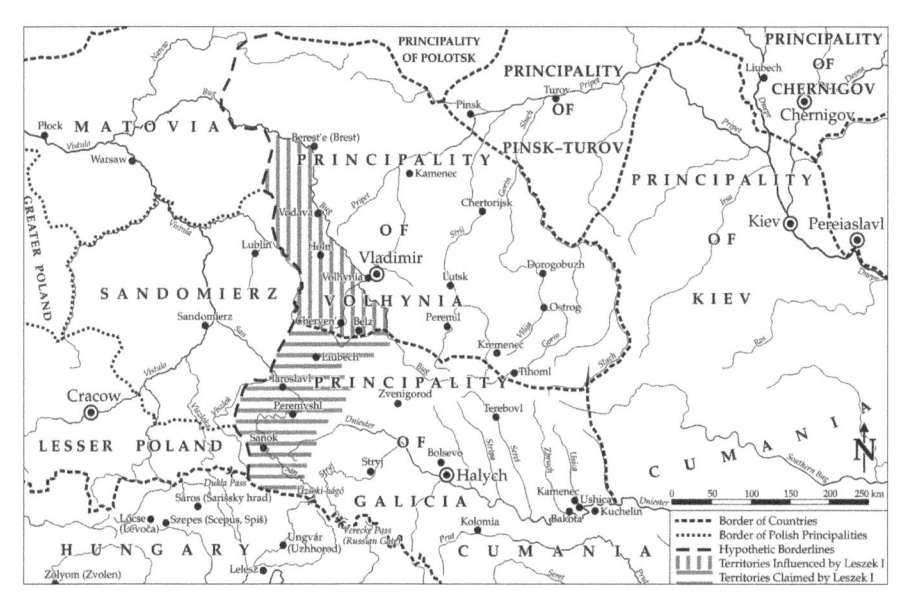

Map 2. The Principality of Galicia–Volhynia and its Vicinity in the Twelfth to Thirteenth Centuries (3_galicia_volhynia).

1206. However, internal struggles within the Polish claimants, each hankering after different territories in Galicia, led to military conflict there.

The most important sites in Galician territory were Peremyshl, Terebovl, Zvenigorod, and Halych (later they were Iaroslavl, Kholm, and Lvov); while Cherven', Vladimir Volynsky, Belz, Berestie, and Lutsk belonged to the Volhynian part. The duke of Kraków, Leszek, claimed rights over the western part of Galicia (Cherven' and Vladimir Volynsky) and certain parts of Volhynia, whereas the rest of Volhynia was of great interest to Conrad, the prince of Mazovia.

In Kraków Leszek "the White" (Biały) was duke (1202–27); it was his father, Casimir the Just, who had earlier helped the Galician ruler, Vladimir (1189–99), to return to the principality after his escape from Hungarian captivity. However, rivalry was developing in 1205–06 between Leszek and his brother, Conrad of Mazovia, concerning the overall rulership of Kraków.

The Hungarian–Polish agreement of 1206 may have been reached during Leszek's stay in Vladimir Volynsky. Mykhailo Hrushevsky believed that a personal meeting took place between the Hungarian king, Andrew II, and Leszek from Kraków.[10] After the departure of the Hungarians, Leszek sent his envoys to Andrew II and proposed joint support for Roman's children.[11] The Polish prince and Andrew II divided up Roman's

---

10 For the events of 1205 see: PSRL, 2:717–18; *Kronika halicko-wołyńska*, 7–9; and Hrushevsky, *Istorija Ukrainy-Rusi*, 3:19. Leszek could have referred to this through his envoy. See also PSRL, 2:719; Leszek agreed with Conrad (see: *Ioannis Dlugossii Annales seu Cronicae*, 6:201–2).

11 PSRL, 2:719–20; *Kronika halicko-wołyńska*, 14–15; Bronisław Włodarski, "Rola Konrada

former principality: Volhynia became Leszek's, while Galicia would now belong to the Hungarian king's sphere of interest. As part of the agreement, Daniil Romanovich was kept in the Hungarian court from 1206 onwards. A planned military campaign in 1207 fell through due to an arrangement with the Galicians, but the division of the spheres of interest probably remained intact. Leszek granted Vladimir Volynsky to his father-in-law in 1209, Berestie became the dominion of Vasilko Romanovich and his mother, while meanwhile in Belz his ally, Alexander Vsevolodich, was in charge.

After the Hungarian campaign of 1207 Andrew II gave none of Galicia to Leszek; on the contrary, as the "guardian" of Daniil he started to use the title *rex Galicie Lodomerieque* in the *intitulationes* of his royal charters.[12] He must have thought that he was able to operate without the cooperation of the Polish ruler. Furthermore, he based his assumption on his agreement with the Igorevich brothers from Chernigov who as leaders of four of the centres of the Galician principality paid taxes to the Hungarian sovereign. But Daniil's presence in the royal court was a stimulus for further actions.

Polish–Hungarian cooperation was also damaged from the Polish side. Leszek's plans for Volhynia were only partially realized and his influence was barely recognized in certain parts of the territory. As a result, Leszek tried to expand in Western Galicia, regardless of his agreement with Andrew II, which caused tension with the Hungarian king.[13] Andrew II tried to pacify the situation by enthroning the child Daniil.

Meanwhile, Leszek granted power in Volhynia, where he held influence due to his father-in-law (Ingvar, prince of Lutsk), to Daniil's brother, Vasilko, and their mother. In 1211 the prince of Kraków joined a Hungarian-led campaign; he sent his captain, Sudisław, and his Volhynian military force (Vasilko from Belz, Alexander from Vladimir, his brother-in-law from Lutsk, and Mstislav Iaroslavich "the Mute" (Nemoj, Немой)) from Peresopnica to Peremyshl. This enormous army could easily take Peremyshl, and after a series of Hungarian–Polish joint victories the young Daniil was inaugurated in the principality. His mother remained with him in Galicia, still fostering her own political ambitions. However, as soon as the Hungarian forces left, the local elite rose up against them and the *boyars* overcame the aspiring regent mother. The princess travelled to Belz in late 1211 and sought help again, probably via her envoys, from the Hungarian court against the *boyars* who were now in power. Andrew II helped her reclaim Galicia in the winter of 1211–12, and Volodislav, the leader of the *boyars*, was imprisoned in Hungary. Nonetheless, the widow and her sons could not retain power and fled to Hungary in late 1212 or early 1213 and later went to Kraków.[14]

Andrew II took off for Galicia anew in September 1213, but the campaign was disrupted because of Queen Gertrude's assassination (September 28). Nonetheless, the conflict at home did not affect the king's intentions towards Galicia. He may have returned home but his army, now led by his appointed *boyar*, Volodislav Kormilichich,

---

mazowieckiego w stosunkach polsko-ruskich [Conrad of Maziovia's Role in Polish–Rus'ian Relations]," *Archiwum Towarzystwa Naukowego we Lwowie*, series 2, 19, no. 2 (1936): 85–138.

12 *Codex diplomaticus Hungariae*, 3/1:31–32.
13 Włodarski, *Polska i Ruś*, 44; Szczur, *Historia Polski*, 260.
14 PSRL, 2:728; *Kronika halicko-wołyńska*, 43; Font, *Árpád-házi királyok*, 200–2.

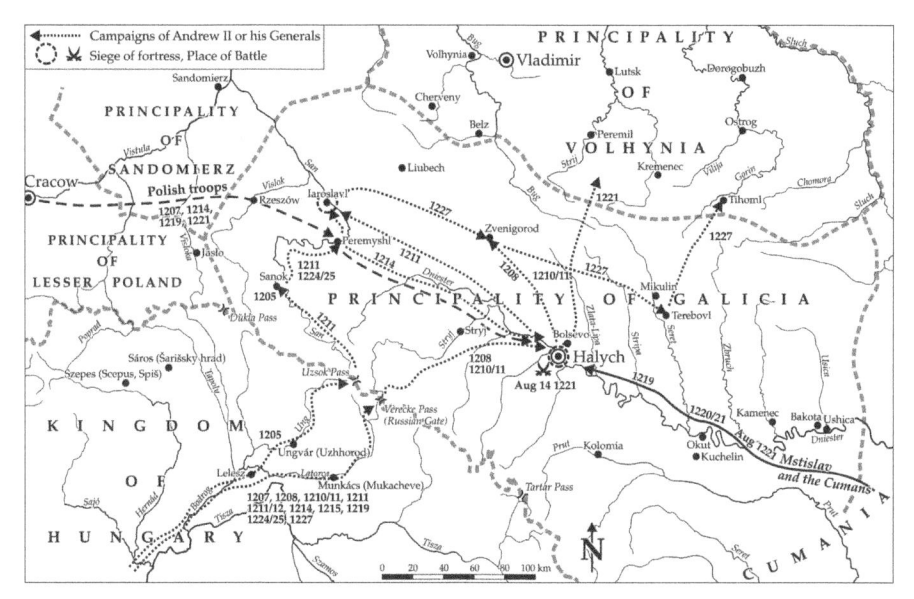

Map 3. The Galician Campaigns of Andrew II in 1205–1227.

continued marching towards the Rus'. Daniil and Vasilko were present in Volhynia in the fall of 1213 and tried to claim the principality. Volodislav might even have received some estates in return for his cooperation, lands that were to become in 1218 the possession of the archbishop of Esztergom.[15]

The Poles then attacked Volodislav, who was seen as representing Hungarian rule in Galicia, a new Hungarian–Polish conflict.[16] Leszek brought together the armies of Volhynia (Alexandr Vsevolodich and Mstislav "the Mute" (Храбрый)) with the elite of Lesser Poland, Daniil and Vasilko, and attacked Galicia. He was triumphant on the battlefield but failed to seize the stronghold of Halych. He was urged to come to an agreement with Andrew II, since probably both of them realized that Volodislav's rule was not favourable for either of them.

---

15 PSRL, 2:729; *Kronika halicko–wołyńska*, 45–46; Font, *Árpád-házi királyok*, 200–2; Włodarski, *Polska i Rus*, 53; *Codex diplomaticus et epistolaris Slovaciae*, 1:180; *Codex diplomaticus Hungariae*, 3/2:310.

16 Volodislav is probably identical with *Ladislaus Ruthenus*, who is mentioned in the Hungarian charters. See Font, *Árpád-házi királyok*, 104, 199–205. The hypothesis that Volodislav might have lived in Hungary until 1231–32 (for which see Jusupović, *Elity ziemi Halickiej i Wołyńskiej*, 286; and Мирослав Волощук, «*Русь*» *в Угорському Королівстві (XI–друга половина XIV ст): суспільно-політична роль, майнови стосунки, міграції* ["Rus" in the Hungarian Kingdom (Eleventh to Second Half of the Fourteenth Century): Social-Political Role, Potencial Conflicts, Migration] (Івано-Франківськ: Лілея НВ, 2014), 145) is not convincing, and similarly his presumed role in the Hungarian elite is also a misunderstanding (Мирослав Волощук, "Володислав Кормильчич: венгерская бытность 1214–1232 гг [Volodislav Kormilichych: in Hungary between 1214 and 1232]," *Древняя Русь. Ворпосы медиевистики* 37, no. 3 (2009): 19–20).

At this juncture, the elite of Kraków was divided on reaching an agreement with the Hungarians; those who favoured it were motivated by the failure of their own endeavours. The other group wished to expand the influence of Kraków over Galicia and wanted no alliance with the Hungarians. Within Leszek's court, the main figures behind the active politics towards the Rus' belonged to the Odrowąż and Awdaniec families, particularly the chancellor, Iwan Odrowąż, and the *castellanus*,[17] Wojewoda Pakosław from the Awdaniec family, who led Leszek's campaigns.

The Polish Dynastic Element: Leszek, Conrad, and their Rus' Wives

Lesser Poland, Sandomierz, and Mazovia were all close to the south-western centres of the Rus', yet the border between the eastern and western Slavs was not fixed at all, as the western endeavours of Roman Mstislavich and Leszek's interests in the east demonstrate.[18]

Members of the Piast and Rurikid dynasties often wed members from the other's families. If we take a look at the ancestors of Leszek the White, we know that the first wife of his grandfather, Bolesław III Wrymouth, was Zbyslava, daughter of Grand Prince Sviatopolk of Kiev (1093–1113). Two of Leszek's uncles also wed princesses from the Rus': Bolesław IV "the Curly" married Verhuslava, daughter of Vsevolod Mstislavich, the prince of Novgorod, while Mieszko III "the Old" wed Eudoksiya, daughter of Iury Dolgoruky (Долгорукий). Likewise, their sister, Agnieszka was married to Mstislav Iziaslavich.[19]

The sources provide no explicit reference to the kinship of Leszek's mother. Recent studies state that Helena, his mother, was the daughter of Conrad II, the prince of Znojmo. This assumption is based on Kadłubek the chronicler's remark that Prince Conrad III of Olomouc was the brother-in-law (*frater iugalis*) of Casimir the Just. Conversely, Balzer believed Helena to be a descendant from the Rurikid dynasty, basing himself on the records of the *Old-Russian Chronicles* in which Leszek is thought to be related to certain princes. According to Balzer, Helena was the daughter of Grand Prince Rostislav Mstislavich of Kiev (1159–67). This replaced his earlier theory that she was the daughter of Grand Prince Mstislav Iziaslavich of Kiev (1167–70). Balzer's argument contradicts Kadłubek, yet the report of the *Old-Russian Chronicles* regarding kinship between certain princes and Leszek is not necessarily false, since Leszek's uncles married within

---

[17] The Polish word *wojewoda* looks similar to the Hungarian word *vajda*, but they have different meanings. The term *wojewoda* means "warlord" and "castellan" (from the Latin word *castellanus*), and it did not become an office with a secure territorial power, like the Transylvanian *vajda* in Hungary, where it is used solely with this meaning.

[18] Rhode, *Ostgrenze Polens*, 103–8; Marcin Wołoszyn, "Grody Czerwieńskie – między fascynacją a zapomnieniem [The Cities of Cherven': Between Fascination and Oblivion]," in *Czerwień – gród między Wschodem a Zachodem. Katalog wystawy*, ed. Jolanta Bagińska et al. (Tomaszów Lubelski: Muzeum Regionalne im. dr. Janusza Petera, 2012), 81–103.

[19] Balzer, *Genealogia Piastów*, 218–20 (Zbyslava); PSRL, 2:313; Balzer, *Genealogia Piastów*, 281–85; Dąbrowski, *Genealogia Mścisławowiczów*, 192–207 (Verhuslava). Balzer's statement was corrected by Dąbrowski, *Genealogia Mścisławowiczów*, 677–86 (Eudoksiya); Balzer, *Genealogia Piastów*, 323; Dąbrowski, *Genealogia Mścisławowiczów*, 216–28 (Agnieszka).

the Rurikid dynasty, and in that respect, following medieval perceptions, he could be seen as being kin to them.[20]

Leszek's own wives came from the Rus', the first one being the daughter of Ingvar Iaroslavich.[21] Ingvar possessed several parts of Volhynia, and he even attempted to gain Kiev, but he could only maintain long-term control of Lutsk in Volhynia. Leszek opposed him and supported Alexandr Vsevolodovich, the ruler of Belz, in trying to seize the core town of Vladimir Volynsky. Eventually they made peace in 1207. Leszek wed Grzymisława, the daughter of Iaroslav Vladimirovich afterwards.[22] It is no wonder, with this in mind that Leszek held some influence in Volhynia, even being in a position to later bestow Belz to Vasilko (Daniil's brother), whilst also gaining control over the territory between the rivers Wieprz and Bug, the so-called border region, or "Ukraine," in the *GVC*.[23]

Leszek's brother, Conrad, also married within the Rus'. His second wife was apparently, Agafia/Agatha, according to Balzer, basing this on Długosz's chronicle and later sources. But his first bride may have been the daughter of Sviatoslav Igorevich, who had interests in the territories of Novgorod–Seversk and Galicia. The dual marriage is largely ignored in recent research.[24]

The Hungarian kings had significantly fewer family ties with the princes of the Rus'. Their primary interest was capturing Galicia, and expended little effort on Volhynia, even if the name of the territory eventually featured among their titles, with Andrew II the first to signal himself as king of Galicia and Volhynia ("Lomoderia"). The Hungarian royal troops (the army of the whole realm) was superior to the forces from Kraków, yet the military contingent they left in Galicia was never sufficient enough to hold onto their gains. Meanwhile, the presence of Daniil in Kraków was to prove disadvantageous for further Hungarian expansion. The solution to this ongoing rivalry and internal struggles was to be the Agreement of Scepus, which we will now describe.

---

20 *Magistri Vincentii Chronica Polonorum*, 4:162; Kazimierz Jasiński, *Rodowód Piastów śląskich. Piastowie wrocławscy, legnicko-brzescy, świdniccy, ziębiccy, głogowscy, żagańscy, oleśniccy, opolscy, cieszyńscy i oświęcimscy [The Genealogy of the Piasts of Silesia]* (Kraków: Avalon, 2007²), 266; *Piastowie. Leksykon biograficzny [The Piasts: A Biographical Lexicon]*, ed. Stanisław Szczur and Krysztof Ożóg (Kraków: Wydawnictwo Literackie, 1999), 179; Szczur, *Historia Polski*, 147–48; Chrzanowski, *Leszek Biały*, 27. The former statements are based on: PSRL, 2:720, 2:731; *Kronika halicko-wołyńska*, 18; see, for example, Rapov, *Kniazheskie vladeniia*, 191; Rhode, *Ostgrenze Polens*, 104.

21 The *GVC* reports on the marriage. See also PSRL, 2:720; *Kronika halicko–wołyńska*, 18. Yet her name is unknown. For Ingvar Iaroslavich see Rapov, *Kniazheskie vladeniia*, 177. For the two marriages of Leszek see Dariusz Dąbrowski, *Genealogia Mścisławowiczów. Pierwsze pokolenia (do początku XIV wieku) [The Genealogy of the Mścisławiczs. The First Generations (Prior to the Start of the Fourteenth Century)]* (Kraków: Avalon, 2008), 334–38, 689.

22 Her name is known only from Polish sources, for instance, from the legend of her daughter, Blessed Salomea. See *Monumenta Poloniae Historica*, 4:776. Balzer, *Genealogia Piastów*, 462–65; Włodarski, "Rola Konrada mazowieckiego," 80–82 (full citation above).

23 PSRL, 2:732; *Kronika halicko–wołyńska*, 60; Rhode, *Ostgrenze Polens*, 105.

24 *Ioannis Dlugossii Annales seu Cronicae*, 6:200; Balzer, *Genealogia Piastów*, 479; Szczur, *Historia Polski*, 260; Henryk Samsonowicz, *Konrad Mazowiecki (1187/88 – 31 VIII 1247) [Conrad of Mazovia (1177/78 – 31 August 1247)]* (Kraków: Avalon, 2014), 50.

Chapter 2

THE AGREEMENT OF SCEPUS

WE HAVE SEEN how, from 1205, the duke of Kraków, Leszek the White, and the Hungarian king, Andrew II, were rivals in the "lordless" territory, even if they had to make compromises from time to time. Their shared priorities were primarily to strengthen their influence, and they supported Daniil and Vasilko while their mother acted as their regent (1205–06). Andrew II came to an agreement with the sons of Igor (Igorevichs), who were given Galicia in return for paying taxes (1207–10). Meanwhile, the young Daniil continued to reside at the Hungarian court. Once the minor Daniil was expelled from Galicia, Hungarian–Polish cooperation reached a new level (1211, 1213), yet soon enough the collaboration faced new problems. It became clear for both parties, as early as 1214, that rule over Galicia would be possible only as the result of Polish–Hungarian cooperation, with a more solid foundation. To this end, the idea emerged to marry their two children, Coloman and Salomea, who would then rule Galicia together.

The Agreement

Leszek and Andrew came to an agreement at a personal gathering in Scepus (Hungarian: Szepesség, today in Slovakia: Spiš).[1] This council was prepared by the duke's envoys, "Lestich"[2] and Pakosław, *castellanus* of Kraków. The GVC credits Leszek with the idea of the dynastic marriage to bind the alliance. Pakosław took an active part in the arrangements, not least because the agreement was favourable for him. The object of the bargaining was the Galician territory, yet Kraków laid claim only to Peremyshl and Liubachev. Those two important settlements belonged to the watershed of the river Vistula (around the San and Bug tributaries) which ran north to the Baltic, whereas all the other rivers belonged to the watershed of the Dniester which headed south towards the Black Sea. It is worth mentioning that Pakosław, not Leszek, gained possession of Liubachev which underlines the political strength of the so-called "Galician party."[3]

---

1 PSRL, 2:732; Pauler, *A magyar nemzet története*, 2:54–55; Włodarski, *Polska i Rus*, 58; Pashuto, *Ocherki po istorii*, 200; Procházková, "Postavenie haličského kráľa," 66; Hollý, "Princess Salomea and Hungarian–Polish Relations," 12, 14–15; Nagirnyj, *Polityka zagraniczna księstw tiem Halickiej i Wołyńskiej*, 171; Dąbrowski, *Daniel Romanowicz, biografia polityczna*, 83–84.

2 "Lestich" is not a given name, but it derives from the word Lestco (the Latin version of Leszek) and is a "paternal name." It was not used by the Poles; still, the eastern-Slavic chronicler could use it referring to some relative of Leszek. It could logically refer to his son, but Leszek married only in 1207, and he had no son by that time. A mystical Polish king also bore the name Lestco (See *Magistri Vincentii Chronica Polonorum*, 18), so the passage could be also interpreted as "someone from the family of the Polish prince." The historiographical sources only name Pakosław and no-one else. The name Lestich as an independent version can be seen in the name register PSRL, 2:xxi. For the origin of the name Leszek and its bearers see Chrzanowski, *Leszek Biały*, 25–26.

3 PSRL, 2:731; *Kronika halicko–wołyńska*, 59–60.

The Polish–Hungarian rule of Galicia was now to be embodied in the children of Andrew and Leszek, respectively the roughly six-year-old Coloman and three-year-old Salomea (probably born around 1211). The agreement was theoretically perfect, but the practice showed its weakness, and several problems emerged. They mostly abandoned the earlier justification and pretence that the combined forces were merely there in support of the sons of Roman Mstislavich. This was dangerous for Leszek, who relied on the Volhynian military force, and an alliance between Daniil and Vasilko supported by the local *boyars* could imperil Polish influence. The autonomy of the siblings was also a threat to Andrew II's Galician chances, since they could offer an alternative to Hungarian rule. The Hungarian army was significantly larger than that of Lesser Poland, so Leszek was almost forced to follow Andrew II.[4] But the prince intended to ease this pressure through the search for new allies.

The date of the Scepus Agreement cannot be ascertained from the *GVC* or any other sources, yet the year of 1214 is not disputed by scholars.[5] A more precise dating is impossible and moves into the realm of possibilities. Most researchers assume the date to be the fall of 1214, with Holovko only opting for a summer meeting of the rulers.[6] The logic behind the date lies in the previous events and the later cooperation. Leszek was still fighting in Volhynia in the spring of 1214, whereas a united Polish–Hungarian force had appeared by the end of the year.[7] The chronicles offer an intense narrative, yet it seems sure that weeks passed by between the journey of Leszek's envoys and the rendezvous of the sovereigns. Implementing the agreement needed further time, and the combined army probably took some weeks to reach Galicia. Therefore, the meeting

---

4 Олександр Б. Головко, *Корона Данила Галицького. Волинь і Галичина в державно-політичному розвитку Центрально-Східної Європи та класичного середньовіччя* [*The Crown of Daniil of Galicia. Volhynia and Galicia in the Political Development of East Central Europe and the Classical Middle Ages*] (Київ: Стилос, 2006), 281.

5 PSRL, 2:732; *Kronika halicko-wołyńska*, 52–53; Balzer, *Genealogia Piastów*, 482–83; Hrushevsky, "Khronologia podij," 337; Pashuto, *Ocherki po istorii*, 200; Крип'якевич, *Галицько-Волинське князівство*, 89; Günther Stökl, "Das Fürstentum Galizien-Wolhynien," in *Handbuch der Geschichte Russlands, I*, ed. Manfred Hellman and Klaus Zernack (Stuttgart: Hersemann, 1981), 484–533 at 500–1; John Fennell, *The Crisis of Medieval Russia, 1200–1304* (Harlow: Longman, 1983), 37; Котляр, *Данило Галицький*, 106; Володимир Александрович and Леонтій Войтович, *Король Данило Романович [King Danilo Romanovych]* (Біла Церква: Пшонківський, 2013), 52–53.

6 Włodarski, *Polska i Ruś*, 58; Font, "II. András orosz politikája és hadjáratai," 126; Font, *Árpád-házi királyok*, 225; Ђура Харди, *Наследници Кијева. Између краљевске круне и татарског јарма [The Successors of Kiev: Between Royal Crown and Tartar Yoke]* (Нови Сад: Филозофски факултет, Еовом Саду, Катедра за историју 2002), 134; Мирослав Волощук, "Вассальная зависимость Даниила Романовича от Белы IV в 1235–1245 гг.: актуальные вопросы реконструкции русско-венгерских отношений второй четверти века [Vassal Dependence of Daniil Romanovych on Béla IV between 1235 and 1245: Actual Questions for Reconstruction of Russian-Hungarian Ties in the Second Quarter of the Thirteenth Century]," *Specimina Nova, Pars Prima: Sectio Mediaevalis* 3 (2005): 83–115 at 98–99; Nagirnyj, *Polityka zagraniczna księstw tiem Halickiej i Wołyńskiej*, 171; Dąbrowski, *Daniel Romanowicz, biografia polityczna*, 83; Chrzanowski, *Leszek Biały*, 72; Головко, *Корона Данила Галицького*, 276.

7 PSRL, 2:730–31; *Kronika halicko-wołyńska*, 54–55.

could have taken place in late summer or early autumn, while the campaign can be dated probably to the late fall of 1214.

Implementing the Scepus Agreement needed military and political preparations, especially the occupation of Galicia. Volodislav, the *boyar* leader, was captured and imprisoned once again, never to escape. This imprisonment has been called into question by Włodarski, as he interpreted the verb *"zatoči"* instead as exile.[8] In the light of later events, this is improbable. On the contrary, Volodislav never appeared again in any of the sources and an exile probably would not have hindered him from some forms of involvement.

From the Polish side, Pakosław must have been present during the negotiations, but we know nothing certain about the Hungarian participants. Several royal officials must have accompanied the king. Among Andrew's key dignitaries were Palatine Nicholas, who was also count (*comes*) of Bodrog County, Marcel, son of Marcel from the Tétény *genus* (for which term I will use kindred henceforward), who was the judge of the royal court (*iudex curiae*) and count of Csanád, Gyula from the Kán kindred, who was the *voivode* of Transylvania and count of Szolnok, and Atyusz, son of Atyusz from the Atyusz kindred, who was the *ban* of Slavonia. The master of the treasury was Miska, son of Solomon, from the Atyusz kindred, later the first master of the horse, a title that only appeared in 1217. If we look at the region where the meeting took place, royal control was clearly still in flux; from 1214 only the counts of Borsod, Újvár, and Zemplén counties are known (Jacob; Alexander, son of Thomas, from the Hontpázmány kindred; and Martin, respectively). The first count of Scepus appeared in sources only from 1216, the one of Gömör (Gemer) from the mid-thirteenth century, while Sáros (Šariš) was merely a royal estate (*predium*) at the start of the fourteenth century.[9]

The presence of Archbishop John of Esztergom (1205–22), one of the prelates of the Kingdom of Hungary, was presumably required for the coronation of Coloman. Marcel, the royal judge, was probably there too, since his career started in 1206, right after the enthronement of Andrew II, and he also playd an important role in leading the realm's military in 1211.[10] Denis (Dénes), son of Ampud, also could have been present; his career started as master of the treasury and count of Scepus in 1216. It can be assumed that the events of 1214 promoted the formation of the royal county in Scepus. Furthermore, Demetrius of the Aba kindred and File (Füle, Filja), who both played a later role in Prince Coloman's rule in Galicia, were presumably present at the meeting.

There would have been no participants who would have also witnessed Andrew II's adventure in Galicia as a child. Palatine Moch (Mog) served under King Béla III: as judge of the royal court (*iudex curiae*) in 1185–86, and in 1188 as count of Nyitra (Nitra). At the beginning of Andrew's reign, he received the palatine's office for the third time (1206) but he was probably dead by 1214.

---

8 PSRL, 2:731; *Kronika halicko–wołyńska*, 53–54; Włodarski, *Polska i Rus*, 65.

9 Zsoldos, *Magyarország világi archontológiája*. For the royal officials in 1214 see pp. 17, 28, 37, 43; For the master of the treasury, the master of the horse, and the master of the stewards, see pp. 56, 62. 71; For the counts: 143 (Borsod), 205 (Gömör), 156 (Sáros), 188 (Scepus/Szepes) 217 (Újvár), 234 (Zemplén).

10 PSRL, 2:724; *Kronika halicko–wołyńska*, 32.

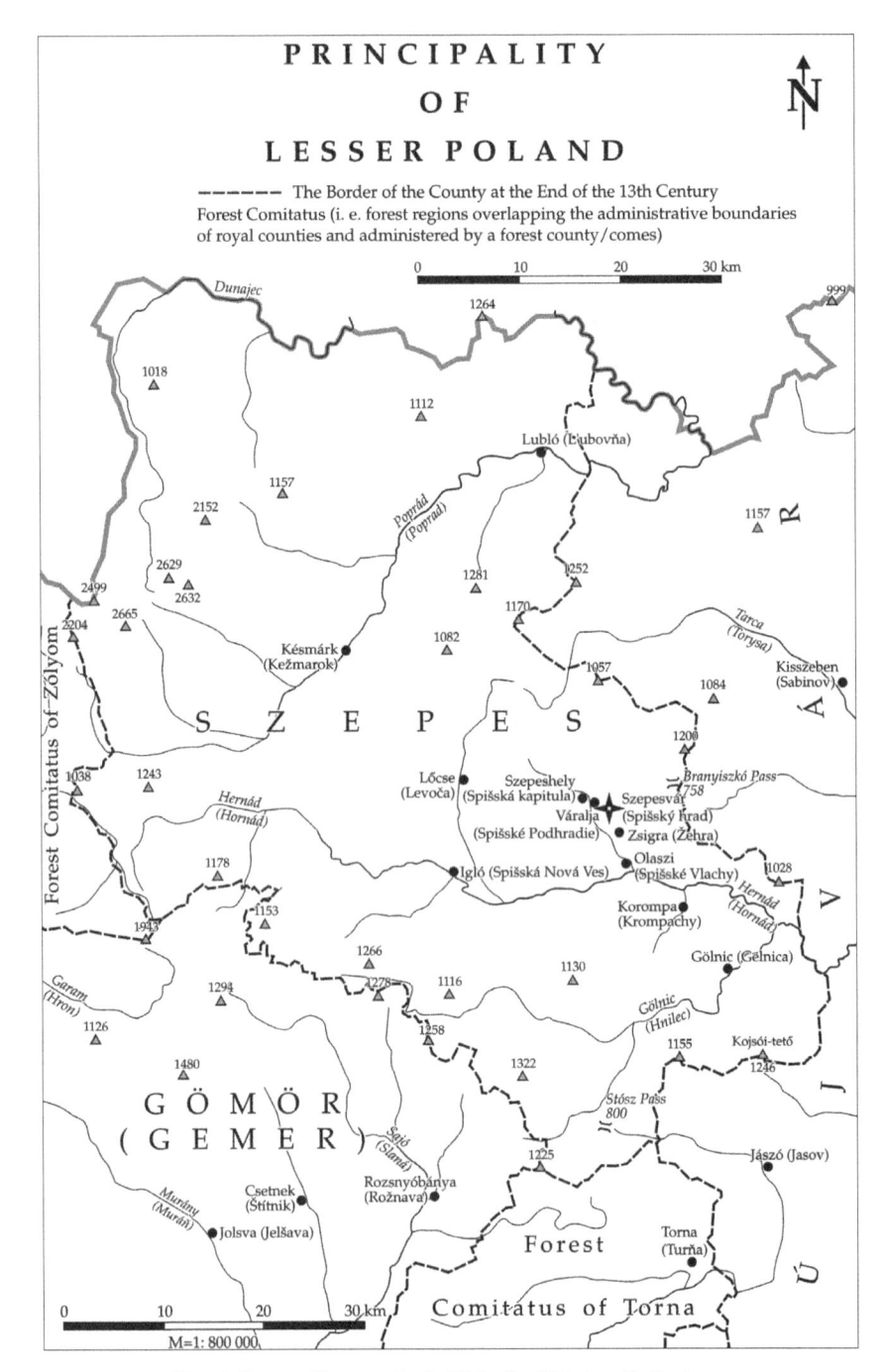

Map 4. Scepus (Szepesség, Spiš) in the Thirteenth Century.

Figure 1. The Castle of Scepus in 2016
(with kind permission of Márta Font).

The Location

It was convenient for the meeting of the Hungarian king and the Polish prince to take place near the common border; it is similarly understandable that the sovereign of lower rank and of younger age, the prince, visited the older king. We do not know where exactly they met in Scepus, or what suitable venue (perhaps a royal residence) could accommodate such a council, a reception, and catering for the king, the prince, and their entourages. The *GVC* refers only to the name of Scepus.

The settlement of the Scepus region happened only in the second half of the thirteenth century, and it must have been quite unpopulated still in 1214. The lack of an established royal county supports this, since across the Kingdom of Hungary royal counties were established to make the inhabitants belong to and depend upon royal power.

The name "Scepus" derives from the Hungarian adjective *szép* ("beautiful"); variations in other languages were based on that (Latin: *Scepus*, German: *Zips*, and later the Slovak *Spiš*).[11] The county of Scepus was a royal county, a kind of structure that first appeared in the thirteenth century. According to Gyula Kristó's categorization of the counties, the region was one of the later formed counties, since records of the first ruling count, Denis, son of Ampud, only appear from 1216; likewise, the earliest dating of the castle is unknown. It can be assumed that development started at the turn of the twelfth and thirteenth centuries from the territories originally belonging to Borsod and Gömör.

---

[11] *Földrajzi nevek etimológiai szótára, I–II [Etymological Dictionary of Geographical Names]*, ed. Lajos Kiss (Budapest: Akadémiai Kiadó, 1978), 609; *Korai magyar történeti*, 636 (entry by Gyula Kristó).

At that time Denis was also count of the neighbouring Újvár County, so it was reasonable to give him jurisdiction over the newly forming county as well. One reason for the separation into two distinct counties might have been the income from the trade route; as data from 1198 shows, it led through the area *terra Scepusiensis* (land of Scepus) from which the royal men took a toll.[12] The next record of the tolls dates to after the attack of the Mongols (1243), at which point the toll-free status of the noblemen of Scepus to the markets of Szepesváralja (*Spišské Podhradie*) was secured.

Research by Attila Zsoldos demonstrates the special nature of the formation of Scepus, and he compares it with other counties. Zsoldos[13] differentiates two types of county formations, the first being based on a close symbiosis between the county and the royal castle (*várispánság*), whereas the other type (the later counties) were based on the kings' personal estates. These were generally formed on the basis of so-called forest-dominions (*erdőuradalom*). But Scepus fits neither group.[14]

The territory's formation was still in flux in the opening decades of the thirteenth century. It is unclear if the construction of the royal castle, which could have been the location of the meeting, was already finished or whether it was even started. The first mention of this stronghold derives from a charter of Béla IV issued in 1249, so the beginning of the construction must have been by the 1230s. The three-storey palace included a freestanding tower and a large hall (22×12 metres) on every floor. Slovak historians believe that these buildings were constructed by Coloman, even if certain investigations date the whole castle to the second half of the thirteenth century. Archaeological finds suggest an earlier construction, yet their interpretation is somewhat doubted. István Feld summarized the history of the research in his recent study; according to him, the round building of twenty-two metres in diameter with a middle pillar on the top of the hill was originally a residential tower, and it was turned into a water tank only after the reconstruction of the building. Other scholars argue that it was originally built for water catchment. The latest Slovak research suggests that the tower was a residential building built in the late twelfth century, whilst its first floor was meant to be a water tank. Martin Homza even stated that Béla III imprisoned Prince Vladimir in the tower after he fled to Hungary from Galicia, but this seems fanciful. A comprehensive monograph on the whole castle, describing the history of the construction, is sorely needed. Notwithstanding, we

---

12 Boglárka Weisz, *A királyketteje és az ispán harmada. Vámok és vámszedés Magyarországon a középkor első felében [The King's Half and the Count's Third: Tolls and Toll-Collecting in Hungary in the First Half of the Middle Ages]* (Budapest: MTA BTK TTI, 2013), 370.

13 Zsoldos, "Szepes megye kialakulása," 19–31.

14 For the formation of the territory of the Scepus region see Gyula Kristó, *A vármegyék kialakulása Magyarországon [The Formation of Counties in Hungary]* (Budapest: Magvető, 1988), 393–95; Zsoldos, "Szepes megye kialakulása." For the first count (*comes*) see *Codex diplomaticus et epistolaris Slovaciae*, 1:165; and Zsoldos, *Magyarország világi archontológiája*, 205. Denis, son of Ampud, held the titles of count of Scepus and Újvár, and he also bore the office of master of the treasury in 1216. Later on he had a major role in Hungarian affairs in the Balkans as the count of Bodrog (1220–22), and subsequently as palatine (1227–28, 1231, 1234). See Zsoldos, *Magyarország világi archontológiája*, 295 (*Regesta regum stirpis Arpadianae*, no. 308); Zsoldos, "Szepes megye kialakulása," 30.

might presume that the tower could have served as a royal court house, like a curia, as Alexander Ruttkay believes, and if not, there could have been a separate "court house without any fortification," as seen at other administrative units on the periphery of the forest county/*comitatus* (*erdőispánság*),[15] which would only be suitable for shorter stays.[16]

The first mention of a provost of the collegiate chapter of Scepus, a certain Adolf, originates from 1209; he was given the estates along the River Poprad "to populate them with people." The building of the provostry is later; according to Ernő Marosi the construction started in the mid-thirteenth century. Attila Zsoldos stated that the foundation of this collegiate chapter meant that ecclesiastical estates must have existed in Scepus at the beginning of the thirteenth century, whilst the royal benefactions presented the possibility for the appearance of private estates.[17]

Whether secular or religious, the formation of Scepus (Szepes) County seems to be dated to the start of the thirteenth century, whilst the buildings were a generation or two later.[18]

The Impact on Dynastic Legitimacy and the Succession

How did the Scepus Agreement affect the legitimacy of the new Polish–Hungarian rulers of Galicia, Coloman and Salomea, in a region where different customary traditions and clans had held sway? We have already noted how Roman Mstislavich's widow, after his death in 1205, attempted to keep his lands together for her small children, tried to wield power herself in the name of the sons, but how this generated great resistance by the *boyars* who forced her into exile.

The statement that "Roman's sons had a legitimate right to the throne" appeared on several occasions in the historiography of the period.[19] In the principalities of the Rus' seniority (*staršinstvo*), as we previously described, was the basic principle,[20] yet as a dynasty grew not even adults were always able to enforce their rights: many times uncles and nephews were not only of the same age, but an uncle could be the younger one. Therefore, traditional seniority was almost impossible to follow. Claimants often had resource to military help of their western neighbours or nomads of the steppe to

---

15 That is, forest regions overlapping the administrative boundaries of royal counties and administered by a forest count (*comes*).

16 *Korai magyar történeti*, 637 (entry by István Feld); Feld, "Az erdőispánságok várai az Árpád-kori," 371, 376–79; Homza, "Včasnostredoveké dejiny Spiša," 1:126–50; Vladimír Olejník, Magdaléna Janovská and Martin Stejskal, "Spišsky hrad ako kráľovské sídlo [The Castle of Spiš as a Royal Seat]," in *Spišský hrad ako kráľovské sídli*, ed. Mária Novotná (Levoča: Slovenské národové múzeum Spišské múzeum v Levoči, 2015), 55–96 at 57. The volume unfortunately gives uncritical support for Martin Homza's statements concerning the Scepus region and ignores key Hungarian research (cf. pp. 55–61).

17 Zsoldos, "Szepes megye kialakulása," 29.

18 *Regesta regum stirpis Arpadianae*, no. 243; *Korai magyar történeti*, 636 (entry by Ernő Marosi).

19 See, for instance, Procházková, "Postavenie haličského kráľa," 64.

20 Font, "Daniil Romanovych of Galicia," 92–93.

support their claims. The chances of the orphans—and as a matter of fact widows—were almost hopeless.

The consequences of *staršinstvo* were obvious. An attempt to formulate the principle took place at the convention of Liubech, as early as the eleventh century, underscoring that everyone should preserve their fathers' heritage, yet its implementation was often only possible with accompanying, often military, force. Local branches of the Rurik dynasty emerged in the course of the twelfth century (for instance, in Chernigov the offspring of Oleg Sviatoslavich, while in Vladimir–Suzdal the descendants of Iury Dolgorukii shared the incomes of the territory). In the south-western part of the Rus', in Galicia, power was passed down from father to son on several occasions: Vladimirko to Iaroslav Osmomysl (Осмомысль) to Vladimir. When the branch died out, however, with the last prince of neighbouring Volhynia, Roman Mstislavich followed his usual process of absorbing Galicia into his Volhynian territory (in 1199). Despite expansion along the river Dniestr between 1199 and 1205, there was no real cohesion between the two principalities, with the Galician *boyars* distrustful. The incomes were more significant in Galicia,[21] so it is no wonder that the local *boyars* sought independence.

Roman's children's right to the succession was rejected after their father's death. The adult Igorevichs from Chernigov[22] also claimed their right to Galicia based on their mother's descent, whilst Roman's distant relatives from Novgorod appeared too, with favourable connections on the steppe: Mstislav "the Brave" (Khrabry, Храбрый), and his son Mstislav "the Successful" (Udaloy, Удалой).[23] In this situation Roman's sons, or rather their mother, chose the obvious solution and tried to make use of their Polish and Hungarian connections. The claims were all based on various titles; yet everyone was being led by the goal of expansion, including the Krakówian and the Hungarian rulers.

Slavic historiography holds, following Shusharin, that Andrew II's purpose regarding Galicia was to form a personal union, as had happened in Croatia in the late eleventh century.[24] Nevertheless, the parallel of the two cases is not just invalid but misleading,

---

21 See the incomes of Vladimirko and later his grandson, Vladimir, in order to hold their power in the twelfth century. The former sent several gifts to the Hungarian kings, whereas the latter promised the Holy Roman emperor two thousand *grivnas* per year. See Font, *Magyarok a Kijevi Évkönyvben*, 228–31, 310–11.

22 The rival sides among the branches of the Rurik dynasties were the descents of Vladimir (Vsevolodovich) Monomakh and Oleg Sviatoslavich. Prince Roman and his son were offsprings of the Monomakh branch, and the princes of Chernigov derived from Oleg. One of the newest branches among Oleg's offsprings was that of the Igorevichs, and they were related to a certain part of Chernigov, Novgorod Severskii. There were several kinships among the various branches at the beginning of the thirteenth century. Unfortunately, the names of the female members are mostly unknown.

23 Rapov, *Kniazheskie vladeniia*, 163, 182.

24 Владимир П. Шушарин, *История Венгрии в трех томах* [*The History of Hungary in Three Volumes*], 3 vols. (Москва: Наука, 1971), 1:143; Dąbrowski, *Daniel Romanowicz, biografia polityczna*, 84; Nagirnyj, *Polityka zagraniczna księstw tiem Halickiej i Wołyńskiej*, 172n143. Nagirnyj has misinterpreted my statement (Márta Font, "Ungarn, Polen und Halitsch-Volhynien im 13. Jahrhundert," *Studia Slavica Academiae Scientiarum Hungaricae* 38, nos. 1–2 (1993): 27–39 at 35), since the reference regarding the territory *banats* did not refer to Croatia.

since Croatia had already begun to form a state in the tenth century, and the Croatian kings had received a crown from the papacy in the eleventh century. The personal union between Hungary and Croatia was emphasized by King Coloman's separate coronation in 1102.[25] The state of Croatia diverged fundamentally from that of Galicia, where the institution of a kingdom and its later tradition was only established by Prince Coloman's coronation at the start of the thirteenth century. We see the plans of Andrew II in Galicia as being far more analogous to Hungarian expansion and administration on the Balkans.[26]

---

25 *Diplomata Hungariae antiquissima: accedunt epistolae et acta ad historian Hungariae pertinenta*, vol. 1, *Ab anno 1000 usque ad annum 1131*, ed. Georgius Györffy (Budapestini: Academia Scientiarum Hungarica, 1992), 330; Font, *Könyves Kálmán és kora*, 64; Sokcsevits, *Horvátország*, 71–83, 95–105.

26 Font, *Árpád-házi királyok*, 267–68.

Chapter 3

COLOMAN'S CORONATION AS KING OF GALICIA: DATE AND PLACE

THE DATE AND location of Coloman's coronation is nowhere mentioned in our sources. We know it happened and a few details are revealed thanks to four charters: two letters of Andrew II written to Pope Innocent III, a diploma of Honorius III, and a grant from the Hungarian sovereign to Demeter of the Aba kindred, one of the officials of the newly crowned Coloman. The last two sources were issued long after the events (in 1222 and 1234), and neither reveal the location nor the date, but do confirm the fact of the enthronement.

The first royal letter sent to Innocent III is dated to 1214 and must have followed the Scepus Council. Andrew II intended to handle several items. First, he requested papal permission for Coloman to be crowned king of Galicia by Archbishop John of Esztergom (*filium nostrum* [...] *in regem inungat*).[1] The second letter[2] was meant to offer thanks for the received licence and formulated a petition for a golden crown for Coloman (*coronam auream Regie dignitati congruentem filio nostri conferre*). Furthermore, the Hungarian king promised to send a clergyman from Galicia to participate at the Fourth Lateran Council. The council started in November 1215, so the royal letter was probably written in August, at the very latest.

Regarding the coronation, while in the Kingdom of Hungary the reigning archbishop of Esztergom had the right to conduct the enthronement,[3] this privilege concerned solely the Hungarian kings and it did not require papal permission. The case of Coloman was different; it was a new phenomenon with no precedent, and therefore papal licence was essential. Innocent III's approval was intended to be secured using the formulation of a request that it was motivated by the local elite and people, who were eager to join the Roman Church (*Galiciae principes et populus, nostri ditioni subiecti humiliter a nobis postularunt*). The Scepus Agreement was not even mentioned in the first letter, whereas the second mentions a matrimonial contract (*contractum*) and asks for papal mediation to convince Leszek to send help for Coloman, who was under siege in the castle of Halych. It is significant that Andrew II also expressed gratitude for the papal approval of Coloman's coronation (*referentes gratiarum actiones, quod postulatio nostra super coronando*

---

1 *Codex diplomaticus Hungariae*, 3/1:163–64; *Regesta regum stirpis Arpadianae*, no. 294.

2 *Codex diplomaticus Arpadianus*, 6:374–75; *Regesta regum stirpis Arpadianae*, no. 302; Pauler, *A magyar nemzet története*, 2:496n55; Włodarski, *Polska i Rus*, 62.

3 The right of the archbishops of Esztergom during the coronation can be documented as early as the eleventh century. Archbishop Berthold of Kalocsa, brother of Queen Gertrude, tried but failed to extend the rights of the prelates of Kalocsa. The quarrel was ended by a charter of Pope Innocent III issued on May 9, 1209 (see László Koszta, *A kalocsai érseki tartomány kialakulása [The Formation of the Archdiocese of Kalocsa]*, Thesaurus historiae ecclesiasticae in Universitate Quinqueecclesiensi 2 (Pécs: Pécsi Történettudományért Kulturális Egyesület, 2013), 109–11; Kiss, *Királyi egyházak*, 46–47; Barabás, *Das Papsttum*, 295–99.

filio nostro in Regem Galicie ad mandatum Apostolicum optatum consecuta est effectum), and it was no longer an anointment with unction, as earlier, but in fact a coronation. The golden crown and letter that were requested were meant to help stabilize Coloman's rule in Galicia (*perpetuam stabilitatem pretendat*).[4] There is no record of the crown's delivery; but, a royal charter of 1234 states: *sepedictum filium nostrum optento ex indulgencia Sedis Apostolice dyademate, Illustrem Regem Gallicie feliciter inunctum fecissemus inclite coronari* ["We made our aforementioned son to be crowned with a diadem and successfully unctioned to be illustrious king of Galicia as the result of the Apostolic See's indulgence"].[5]

Despite the limited evidence, several theories have emerged on the date and location of the coronation.[6] It seems certain that the crown had been sent in advance by Innocent III, therefore the *terminus ante quem* is dated to July 16, 1216; whereas the *terminus post quem* was August 1215. In our opinion, it is reasonable to make a distinction between the acts of unction and coronation, as the Hungarian Gyula Pauler and Ubul Kállay had done over a century ago.[7] Using the extant charters we can reconstruct the following course of events: having gained the papal licence Archbishop John of Esztergom anointed and crowned Coloman in Hungary, and the prince left for Galicia only afterwards. The ritual of the unction was meant to express the power of God's grace on the sovereign, yet the crown was also necessary for the ceremony. Based on Andrew II's earlier difficulties, it was essential to demonstrate Coloman's royal status for the Galicians, and that is why he needed the requested golden crown. In our view, the coronation happened in late 1214 or early 1215 at the very latest, probably before the departure of the Hungarian army (we have no reason to doubt that the newly crowned king then joined the royal force from Hungary). The first ceremony—the unction and the coronation—must have taken place in Esztergom, the royal centre at that time; which would not have fulfilled the requirements if it were a Hungarian royal enthronement since it would have had to have taken place at Székesfehérvár, the sacral centre for the kingdom, fifty kilometres south-west of today's capital, Budapest. It is also assumed that Andrew II appointedd the future officials of the new king's royal court, though just one of them is known, Demeter of the Aba kindred, the master of the stewards (*dapiferum eidem instituentes* [...] *fecimus*).

The second coronation was probably a ceremony presented for the locals in Galicia itself. Andrew II, despite his request to the pope, received no help from his ally, Leszek the White, so he invaded Peremyshl (despite the Scepus Agreement) at the turn of 1215 and 1216. In our opinion, the second enthronement would have happened in relation to this move and took place in early 1216; it is even possible that Andrew II and Archbishop

---

4 *Codex diplomaticus Arpadianus*, 6:374–75, *Regesta regum stirpis Arpadianae*, no. 302.

5 *Codex diplomaticus Arpadianus*, 6:546, *Regesta regum stirpis Arpadianae*, no. 529.

6 Arguing for the year 1214: Ludwik Droba, "Stosunki Leszka Białego z Russią i Węgrami [The Relations of Leszek the White to the Rus' and the Hungarians]," *Rozprawy Akademii Umiejętności* 13 (1881): 361–429; arguing for 1215: Pashuto, *Vneshniaia politika*, 246; and on the first half of 1215: Włodarski, *Polska i Rus*; Chrzanowski, *Leszek Biały*, 72; and arguing for winter 1215 to spring 1216: Kállay, "Mikor koronázták meg Kálmánt"; and finally an argument for 1217: Pauler, *A magyar nemzet története*, 2:57.

7 Pauler, *A magyar nemzet története*, 2:57, 496n55; Kállay, "Mikor koronázták meg Kálmánt," 672–73.

John of Esztergom both also participated. A new wave of Polish–Hungarian conflicts started at this time with Andrew II's occupation of western Galicia, territory that had earlier been conceded to Leszek. If we are looking for the cause of the change, we have to look again at the Scepus Agreement. While both the Hungarian king and the prince of Kraków *de facto* ceased support of the sons of Roman, it could have been also required *de iure* in the agreement. Leszek went back on the deal when he handed over Vladimir Volynsky, one of the key—and at that time most prestigious—settlements in Volhynia, to Daniil and Vasilko. Leszek's action provided enough support to the Romanovich siblings for them to realize their Galician aspirations. This turn of events meant more enemies for Coloman. In our opinion, Andrew II was motivated by fear of a possible coalition of Peremyshl, Kraków, and Volhynia into occupying the western part of Galicia. By the first half of 1216 the Hungarian king and Coloman controlled the whole of Galician territory and must have possessed the crown too, so nothing would have prevented them holding a coronation in Halych, the only episcopal see in the area.[8] The ceremony served as a firm declaration of the Hungarian rule in Galicia.

While we agree with Pauler concerning the two coronations, we disagree with his chronology (1217). The dating by Ubul Kállay of the coronation in Hungary at the turn of 1215–16 does not work either. In most other publications, a single coronation is traditionally accepted, but in several cases the authors assume an earlier dating.[9]

Droba stated, based on the later account by Długosz, that Bishop Wincenty Kadłubek of Kraków was also present at the enthronement. We do not consider this version realistic; it seems unlikely that any prominent Polish figure, not even the bride, Salomea, attended Coloman's Galician coronation. The whole episode seems to be about initiating ideal circumstances for the union with the Roman Church, and the account in the *Voskresensk Chronicle* supports this reading: "the Hungarian king sent his son into Galicia, he expelled the bishop and the priests from the church and brought a Latin priest there."[10]

---

[8] The first mention of a bishop of Galicia dates from 1153. In Peremyshl a local bishop appeared first in 1220, and he came from Novgorod. See Ярослав Н. Щапов, *Государство и церьковь Древней Руси X–XIII вв. [State and Church of Old Rus' in the Tenth to Thirteenth Centuries]* (Москва: Наука, 1989), 212.

[9] For instance, Nataša Procházková ("Postavenie haličského kráľa," 67) and Ђura Hardi (Ђура Харди, *Наследници Киева. Између краљевске круне и татарског јарма [Successors of Kiev: Between the Royal Crown and Tartar Yoke]*, Monographs 41 (Нови Сад: Филозофски факултет у Еовом Саду, Катедра за историју 2002), 138) opted for the dating of Ubul Kállay, and Mikola Kotliar (Котляр, *Данило Галицький*, 106) only presented the year (1215); Marek Chrzanowski (*Leszek Biały*, 72) and Witalii Nagirnyj (*Polityka zagraniczna księstw tiem Halickiej i Wołyńskiej*, 172) dated the coronation to the first half of 1215; Martin Homza ("Včasnostredoveké dejiny Spiša," 1:147) emphasized the role of the archbishop of Esztergom; meanwhile Karol Hollý referred only to the fact that the coronation is indisputable: : Karol Hollý, "Kňažná Salomea a uhorsko-poľské vzťahy v rokoch 1214–1241 [Princess Salomea and Hungarian – Polish Relations in the Period 1214–1241]," *Historický Časopis* 53 (2005): 3–28, 14–15. See further Gábor Barabás, "Coloman of Galicia and his Polish Relations. The Duke of Slavonia as the Protector of Widowed Duchesses," in *Hungaro-Polonica. Young Scholars on Medieval Polish-Hungarian Relations*, ed. Dániel Bagi et al. (Pécs: Történészcéh Egyesület, 2016), 89–117 at 92–94.

[10] *Ioannis Dlugossii Annales seu Cronicae*, 6:204; Droba, "Stosunki Leszka Białego," 400–18 (full citation just above); PSRL, 7:119.

Despite his royal title, Coloman remained under the authority of Andrew II, and not only because of his minor age. The Hungarian king still and continuously considered himself to be the *real* sovereign of Galicia and Volhynia, as the royal chancery demonstrates, since with this title constantly employed in the royal charters, even after the coronation of Coloman.[11]

Queen Salomea

We know little about Coloman's wife, Salomea; even her date of birth is ambiguous, and the years 1211–12 are only hypothetical and based on her hagiographical legend, according to which she was three years old when she arrived in Hungary. These dates imply that Salomea was sent to Andrew II's court right after, or not much later, than the Scepus Council, yet there is no evidence to support this assumption. The end of Salomea's life is better known, since both her legend and various Polish chronicles give the exact day of her death: November 10, 1268. Unfortunately, her age is not revealed then.[12]

Polish chronicles from the thirteenth century mention the names of Salomea's parents (Leszek and Grzymisława) and record the cult of Blessed Salomea, yet the Scepus Council and the marriage of the princess are not mentioned. In the Polish context she became relevant only after she returned home after the death of her husband and introduced the Poor Clare order to Poland. She not only joined the order but also gave donations to their nunneries in Sandomierz and Skała.[13] She is illustrated in her legend—following hagiographical norms—as a person destined from her childhood to be a nun; she was wed to Coloman only because of the insistence and the threat of the Hungarian king. The marriage had a positive effect in the eyes of the legend's author: Salomea contributed to the marriage of her younger brother, Bolesław V "the Chaste," to King Béla IV's daughter, princess Kinga—later Saint Kinga of Poland—and as a result the latter saint moved to Kraków.[14]

Salomea became very "valuable" in the light of the new Polish–Hungarian pact of 1214. By custom, engaged girls were often sent to the court of their future family after treaties had been sealed, so the same may have happened to Salomea. But marriages traditionally took place only after the parties reached maturity; around the ages of fourteen

---

[11] Barabás, "The Titles of the Hungarian Royal Family," 30–33.

[12] *Piastowie. Leksykon biograficzny*, 189–91 (entry by Andrzej Marzec) (full citation above); *Vita et miracula sanctae Salomeae*, in *Monumenta Poloniae Historica*, 4:776–96; According to her legend, she died on the vigil of St. Martin (November 10), but certain chronicles (for instance, the *Chronica Poloniae maioris* and the *Chronica principum Poloniae*) state November 17. Based on a close reading of the sources, November 10 seems genuine (see Kürbisówna, "Żywot bł. Salomei," 238).

[13] *Monumenta Poloniae Vaticana*, vol. 3, (*1202–1366*), ed. Joannes Ptaśnik (Cracoviae: Academia Litterarum Cracoviensis, 1914), 38, no. 71; *Monumenta Poloniae Historica*, 4:784; *Kodeks dyplomatyczny Małopolski*, ed. Franciszek Piekosiński, 4 vols. (Kraków: Akademia Umiejętności, 1876–1905), 1:90–93, nos. 75–76.

[14] On the marriage of Coloman and Salomea: *Monumenta Poloniae Historica*, 4:777. Further on Kinga, see: *Vita et miracula sancti Kyngae*, in the *Monumenta Poloniae Historica*, 4:682–774. Kinga was canonized by Pope John Paul II in 1998.

to sixteen. Coloman's and Salomea's engagement was primarily a diplomatic arrangement, as happened to Coloman's sister, Elizabeth of Thuringia, or later to the aforementioned royal princess, Kinga. It would have been normal practice were Salomea to have been sent to Hungary as early as 1214, but we should remember that Salomea's father, Leszek the White, was resistant to fulfil the requirements of the Scepus Agreement. So, on balance, she may not been sent to Hungary in 1214.

The legend of Salomea states that their reign lasted twenty-five years in Galicia. This is clearly wrong, but if we it was her marriage that lasted twenty-five years, it gives us 1217 as a date of Salomea's arrival to Hungary, working backwards from Coloman's death in 1241. If the twenty-five years were to refer to the princess's stay in Hungary, then given the time of her return to Poland in 1245, we get 1220. On this flimsy evidence, we might date Salomea's arrival in Coloman's court between 1217 and 1220. Certain Polish and Ukrainian authors state 1218 or 1219,[15] in our opinion, the Hungarian–Polish campaign in the fall of 1219 gave the perfect opportunity for Salomea's arrival, with her being sent direct from Kraków to Galicia, not to Hungary.

Coloman, being a child was not in control of events in Galicia, nor was his young wife. Their adult life started in Hungary only after they were released from captivity (1221/22), and their marriage might have taken place at this time. Salomea is called *regina* (queen) in her biography, which is why historians have asked where and when was she crowned? Evidence for this event is based on the chronicle of Długosz, but not all of his statements are authentic (for instance, he wrote about Leszek's and Grzymisława's marriage in 1220).[16] The term *regina* in the legend and in later Polish chronicles does not necessarily mean that she was indeed crowned but may simply refer to her marital status to King Coloman. Whether or not Salomea was in fact crowned is probably irrelevant, as Karol Hollý argued.[17] She was not the queen of the Hungarian Kingdom, nor bound by the customs of the realm; nor were there any complicated Hungarian royal regulations to fulfil for a queen, as we saw had been the case with Coloman. A single charter of Pope Gregory IX refers to Salomea as the wife of King Coloman (*uxor Colomani regis*).[18] Summarizing the evidence, the coronation of Salomea is plausible.[19] Only one particular point of time leaps out as more than a possibility: her assumed arrival in Galicia in the fall of 1219; yet the constant wars do not seem to support this theory. The coronation was—in our view—no longer needed after they settled down in Hungary after being released from captivity.

---

15 Włodarski, "Salomea królowa Halicka," 70; Niezgoda, "Między historią, tradycją i legendą," 237; Nagirnyj, *Polityka zagraniczna księstw tiem Halickiej i Wołyńskiej*, 178; Dąbrowski, *Daniel Romanowicz, biografia polityczna*, 102.

16 *Ioannis Dlugossii Annales seu Cronicae*, 6:204, 6:231–32.

17 Włodarski, "Salomea królowa Halicka," 71; Niezgoda, "Między historią, tradycją i legendą," 241; Barabás, *Das Papsttum*, 301–2; Hollý, "Kňažná Salomea", 14–15.

18 *Codex diplomaticus regni Croatiae*, 3:360; "*Salomee regine, uxori Colomanni regis, nati [...] illustris regi Ungarie, salutem*," in *Registres de Grégoire IX*, no. 2126.

19 Font, *Árpád-házi királyok*, 212.

Salomea's years in Hungary remain completely obscure; and maybe that was the intention of the author of her legend. She would have been a constant member of the royal court, and she might have had some positive role in the good relationship between Béla and Coloman. This is a hypothetical background to the aforementioned engagement of Béla's daughter, Kinga, and Bolesław V, Salomea's brother, in 1239.[20]

The Royal Court in Galicia

Despite his title *rex Galiciae* (king of Galicia), Prince Coloman was only able to lay claim to a part of Galicia, as the western segment belonged to Leszek, according to the Scepus Agreement. The land promised to Leszek lies in the watershed area of the north-bound river Vistula, whereas the other rivers of Galicia are running south towards the Dniester. Their valleys were densely populated, yet archaeological excavations have not focus on this area, and not even the princely residences have been properly examined.[21] Of the main settlements, Peremyshl is located on the bank of the river San, which flows into the Vistula above Sandomierz. Sanok, a smaller settlement in western Galicia, lay on the upper San, while Iaroslavl is located south from Peremyshl. The other key settlement claimed by Leszek, Liubachev, lies next to the route between Belz in Volhynia, near the source of the river Bug, and Iaroslavl.

The most significant settlement in the territory ruled by the Hungarians was Halych, located on the right (or west) bank of the Dniester near the rivers Limnica and Lukva on about sixty square kilometres. The stronghold stood near the mouth of the Lukva on a hill, and it controlled the Dniester. On the other side of the hill a stream gave some natural defence, and on the western and north-eastern side it ended in a slope. From the south the castle was protected by a moat; the road went around it and reached the gate on the south-eastern side of the hill. The residential tower was built at the turn of the thirteenth century, and several watchtowers served to control the road. Today only a part of the residential building remains, and its layers have not been examined with contemporary methods of archaeological building research ("Bauforschung"). Today's reconstruction depicts the fourteenth-century version of the building instead. Archaeologist Zenoviy Fedunkiv believes the stronghold to be the residence of Boyar Sudislav; while Bohdan Tomenchuk calls it "the Hungarian court" and associates it with Prince Andrew. Written sources support neither theory.[22]

---

20 *Vita et miracula sancti Kyngae*, in *Monumenta Poloniae Historica*, 4:685.

21 See Богдан Томенчук, *Археологія городищ Галицької землі. Галицько-Буковинське Прикарпаття. Матерали досліджень 1976–2006* [*The Archaeology of Settlements in Galicia: The Carpathian Region of Galicia and Bukovina*] (Івано-Франківськ: Прикарпатський національний університет ім. В. Стефаника, 2008); Михайло Фіголь, *Мистецтво стародавнього Галича* [*The Art of Old Halych*] (Київ: Мистецтво, 1997).

22 For the excavations in the centre of Halych in 1976–2006 see Томенчук, *Археологія городищ Галицької землі*. For the process of the constructions on the castle hill see: Fedunkiv, "Galickyj zamok," 45; Томенчук, *Археологія городищ Галицької землі*, 536; Богдан Томенчук, "Давній Галич у новітніх досягненнях Галицької археологчної експедиції" [Old Galicia in Recent Results of Galician Archeological Expeditions], in *Галич. вып. 1*, ed. Мирослав Волощук, (Івано-Франківськ: Лілея НВ, 2016), 11–34 at 17.

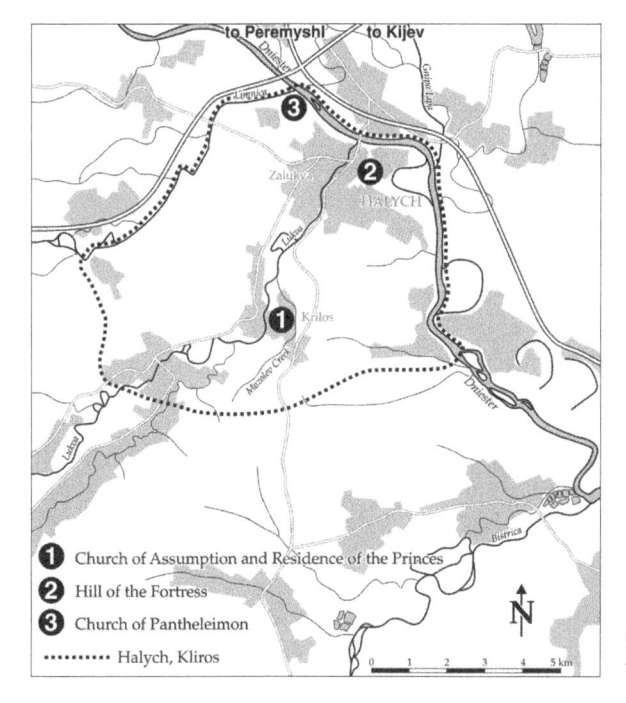

Map 5. Halych, the Centre of the Galician Principality.

① Church of Assumption and Residence of the Princes
② Hill of the Fortress
③ Church of Pantheleimon
·········· Halych, Kliros

The existence of several residential sites is assumed in Ukrainian research. The residence of Prince Vladimirko Volodarevich (1141–53), who established the site of Halych, might have been near to the church of the Pantheleimon ("Almighty") which is dated to the mid-twelfth century, as the burial chapel's wall remains reveal. The church was probably built at the turn of the twelfth to thirteenth centuries by the Galician–Volhynian prince, Roman Mstislavich (1199–1205). The Pantheleimon patronage of the church leads us to Roman's grandfather, Kievan Grand Prince Iziaslav Mstislavich (1146–54). The enormous church at the crossing of the Lukva and Mozolev streams, mentioned in chronicles, is considered to be the cathedral of the Dormition or Assumption of Mary into Heaven (*Uspenskii sobor*). The remains of a building next to it are thought to be the residence of Vladimirko's son, Prince Iaroslav Osmomysl (1153–87).[23]

Coloman's royal residence can be located in this latter area.[24] The *GVC* talks about where the prince was living: "Filja [...] left Coloman in Galicia where he had fortified the Church of Our Lady, the Blessed Virgin Mary."[25] Długosz's statement is almost identical:

---

[23] Богдан Томенчук and Олег Мельничук, "Собор Успіння Пресвятої Богородиці та заснування Галицького єпископства [The Church of the Assumption of Mary and the Foundation of the Galician Bishopric]," in *"Слово о полку Ігоревім" та його доба*, ed. Любов Бойко, и інни (Галич: Національний заповідник «Давній Галич», 2007), 167–71 at 169–70.

[24] Володимир Дідук and Руслана Мацалак, "Пам'ятки Крилоської гори [The Memories on the Church-Hill]," *Пам'ятки України* 189, no. 6 (2013): 4–11 at 7.

[25] PSRL, 2:737; *Kronika halicko-wołyńska*, 75–80; translated in the *The Galician–Volhynian Chronicle*, 27.

"The Hungarians and the Poles first fortified the castle of Halych—as they could—after they went to war in unity against the Ruthenians, then they did the same with the church of Holy Mary in the castle, and it served as a second stronghold."[26] Coloman's court can be located within the defensive ramparts on a field of fifty hectares. The fortified monarchical site "*detinets*" (*детинец*) was located on the plateau above a seventy-metre-high cliff. The excavations of 1998 to 2007 revealed the three-cusped fortifications between the Lukva and the Mozolev, as well as other ramparts suited to this natural environment.

The oldest part of the hill is traditionally called the Golden Lawn (*Zolotoi Tik*), the church of the Dormition being built on its south side, with its foundations still visible. The residence of the prince could not have been too far away. During the excavations in 1998 west of the church a pillar was found, which might have been the base of a wooden structure. The presumed building was identified as the residence of the prince, recorded in chronicles from the 1140s.[27] The importance of the twelfth-century church is clearly shown by the title "sobor" (*собор*).[28] The seat of the bishopric established in the second half of the twelfth century must have been there too. Churches were built usually by the residence of the prince, also monasteries can be located next to some of them. The excavations unearthed the foundations to the basilica of the Resurrection (*Voskresenie*) and the church of the Annunciation (*Blagoveshchenie*).

The church of Pantheleimon (the Almighty) stood to the west of the residence on the hill above the Limnica, and several structural elements suggest Hungarian architectural influence.[29] The church's structure fundamentally reflects local traditions, yet the southern and western gates indicate Hungarian influence.

The residential tower of the royal palace and its counterpart in Esztergom can be characterized with friezes constructed with curved palmette motifs, a common design around Pécs. The rose window of the castle-chapel of Esztergom, the western gate of Halych, probably constructed under the reign of Coloman, and the southern gate of the cathedral of Gyulafehérvár (Alba Iulia) all bear these characteristics.[30] Hungar-

---

26 *Ioannis Dlugossii Annales seu Cronicae*, 6:206 (my translation).

27 Томенчук, *Археологія городищ Галицької землі*, 504–31; Юрій Лукомський and Василь Петрик, "Нові матеріали до відтворення елементів містобудівельної структури Галича XI–XIII ст. [New Material for the Architectural Structure of the Settlements of Galicia in the Eleventh to Thirteenth Centuries], in *До 800-річчя з дня народження Данила Галицького*, ed. Ярослав Ісаєвич (Львів: Інститут Українознавства, 2001), 166–82 at 178–79.

28 The word *sobor* derives from the verb *sobirat(sia)* and means "to gather." Ecclesiastical councils were called *sobor* as well, and the meaning was later applied to (major) churches where synods were held; in addition, large churches could also be called a *sobor*. See Márta Font, *Oroszország, Ukrajna, Rusz [Russia, Ukraine, and the Rus']* (Budapest: Balassi, 1998), 93.

29 Олег М. Иоаннисян, "Польско-русская и венгерско-русская границы в XI–XIII веках и их отображение в развитии средневековой архитектуры [The Polish–Russian and Hungaro-Russian Borders in the Eleventh to Thirteenth Centuries and their Role in Medieval Architecture]," in *Początki Sąsiedztwa. Pogranicze etniczne polsko--rusko–słowackie w średniowieczu*, ed. Michał Parczewski (Rzeszów: Muzeum Okręgowe w Rzeszowie / Instytut Archeologii Uniwersytetu Jagiellońskiego w Krakowie, 1996), 157–182 at 172–75.

30 Marosi, *A romanika Magyarországon*, 51.

Map 6. The Church of the Assumption and its Surroundings.

ian influence have long been identified by the Hungarian and Polish art historians, and the parallel between the "princely gate" of Gyulafehérvár and the western and southern gates of the church of Pantheleimon have been described and emphasized by Ernő Marosi.[31] The changes to the church at the start of the thirteenth century, originally built in local style, probably did not require much time, and one single stonemason could have done the necessary work. The fortifications prior to the campaign of 1221 prove that major constructions could have been managed between military campaigns. The construction of the new, ornamental gate intended to create the right image for Coloman's coronation with the crown sent by the pope, while emphasizing the relationship to the Roman Church.

---

[31] József Peleński, *Halicz w dziejach sztuki średniowiecznej. Na postawie badań archeologicznych i źródel archiwarnych* [Halych in the History of Medieval Art. Based on Archeological Reseach and Written Sources] (Kraków: Akademia Umiejętności, 1914); Sándor Tóth, "A gyulafehérvári fejedelmi kapu jelentősége [The Significance of the Princely Gate in Alba Iulia]," *Építés-Építészettudomány* 15 (1983): 391–428; Marosi, *Die Anfänge der Gotik in Ungarn*; Фіголь, *Мистецтво стародавнього Галича*, 16–20, 79. Krisztina Havasi, "Román kori emlék Európa peremén. A halicsi Szent Pantaleon-templom és a magyarországi művészet [Romanesque Remain on the Border of Europe. The Pantheleimon-Church of Halych and Hungarian Art]," In *Művészettörténeti tanulmányok Tóth Sándor emlékére*, ed. Imre Takács (Budapest: Martin Opitz Kiadó, 2019) 43–64. (Thesaurus mediaevalis) at 52–58.

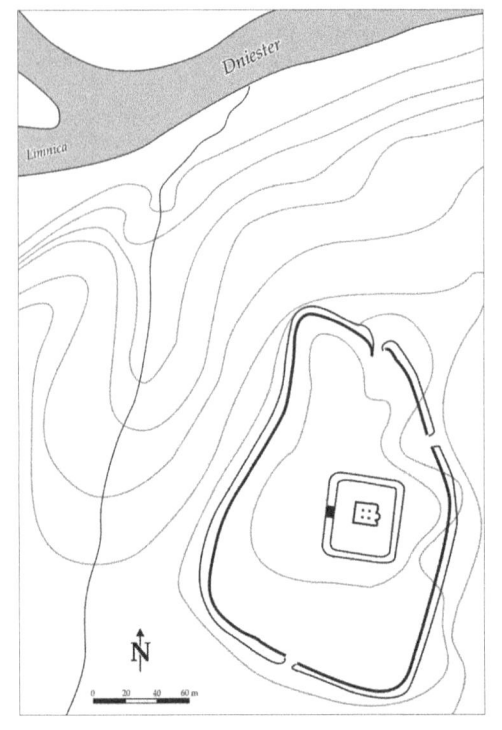

Map 7. The Hill of the Church of Panthaleimon.

Figure 2. The Church of Pantheleimon (with kind permission of Myroslav Voloshchuk) (IMG_6771).

Figure 3. The Western Gate of the Church of Pantheleimon (with kind permission of Myroslav Voloshchuk) (IMG_0741).

Figure 4. The Southern or "Princely" Gate of the Cathedral of Gyulafehérvár (Alba Iulia) (with kind permission of Ernő Marosi) (Gyulafehérvár_MarosiErnő).

Chapter 4

THE HUNGARIAN ELITE AND COLOMAN'S COURT

THE SONS OF the royal family had the right to bear the princely title (*dux*) and to possess the necessary estates to supply their needs. These lands were, like the queens', scattered around the realm. Courts were organized around the princes, following the kings' examples, despite their age. The coronation of minor-age heirs happened as early as the eleventh century,[1] even though they may not be given a territory to rule over, or the kingdom could be divided. Andrew II was forced against his will to allow the coronation of his first-born, the eight-year-old Béla ([...] *omnes conspiratores, et infidelitatis machinatores* [...] *filium nostrum* **nobis viventibus et nolentibus** *in regem sibi praeficere, vel coronare attentauerint* / [...] all conspirators and unfaithful machinators [...] tempted our son to get on the top of the realm or to be crowned **despite our objection**).[2] Nevertheless, Prince Béla had no actual power in the government of the realm until he reached adulthood in 1220, and this was also the case in Galicia for Coloman. Coronation and an active role in the government were independent from each other, and every decision remained in the king's gift.[3]

The court established in Halych after Coloman's coronation consisted of local and Hungarian noblemen. They were entrusted by the Hungarian king, and furthermore, the officials of the queenly court were appointed by him too.[4] A few members of Coloman's court are known to us since they also supported him later in Slavonia. One of them was Demeter of the Aba kindred, the master of the stewards of Coloman (1216–40). He was count of Bodrog between 1235 and 1240, and still alive in 1247, but his other offices are unknown.[5] The *GVC* confirms his presence in Galicia at Coloman's side once before their captivity when File led the Hungarian army to Volhynia. After his departure, Coloman remained in Galicia with a smaller group in his court, and they are even named: "Ivan, Lekin, and Dmitr."[6] We agree with Antal Hodinka, who identified Dmitr with Demeter, yet the other two names refer to just one individual, in our opinion: Ivan Lenkin. It is entirely hypothetical, but it could refer to Ivakhin (Iwachin), count of Szeben (Sibiu).[7] Uz, someone with such a rare name, shot in the eye in battle, is perhaps the same person

---

1 For the princely court see Zsoldos, *Az Árpádok és alattvalóik*, 77; Zsoldos, "Hercegek és hercegnők," 12–19. For Solomon's coronation in 1058 see *Scriptores rerum Hungaricarum*, 1:353.

2 *Codex diplomaticus Hungariae*, 3/1:164 (my emphasis).

3 Zsoldos, *Az Árpádok és alattvalóik*, 79.

4 Zsoldos, *Az Árpádok és asszonyaik*, 179.

5 *Codex diplomaticus Arpadianus*, 6:545; Zsoldos, *Magyarország világi archontológiája*, 71, 294.

6 PSRL, 2:737; *Kronika halicko-wołyńska*, 78–79; Hodinka, *Az orosz évkönyvek*, 344–45.

7 He has been identified (Jusupović, *Elity ziemi Halickiej i Wolyńskiej*, 250) as a Hungarian captain but he was not the focus of the research. Font, *Árpád-házi királyok*, 110, 114; Zsoldos, *Magyarország világi archontológiája*, 204, 312.

as the *bowl bearer* ("tálhordó") count from 1219;[8] his death might explain why he was never mentioned again. According to the text of *GVC* in Hlebnikov's Codex a certain Bot was to be found around Coloman, and the editors of the text identify him as Both, *comes* of Érsomlyó. The person in question, however, was not a *ban*, as the editors state, but an ispán (*comes*), and he appears only one single time in the sources in the mid-thirteenth century, so he was perhaps never present in Galicia. It is far more likely that the text refers to Palatine Pat, the *comes* of Moson at that time and who had been in Galicia (Halych).[9]

Another known member of Coloman's court was File, later master of the queen's stewards (1231–32) and count of Sopron (1237–40). He was referred to as *ban* in a charter issued for his sons in 1250, yet the time span is ambiguous. Długosz thought him to be the palatine (*palatinus*), and this mistake has been regurgitated by many historians.[10] The *GVC* states that he was the leader of the Hungarian army in 1221, when Coloman and Salomea were captured after Mstislav had seized Halych. File's troops abandoned the town's defence and left to fight Leszek in Volhynia. File was eventually attacked and defeated by Mstislav "on the vigil of Mother Mary's festivity."[11] File was probably the leader of the royal army, which arrived in 1219, and the last known Hungarian force before 1221. File must have returned to Hungary alongside Coloman and Salomea after they were released from their captivity. There is no further data regarding File's activity, not even under Prince Andrew's rule in Galicia, yet it cannot be excluded that he received a new position there, since the sources show him in Galicia again in 1245, killed in the battle of Iaroslavl.[12]

Among the members of Coloman's court we might expect to find people who had participated before 1214 in Andrew II's campaigns. Most of the key members took part in the campaign of September 1211, and Andrew II himself was present there.[13] The

---

8 Zsoldos, *Magyarország világi archontológiája*, 356.

9 *Kronika halicko–wołyńska*, 79n265. For support for our view see: Zsoldos, *Magyarország világi archontológiája*, 169, 343; Márta Font, "A halicsi magyar uralmat támogató elit [The Elite Supporters of Hungarian Rule in Galicia]," *Világtörténet* 7 (39) (2017): 33–52 at 38.

10 Zsoldos, *Magyarország világi archontológiája*, 302; the incorrect date derives from *Ioannis Dlugossii Annales seu Cronicae*, 6:206; for its survival in historiography see, for instance, Bartnicki, *Polityka zagraniczna księgcia*, 47.

11 PSRL, 2:737–38; *Kronika halicko–wołyńska*, 79. Mstislav's victory is dated to the vigil of a feast of Mary. Four Marian festivals belong to the so-called "twelve festivals" (*dvunadesiatie prazniki*): the Annunciation (*Blagoveshchenie*, March 25), the Assumption (*Uspenie*, August 15), her Nativity (*Rozhdestvo Bogorodicy*, September 8), and the Presentation (*Vvedenie v hram Bogorodicy*, November 21). Mstislav's victory and Coloman's captivity was previously dated to August 14 or September 7 (Font, *Árpád-házi királyok*, 213). Recently, Dariusz Dąbrowski and Mariusz Bartnicki argued for March 24 based on the sequence of the military events (Dąbrowski, *Daniel Romanowicz, biografia polityczna*, 106; Bartnicki, *Polityka zagraniczna księgcia*, 47–48). We still prefer August based on the fortification after the Hungarian army's victory in the winter of 1221–22, since it required several months. Based on the sources, we also know that the people in the stronghold lacked water, were probably suffering from thirst, and this forced them to surrender.

12 Font, *Árpád-házi királyok*, 212–13, 248.

13 PSRL, 2:724; *Kronika halicko–wołyńska*, 54; Font, *Árpád-házi királyok*, 228–29; For September 1211 see Hrushevsky, "Khronologia podij," 10–11; Pashuto, *Ocherki po istorii*, 197; Włodarski, on

sovereign gave the military leadership to Palatine Poth (Pat) from the Győr kindred (1209–12), but the chronicles list seven other officials alongside him. Peter, son of Turoy (Töre), was the count of Bács between 1210 and 1212; Banko (Bánk, possibly from the Bárkalán kindred) was count of the queen's court (1210–12) and count of Bihar at the same time (1209–12); Mica (Mika) "the Bearded" (*Mica barbatus, Mika brodatyj*) held no office in 1211, and his career must have started later since he succeeded Bánk as count of Bihar by 1212. The *GVC* also mentions Lotard from the Gutkeled kindred, who later became count of Szabolcs (1213); a count in the court, Marcel (1211–12); and Tiborc, count of Nyitra (1211). The name Mokyanus (Makján) appears only at the end of the thirteenth century and the statement may be referring to one of his ancestors.[14] Despite the relatively long list, not every one of these men held an office in Coloman's court. For instance, the latest evidence on Palatine Pat derives from 1214–15, when he was count of Moson; he probably died not long afterwards. The same can be stated regarding Marcel, as he disappears from the sources after 1214. In the case of Mokyanus and Lotard we have no evidence so might make the same assumption. Peter, son of Turoy, was one of the assassins of Queen Gertrude in 1213, for which crime he was impaled by the king. Bánk held no offices between 1213 and 1217, and this hiatus is quite odd, since from 1199 onwards he had constantly filled important posts. His role in the queen's assassination was disproved by Tamás Körmendi,[15] as Bánk held key offices between 1217 and 1222 (*ban* of Slavonia (1217), court count and count of Fejér (1221–22), Bodrog, and Újvár (1222)). The assumed roles of the counts of Újvár, Szabolcs, and Bihar in Galicia are based simply on geographical considerations. Bánk might have had a role in Coloman's release from his captivity based on his experiences from previous duties. So, it would appear that people who had been leaders in military campaigns in Galicia before his coronation, generally did not seem to have played any role in Coloman's court.

During his minority, for a short while, Benedict, nicknamed "the Bald" (*lisyi*) in the *GVC*, became the real leader of Galicia. He has been identified as Benedict, son of Korlat, by Pashuto and Hrushevsky. We agree with Włodarski, who emphasized that there are many Benedicts in the period and so any identification is premature. The *GVC* says little beside his name, yet he is described with certain repulsion and compared to the Antichrist. In Hungarian charters there is no Benedict to find with the attribute *calvus* (bald). With no definitive evidence, we conclude it is prudent not to equate Benedict, son of Korlat with some Benedict the Bald.[16]

---

the contrary, believes the date to be September 1210, since he dates Benedict's activity in Galicia to 1208. See Włodarski, *Polska i Rus*.

14 Zsoldos, *Magyarország világi archontológiája*, 286–87 (Bánk), 323 (Lotard), 326 (Mokyanus, Marcell), 332 (Mika), 343 (Pat, Peter).

15 Tamás Körmendi, "A Gertrúd királyné elleni merénylet körülményei [Circumstances of the Assassination of Queen Gertrude]," in *Egy történelmi gyilkosság margójára. Merániai Gertrúd emlékezete, 1213–2013*, ed. Judit Majorossy (Szentendre: Ferenczy Múzeum, 2014), 95–124 at 107–8 (Peter, son of Turoy), 112–15 (Bánk). See also Zsoldos, *Magyarország világi archontológiája*, 286–87.

16 For Benedict "the Bald" see PSRL, 2:732; Hrushevsky, *Istorija Ukrainy–Rusi*, 3:31; Pashuto,

In Hungary, thanks to Pauler's research, it is generally held about a Benedict who was active in Galicia around 1208 that he was the son of Korlat from the Bor kindred, and *voivode* of Transylvania (1205–06, 1208–09), and he it was who took over the reins of government in Galicia. The campaign of Benedict, son of Korlat, is dated to 1210 by Pashuto and Lammich (drawing on Hrushevsky's work), and to 1209 by Włodarski.[17] It is certain that Benedict's rule was not popular, nor was the forcing of the ecclesiastical union; a papal letter from 1207 refers to the endeavour.[18] It is no surprise that the unpopular Benedict was called "Antichrist" in some chronicles, and opposition to him led to him being expelled in the first half of 1211. It is interesting that he was called *dux* (prince) in a charter from 1221,[19] probably because of his high status in Galicia. It is difficult to reconcile Benedict's life: at one level an exile in 1209 and then again someone with a big role in Galicia, while his *dux* title is also questionable, since he did not belong to the ruling dynasty.

Recently, Toru Senga tried to distinguish and identify the two Benedicts; his task was not particularly easy because of old errors and misunderstandings in the—particularly Slavic—historiography.[20] He found the original source of the mistake in the work of Sergei M. Soloviov (1820–79) on the history of Russia. Soloviov based his assumption on a German work by Christian Engel (1770–1814). So, an erroneous statement from 1813 has transmitted itself into the latest Russian, Ukrainian, Serbian, and Polish publications. Senga went instead to the biographies of Attila Zsoldos: he explained the disappearance after 1209 of Benedict, son of Korlat, *voivode* of Transylvania (1202–06, 1208–09), with the idea that he participated in the plot against Andrew II, so he was expelled by the king, as stated in the 1221. Zsoldos thinks Count Benedict of Sopron (1206–08) was

---

Ocherki po istorii, 200; Włodarski, *Polska i Rus*, 65n25; Angelika Herucová, "Palatine then Antichrist. Benedict in the Chronicle of Galicia-Volhynia," in *Rus' and Central Europe from the Eleventh to the Fourteenth Century. Publication after the 5*th *International Conference, Spišská kapitula, 16–18*th *October, 2014*, ed. Vitaliy Nagirnyy and Adam Mesiarkin, Colloquia Russica ser. 1, 5 (Kraków: Jagiellonian University, 2015), 117–27. An earlier summary regarding information on Benedict is offered by Font, *Árpád-házi királyok*, 206.

17 PSRL, 7:116; Pauler, *A magyar nemzet története*, 2:50; Hrushevsky, "Khronologia podij," 10–11; Pashuto, *Ocherki po istorii*, 196; Pashuto, *Vneshniaia politika*, 243; Lammich, *Fürstenbiographien des 13. Jahrhunderts in den Russischen Chroniken*, 7–12; Włodarski, *Polska i Rus*, 42.

18 *Documenta Pontificum Romanorum historiam Ucrainae illustrantia*, 12. For the activity of Gregorius de Crescentio in Hungary see Barabás, *Das Papsttum*, 42–43.

19 *Codex diplomaticus Hungariae*, 3/1:316.

20 Let me recap some recurrent errors. Use of the term "Benedikt Bor" is incorrect because no one with this name existed in early-thirteenth-century Hungary. Others do not know the kindred of Bárkalán and explain it with the form "Bor" from the Hungarian word "bor" (wine) (Леонтій Войтович, *Галицько-Волинські етюди [Galician-Volhynian Studies]* (Біла Церква: Пшонківський, 2011), 236–37). Some authors confuse Benedict with Palatine Pat (Poth) (Головко, *Корона Данила Галицького*, 266) by missing the distinction between the Hungarian office of *voivode* ("vajda") and the Slavic "vojevoda." Unfortunately such errors are embedded now in the source editions and scholarly research. See the correction: Toru Senga, "'Benedikt Bor', Benedek és Bankó Halicsban 1210 körül ['Benedict Bor': Benedict and Bankó in Galicia around 1210]," *Magyar Nyelv* 112 (2016): 32–49, 183–206 at 34.

another individual; it was the son of Korlat—according to him—who was governor of Galicia. Klatý thinks that the contradiction could be explained by Benedict receiving a royal pardon and that is how he came to be in Galicia in late 1210. No evidence supports this assertion, so we tend to agree with Senga that the "Antichrist–Benedict" cannot be Benedict, son of Korlát. Nevertheless, his *dux* title is hard to justify this way, although Senga tried to explain it with the help of his marriage. Senga's main conclusion seems reasonable, that Benedict, son of Korlát, and the "Antichrist–Benedict" are not one person. He believes that this "Antichrist–Benedict" who otherwise has no nickname and the "bald" Benedict might be one person, someone whose career started with Andrew II's enthronement in 1205. He first became count of Bodrog (1205), then later count of Sopron (1206–1208), and then Újvár (1209). He held no office in Hungary between 1209 and 1214, this hiatus making his stay in Galicia in 1210–11 plausible, just like his activity as count of Ung in 1214. Senga presumes, furthermore, that this Benedict tried in 1212–14 to prepare his return to Galicia after the Scepus Agreement by presenting himself as a seasoned expert in local affairs within the entourage of the young Coloman,[21] and this led him to being a member of the new royal court as well.[22]

Długosz merely stated that Coloman's court contained several men, but he did not know any names. The royal charter regarding Andrew II's donation to Demeter from the Aba kindred does give information on Demeter's relatives; some of them were captured alongside Coloman, whilst Demeter's siblings, Mikola and Ladislaus, were also injured. Demeter's half-brother, Aba, and relatives from his mother side, Thomas and John, sons of John, Juda, son of Otto, Matthias, son of Vid, and Mojs, son of Pexa, also participated in these conflicts. They held no offices, yet they did represent the Hungarian army in Galicia.

Coloman's Circle of Supporters in Galicia

Andrew II was probably motivated by his personal experiences back in 1188–89 when he contacted the princes of Galicia from 1205 for their support in recognizing Hungarian rule. The communication with Prince Vsevolod of Vladimir–Suzdal (1178–1212) happened via his son, Iaroslav Vsevolodich, who controlled Pereiaslavl Russkiy between 1201 and 1208.[23] The balance of power had by then changed in the Rus', and the local branches of the dynasty had grown stronger; with the grand prince of Vladimir–Suzdal having no influence over them anymore. The *boyars* gained power especially in the western and south-western parts of the Rus', and they as the elite played increasingly important roles in underpinning the power of the prince.

The *GVC* reveals the names of several *boyars*, yet the courses of their lives and motives are unclear, especially when drawn from a single narrative source, and some names are

---

21 Senga, "'Benedikt Bor'," 48.

22 Zsoldos, *Magyarország világi archontológiája*, 288; Hodinka, *Az orosz évkönyvek*, 312–13; Marek Klatý, "Vojvoda Benedikt v kontexte uhorsko-haličkých vzťahov prvej tretiny XIII. storočia [Voivode Benedikt in the Context of Hungarian-Galician Relations in the First Third of the Thirteenth Century]," *Medea* 2 (1998): 76–90 at 82–86; Senga, "'Benedikt Bor'," 48–49.

23 Rapov, *Kniazheskie vladeniia*, 170; Pashuto, *Ocherki po istorii*, 194.

mentioned merely once. In the *GVC* there are thirty of these people, and fourteen other names are mentioned just twice. In twenty-one cases the chronicler gave the patronymic (*otchestvo*) too, which helps reconstruct the kinships. Three *boyar* clans played leading roles—the Arbuzovichs, Molibogovichs, and the Kormilichichs—but no individuals are named. Sometimes names are known, whilst the family ties between others can only be suspected based on their common activities.[24]

Individuals who talked with the Hungarians had various backgrounds. Some of them were only mediators, mostly for Daniil or originally for his mother. For instance, Demian, Viacheslav Tolstoy (Толстой), and Miroslav participated in negotiations between Andrew II and Roman's widow in 1211, and they followed the fleeing mother and her sons to Hungary and later to Poland. Two of them took part in military actions (1219) when Coloman was in Galicia: Vladislav Vitovich and Lazar Domazhirec. Their connection to Hungarian rule was indirect: Vladislav was expelled from the circle of Daniil, even his horse was taken, whereas Lazar was captured by Mstislav Mstislavich.[25]

Let us now focus on what we can decipher about three people who were evidently on the side of the Hungarian king, taking part in several actions and even visiting Hungary: Filipp, Sudislav, and Volodislav Kormilichich. Filipp and Sudislav appeared regularly alongside members of the Kormilichich kindred, and they were probably counted among their supporters. The leader of the Kormilichichs was Volodislav, and we know of two brothers of his, Iavolod and Iaropolk. They held a consistent line against the sons of Roman (Daniil and Vasilko), yet they did not always support Hungarian rule. For instance, in 1208 they lined up behind the Igorevichs of Chernigov (Roman, Sviatoslav, Vladimir), when they made an appearance in Galicia. The Kormilichichs later turned against the Igorevichs led by Volodislav and his followers (Sudislav, Filipp), perhaps due to the enormous number of executions the Igorevichs engaged in against their opponents. Volodislav and his circle fled to Hungary to escape this fate and seek shelter. Andrew II made the decision only later, after the successful campaign of 1211, that Volodislav was a danger to his aspirations, so he took him to Hungary by force and imprisoned him. Sudislav managed to redeem his captivity, while Filipp's fate is unknown, though he may have managed to escape "only" with torture.[26]

Sudislav and Volodislav, the *boyar* leader, both played important roles in Galician affairs for decades; Sudislav from 1211/12 until his death in 1234, and Volodislav from 1206 till his final hours. A figure called Sudislav took part in the campaigns of the Coloman era and later became a supporter of Prince Andrew. He is mentioned once in the

---

[24] See Jusupović, *Elity ziemi Halickiej i Wołyńskiej*, 60–79; Font, "A halicsi magyar uralmat támogató elit," 43–44 (full citation above); Фонт, Марта: "Венгры на Руси в XI – XIII вв [Hungarians in the Rus in the eleventh thirteenth Centuries]," in *«А се его сребро» Збірник праць на пошану члена-кор. НАН України М.Ф. Котляра з нагоди його 70-річчя*, ed. Валерій Смолій et al. (Київ: Інститут історії України НАНУ, 2002), 89–98.

[25] PSRL, 2:725, 2:727–28, 2:734, 2:736; *Kronika halicko-wołyńska*, 44–45, 50, 63, 66, 81; Jusupović, *Elity ziemi Halickiej i Wołyńskiej*, 118–19, 198–99, 211, 268–69, 288.

[26] PSRL, 2:723–24, 2:727–28; *Kronika halicko-wołyńska*, 43, 143; Hrushevsky, "Khronologia podij," 11–12; Font, *Árpád-házi királyok*, 199–201; Jusupović, *Elity ziemi Halickiej i Wołyńskiej*, 139–41, 243–62.

GVC while leading the troops of Leszek as Sudislav Bernatovich, which seems to make his Polish background conclusive. Coming from the eastern border region he might have belonged to the group that was interested in the expansion under the Piasts. Jusupović compared Sudislav with Sulisław, the *castellanus* of Sandomierz in Poland, and stated that although their names are similar (Sudislav / Sulislav), they are not the same person.[27] Voloshchuk has argued that the name Sudislav is linked to the Hungarian personal name, Sebes (according to him: Sebeslav and Szoboszló), and that he was connected to the Ludan' kindred. However, Hungarian Sebes (and its variations: Sebe, Sebők) derives from Sebastian (Sebestyén) and cannot be the basis for some form Szoboszló/Sudislav, so this Ukrainian theory should be discounted.[28] Whatever his origin, the Galician Sudislav was certainly committed to the Hungarian cause, perhaps motivated by marriage, as his daughter could have been the spouse of File, since on one occasion he is called File's father-in-law.[29] Sudislav was certainly one of the most prominent *boyars*. He was influential across Galicia and had contacts with several members of the Hungarian elite. His wealth must have been significant since he could redeem his captivity. Last but not least, even Prince Mstislav Mstislavich needed his services. However, even though both Sudislav and File were leaders of the Hungarian cause in Galicia, they possessed little influence over the Hungarian elite. File is perhaps identical with the vice-palatine in 1220,[30] yet he had no part within the elite.

The clan name, Kormilichich, for Filipp, Sudislav, and Volodislav is interesting, since it does not derive from a given name, but refers to an office. The verb *kormiti* meant originally meant "to feed" and the concept *kormlenie* ("feeding") is already known from the eleventh century. It refers to the natural allowance ordered by the prince, whilst *kormilec* meant an official in the court of the prince whose task was the organization of the provision and occasionally the education of children. In several regions of the Rus' this office merged with the duties of the educator (*diad'ko, дядько*). In Latin Europe the terms *tutor*, *nutritor*, *paedagogus*, or *magister dapiferorum* could be equivalent to it. It became the most important role in the prince's court.[31] In this light, these brothers can

---

27 PSRL, 2:725; *Kronika halicko–wołyńska*, 34–35; Майоров, *Галицко-Волынская Русь*, 362–66; Jusupović, *Elity ziemi Halickiej i Wołyńskiej*, 243–62, 276–87; Adrian Jusupović, "Wpływ Halickiego otoczenia książęcego na 'władzę' w pierwszej połowie XIII wieku, na przykładzie Sudysława [Sudyslaw, Influential Example on 'Power' of the Galician Princely Circle in the First Half of the Thirteenth Century]," *Княжа доба* 5 (2011): 145–62 at 147.

28 Волощук, *«Русь» в Угорському Королівстві*, 284–301; Мирослав Волощук, "Iobagio Zubuslaus de villa Chercher castri de Ung, онуки боярина Судислава та проблема етнично ідентіфкацrгandії населениня сіхдних комитатов Угорщини в XI–XIII століттях [Iobagio Zubuslaus de villa Chercher castri de Ung, Grandchild of Boyar Sudislav, and the Problem of Ethnic Identity in the Eastern Counties of Hungary in the Eleventh to Thirteenth Centuries]," *Княжа доба* 7 (2013): 39–48; Katalin Fehértói, *Árpád-kori személynévtár (1000–1301) [Compendium of Given Names of the Árpádian Era]* (Budapest: Akadémiai Kiadó, 2004), 700–701.

29 PSRL, 2:736; *Kronika halicko–wołyńska*, 77; See Pashuto, *Ocherki po istorii*, 143; Hardi, *Naslednicy Kieva*, 143; Jusupović, *Elity ziemi Halickiej i Wołyńskiej*, 245–46.

30 Zsoldos, *Magyarország világi archontológiája*, 302.

31 И. Я. Фроянов, *Киевская Русь. Очерки социально-экономической истории [Kievan Rus':*

be seen as descendants of previously influential members of the court, probably keen to hold similar positions.

The role of Volodislav has been reinterpreted by Alexander Maiorov, critically unpicking the sources and modern research.[32] He traces Volodislav's influence to his inherited office, and from this Volodislav became the leader of the Galician *boyars* against the *boyars* of Peremyshl. Majorov also emphasized that Volodislav and other members of the Galician-Volhynian elite did not aspire to become princes themselves and were satisfied with supporting one or another princely aspirant, even the Hungarian king. Pashuto formulated the theory that Volodislav could have been identical with *Ladislaus Ruthenus*, mentioned in the Hungarian charters,[33] whose vineyards became Archbishop John of Esztergom's property after 1218. The charter on the grant was issued some time later, between 1221 and 1225, delayed by the king's crusade, according to Imre Szentpétery's analysis.[34] After this episode no record of *Ladislaus Ruthenus* appears until 1232, by which time he was "deceased," a *terminus ante quem* for Volodislav's/Ladislaus's death.[35]

We have seen how Coloman's inner circle of supporters from the local Galician *boyars* contained many people of which we know nothing, but mainly Filipp, Sudislav, and Volodislav Kormilichich. Filipp is mentioned three times in documents but otherwise we know little. Sudislav and Volodislav both took part in military actions during the period that Coloman was active in Galicia and both supported the Hungarian claims, and we know about their dynastic heritage through the key princely office of *kormilec*.

Studies on Social-Economic History] (Ленинград: Ленинградский университет, 1974), 64–65; Uwe Halbach, *Der russische Fürstenhof vor dem 16. Jahrhundert*, Quellen und Studien zur Geschichte des östlichen Europa 23 (Stuttgart: Steiner, 1985), 146–59, especially 155, 159; Font, *Oroszország, Ukrajna, Rusz*, 74–75 (full citation above); Майоров, *Галицко-Волынская Русь*, 419.

32 Майоров, *Галицко-Волынская Русь*, 408–36.

33 *Codex diplomaticus et epistolaris Slovaciae*, 1:180; for the dates see *Regesta regum stirpis Arpadianae*, no. 350; *Codex diplomaticus Hungariae*, 3/2:310; Pashuto, *Vneshniaia politika*, 244; Font, *Árpád-házi királyok*, 104–5.

34 *Codex diplomaticus Hungariae*, 3/2:310; *Codex diplomaticus et epistolaris Slovaciae*, 1:180; for the dating see *Regesta regum stirpis Arpadianae*, no. 350; for the identification: Pashuto, *Vneshniaia politika*, 244; Font, *Árpád-házi királyok*, 104–5.

35 Jusupović, *Elity ziemi Halickiej i Wołyńskiej*, 276–87; Волощук, «*Русь» в Угорскому Королівстві*, 145–74.

Chapter 5

COLOMAN'S POSITION IN HALYCH, 1215–22: CAMPAIGNS AND OPPONENTS

WE HAVE SEEN what resources Coloman had available: the impact of a papally-approved coronation in Galicia, a queen, Salomea, who linked the Polish Krakówian powers to Hungary through the pact entered into at Scepus, his royal court at the impressive city of Halych, the Hungarian elite on whom he could call, and those local *boyars* who supported him. Now let us examine what Coloman could accomplish in this situation.

The military campaign that Leszek and Andrew II agreed upon at the Scepus Council probably started as early as the end of 1214. Leszek, prince of Kraków, likely occupied only the lands to which he laid claim (Peremyshl and Liubachev), and he provided no assistance to the Hungarian army. Andrew II's letter to Pope Innocent III from 1215 mentions this lack of support, and the king requested papal mediation on behalf of Coloman.[1] Leszek's resistance probably led to Andrew II's counter-move, and as a result, he occupied Volhynia in 1216.

The agreement of the Scepus in effect expelled the minor sons of Roman Mstislavich from Galicia. Leszek probably intended to rectify this situation, so the sons received Vladimir Volynsky from the prince of Kraków, while he retained some influence through his father-in-law. Leszek also tried to contact Mstislav Mstislavich, to gain further support against the Hungarian rule. At that time Mstislav controlled Trepol' and Torchesk, insignificant towns located at the edge of the steppe. He came into possession of Novgorod in 1210 but abandoned it permanently in 1218 when he tried to occupy Halych. His ties to the steppe were secured through his Cuman marriage. Before his attempt in Galicia, he made a failed attempted to seize Kiev in 1215 and could only escape with great losses in 1216.[2] Leszek's plans concerning Daniil went nowhere; the son of Roman wanted to stay independent from Kraków and so he entered a pact with Mstislav, sealed by his marriage to Mstislav's daughter.

Leszek had failed to find an ally in the Rus' by 1215–16. Perhaps it was the result of this failed eastern policy that he dismissed *castellanus* Pakosław, sent him to Sandomierz, and appointed Marek Gryfita instead. A change also happened in the bishopric of Kraków in 1217; Kadłubek resigned and was replaced with Iwan from the Odrowąż kindred.[3] Leszek was also involved in the conflict of the Piasts in Greater Poland (Władysław

---

[1] "Ad presens vero rogamus Paternitatem vestram, ut cursorem eum litteris vestris ad cognatum nostrum L. Ducem Polonie diriger dignemini, commendantes cognationem inter nos et ipsum mediante filii nostri et filie sue matrimonio contractam, [...] una nobiscum ad defensionem Galicie contra impugnatores ipsius sit sollicitus" (*Codex diplomaticus Arpadianus*, 6:374); *Regesta regum stirpis Arpadianae*, no. 302.

[2] For the course of his life see Rapov, *Kniazheskie vladeniia*, 182; for his family ties: Dąbrowski, *Genealogia Mścisławowiczów*, 506–12, table 3; for his role in Novgorod: NPL, 57–58.

[3] Włodarski, *Polska i Rus*, 71.

Laskonogi and Władysław Odonic), because Laskonogi supported Daniil against him and the Prussians against Leszek's brother, Conrad. As a result of all this Daniil devastated many Polish lands in 1218.[4]

As we just mentioned, Mstislav Mstislavich Udaloy, then prince of Novgorod, attacked the city of Halych on the prompting of Leszek, at least according to the *First Novgorodian Chronicle*, and this event is also found in the *GVC*.[5] The theory that Coloman was expelled and restored to power in 1215[6] in Hungarian historical works is wrong. The mistake lies in the fact that Mstislav Udaloy led his army three times against Halych, and only the first and third were successful.[7] Długosz also mentions three campaigns, but with ten years between them.[8] The *First Novgorodian Chronicle* and the *Moscovite Chronicle Compilations* of 1479 date Mstislav's preparations to 1218, and his first victory in 1219, and this was when Coloman and Benedict were forced to escape to Hungary. The remaining two campaigns are dated to 1220 and 1221.[9] Pashuto follows Hrushevsky, Kripiakevych, Kotliar, and Lammich in accepting this sequence of dates and events. Włodarski however dates the first attack to early 1215, the second to 1215–19, and the third to 1219.[10]

Notwithstanding, we can be sure that Coloman's reign in Galicia took effect and existed continuously from 1215–16 to early 1219.[11]

Mstislav's Successes

Mstislav Mstislavich Udaloy gathered key forces from the Rus' during early 1219 and he seized Halych. His cause was supported and aided by his ally and son-in-law, Daniil, and other Galicians. Coloman and Benedict, as the representatives of the Hungarian rule, had to leave the principality after this attack.[12]

---

4 *Annales Poloniae Maiores*, in *Monumenta Poloniae Historica*, 3:7; Bartnicki, *Polityka zagraniczna księcia*, 42–48.

5 NPL, 53; PSRL, 2:731; *Kronika halicko–wołyńska*, 55–56.

6 Pauler, *A magyar nemzet története*, 2:56.

7 PSRL, 15:329; 25:116–18; NPL, 53, 57–58, 252, 258–59.

8 *Ioannis Dlugossii Annales seu Cronicae*, 6:204–5, 6:206–9.

9 NPL, 57–58; PSRL, 25:116.

10 Hrushevsky, "Khronologia podij," 13–14; Hrushevsky, *Istorija Ukrainy–Rusi*, 3:35–41; Pashuto, *Ocherki po istorii*, 203–4; Pashuto, *Vneshniaia politika*, 247–49; Lammich, *Fürstenbiographien des 13. Jahrhunderts in den Russischen Chroniken*, 29–40; Крип'якевич, Галицько–Волинське князівство, 90; Котляр, Формирование территории и возникновение городов Галицко-Волынской Руси, 140–41; Bronisław Włodarski, "Polityka ruska Leszka Białego [The Rus'ian Policy of Leszek the White]," *Archiwum Towarzystwa Naukowego we Lwowie*, series 2, 3, no. 1 (1925): 239–322 at 300–9; Włodarski, *Polska i Rus*, 67–68; Bartnicki, *Polityka zagraniczna księcia*, 48–54; Nagirnyj, *Polityka zagraniczna księstw tiem Halickiej i Wołyńskiej*, 183–84; Dąbrowski, *Daniel Romanowicz, biografia polityczna*, 109–14.

11 Holovko dates the period more narrowly to 1214–18, see Головко, Корона Данила Галицького, 282–83.

12 PSRL, 2:731–32; 25:116; *Kronika halicko–wołyńska*, 55–56; NPL, 53; Pashuto, *Ocherki po istorii*, 201.

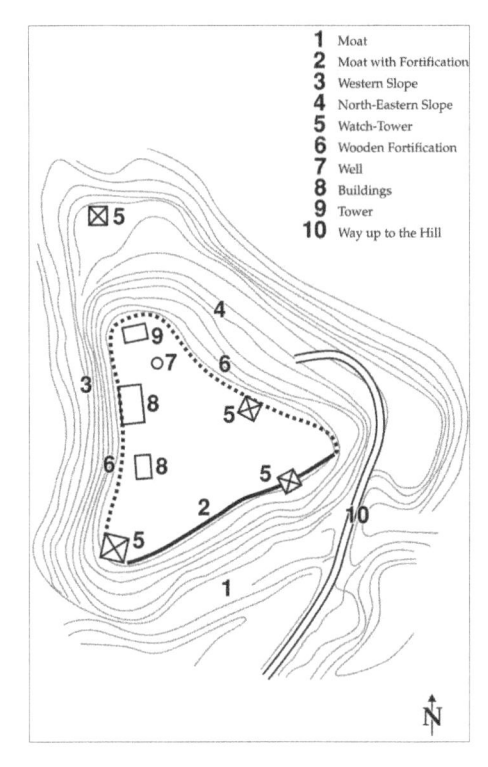

```
1  Moat
2  Moat with Fortification
3  Western Slope
4  North-Eastern Slope
5  Watch-Tower
6  Wooden Fortification
7  Well
8  Buildings
9  Tower
10 Way up to the Hill
```

Map 8. The Hill of Halych in the Twelfth to Thirteenth Centuries.

The summer of 1219 had now put an end to Leszek's hopes in Volhynia and Andrew II's in Galicia, and their political rapprochement was only a matter of time. A joint campaign started afresh in late autumn, in October 1219[13] (according to the *GVC* it also snowed). The Poles took Peremyshl without hindrance, and then the combined forces won a battle at Gorodok against Dmitr, the captain of Mstislav. On their way to Halych they had to fight two more battles, one at Krivavy Brod (Bloody Ford), and the second at Rogozhino. These victories forced Mstislav to retreat, forcing Daniil to surrender in the castle of Halych.

Coloman once more ruled over whole Galicia, and Salomea's arrival was probably the result of these events. In our opinion, File was still the leader of the Hungarian army by this time, even if the sources say nothing, because he later managed an attack on Volhynia. Since there is no evidence of reinforcements sent by Andrew II, it is likely that File had arrived in Galicia by the fall of 1219.

Mstislav Udaloy turned to the Cumans for help after his defeats to the Hungarian-Polish forces. Daniil took a circuitous path back to Volhynia in early 1220 and reclaimed the land occupied by Leszek, and then fought against the Lithuanians. In the winter of

---

[13] PSRL, 2:733–35; *Kronika halicko-wołyńska*, 58–70; Dąbrowski, *Daniel Romanowicz, biografia polityczna*, 101–2.

Figure 5. The Medieval Tower on the Hill Today
(with kind permission of Myroslav Voloshchuk).

1220–21 Mstislav made a second attempt to seize the city but failed again[14] because of an inadequate army and no support from Daniil. A new success for the Hungarians in Galicia simply encouraged them to a new attack, or so we assume from later events. With this intent, File left the royal couple behind in the fortified settlement of Halych while he accompanied Leszek to Volhynia. Taking advantage of the lack of presence in Halych, Mstislav and his Cuman allies then defeated File's army on open land, on the vigil of the Assumption of Mary (August 14), and seized Halych, capturing the young royal couple.[15]

---

14 PSRL, 7:126; 15:329; *Monumenta Poloniae Historica*, 3:132; Hrushevsky, "Khronologia podij," 16-17.
15 PSRL, 1:445, 2:737–738; *Kronika halicko-wołyńska*, 77–83. Based on File's activities in Galicia in

Events are hard to follow and the *GVC* gives only a short description, yet it talks about the suffering of the survivors in the castle due to lack of food and drinking water; they possibly surrendered after the lost battle. The chronicle of Długosz is richer in information but contains several inaccuracies. For instance, its chronology is incorrect (1209!), and according to the chronicler, the Hungarian army was led by a certain Palatine Attila, even though no officer of that name is known from other sources. Furthermore, the events of 1219–21 are interspersed within the text. But, just like the description in the *GVC*, Długosz's chronicle informs us of a battle involving great losses and devastation, where the Cumans raised fires, took prisoners, and murdered a great many people. It is not obvious from the descriptions how Mstislav managed to seize the castle. Based on Długosz, one might even suspect treachery (he stated that several Hungarian rulers and their wives were present in Halych). It is probably unlikely that the Hungarian king's wife sent an envoy to Mstislav named Iarosh, who is probably a fictitious character, or at least he is impossible to identify.[16] It is unlikely that the negotiations with Mstislav and the release of the prisoners happened much later; it could have happened in late 1221 or early 1222 at the latest. Coloman's captivity could not have lasted eighteen months, as Pauler suspected,[17] maybe only a few, as later events suggest.

Pressure for Compromise

Andrew II spent the months during which these events occurred in Poland and Volhynia in the Holy Land. Perhaps he was accompanied on his crusade by Władysław Odonic— or, according to recent research, by Casimir of Opole or Henry II the Pious (Henryk Pobożny)—and several Polish nobles.[18] The king found a desperate situation at home after his return in 1218, as per his report to the pope.[19] The imprisonment of the still young Coloman must have motivated the king to immediate action. Despite initial success, the campaign which started in the fall of 1219, by 1221 turned out to be a failure. The imprisonment of the still young Coloman must have motivated the king to immediate action. In this tense situation, besides the need to free the captives, a Hungarian social movement was developing, one that would lead to the Golden Bull of 1222 in which, it was conventionally thought, Andrew II felt forced to confirm or grant rights and privileges to the secular and ecclesiastical powers. According to recent reseach by Attila Zsoldos, Andrew seems to have been the instigator and the Golden Bull was in fact favourable for him.[20] So, the king wanted peace swiftly and Andrew II accepted Mstislav's terms: Coloman had to rescind all claim on Galicia, but he could keep his royal title.

1219–21, his position as vice-palatine in Hungary in 1220 can be rejected, as we have shown above.

16 *Ioannis Dlugossii Annales seu Cronicae*, 6:206–9.

17 Pauler, *A magyar nemzet története*, 2:73.

18 Bronisław Włodarski, "O udziale Polski w wyprawie krzyżowej Andreja II w 1217 roku [On Polish Participation in Andrew II's Crusade of 1217]," *Kwartalnik Historyczny* 38 (1924): 29–36; Gładysz, *Zapomniani krzyżowcy*, 158–67; Barabás, "Prinz Koloman," 10.

19 *Vetera monumenta historica Hungariam*, 1, no. 32.

20 Zsoldos, "II. András Aranybullája," passim.

Coloman's role passed to Andrew II's third son, Prince Andrew (a child of eleven or twelve years), who became engaged to Mstislav's daughter. Not long after the agreement Andrew II tried to get a papal dispensation from these terms and he also requested the transfer of Coloman's royal title to Prince Andrew. The papal response informs us of the royal petition, yet Honorius III rejected the appeal: "*regia serenitas non turbatur* (The royal majesty is not to be disturbed)."[21]

Parallel to the treaty between King Andrew and Mstislav, Leszek and Daniil also came to an agreement.[22] The Hungarian king's peace with Mstislav only lasted until 1225, although later revisions took place. The king tried to change his vague promises for the future promises and help Prince Andrew consolidate control of the territories. So started another phase in the struggle for rule over the region, and this one lasted until Prince Andrew's death in 1234.

---

[21] See the letter from January 25, 1223: *Vetera monumenta historica Hungariam*, 1, no. 65.

[22] PSRL, 2:739; *Kronika halicko-wołyńska*, 83–85; *Regesta Pontificum Romanorum*, no. 6777; *Regesti del Pontefice Onorii papae III*, no. 3764; for the course of events see Hrushevsky, *Istorija Ukrainy–Rusi*, 3:35–41; Włodarski, *Polska i Rus*, 74–81; Bartnicki, *Polityka zagraniczna księcia*, 48–54; Nagirnyj, *Polityka zagraniczna księstw tiem Halickiej i Wołyńskiej*, 185–88; Dąbrowski, *Daniel Romanowicz, biografia polityczna*, 122–30.

Chapter 6

UPHOLDING THE GALICIAN CLAIM: COLOMAN'S PLACE IN HUNGARY

IT IS NOT known where exactly in Hungary Coloman went after his release from capture in Halych by Mstislav. Conceivably Coloman may have spent time in Scepus, if we assume the existence of a royal *curia* there; but we lack any supporting information. Coloman, as a royal prince—regardless of his current status in Galicia—must have had personal estates in the realm; perhaps Scepus was one since he also initiated the construction of the castle in the 1230s. Residence in Scepus was probably driven by its security and not by the geographical closeness to Galicia, since the Scepus adjoined Lesser Poland as opposed to the principality of the Rus'. From the Carpathians to Galicia by saddle was a great distance; nor was the location ideal for a ride to Galicia. We assume that Coloman possessed a princely *curia* in Scepus but no territorial rule which contradicts Slovak historians who read the situation of the second half of the thirteenth century back into the 1210s and 1220s.[1]

If Coloman indeed stayed in Scepus from 1222 onwards (for which theory we only have indirect evidence), then he probably left there for Slavonia in 1226. 1224–25 must have been a turning point for Prince Andrew's situation in Galicia, since that year he was given his own land in Peremyshl. King Andrew probably believed his third son's place to be stable enough, one assumes, which is why he decided to shuffle his sons' positions in Hungary. Coloman lost his lands in Galicia for good and was sent to Slavonia, where he took over from his older brother, Béla, who was ordered to Transylvania. The decisions were made by Andrew II, since he did not involve his sons in the preparations for these changes. The difference between royal and ducal decision-making is shown by the case of Prince Béla, who had to seek papal support in order to investigate the legality of earlier royal benefactions. Each son of Andrew II was a minor when they were each engaged for marriage, so probably had no say whatsoever.

Prince Andrew in Galicia

Andrew II continued his foreign actions even after the Golden Bull of 1222, despite the continuing tense situation within his realm; his relationship with Prince Béla also remained troubled. Hungarian expansion in the Balkans continued and led to the formation of the banate of Macho (Macsó, Mačva), an area in Serbia at the southernmost tip of territory directly controlled by Hungary, adjacent to Bosnia.[2]

King Andrew's plans for Galicia by seeking peace with Mstislav Udaloy were opposed by Prince Daniil since he thought himself the rightful owner of Galicia, being the eldest

---

[1] Homza, "Včasnostredoveké dejiny Spiša," 1:148–50; Procházková, "Some Notes on the Titles of Coloman," 105–8.
[2] Font, "Prince Rostislav," 497–98.

son of Roman Mstislavich and the son-in-law of Mstislav. This led to rapprochement between Daniil and the elite of Lesser Poland to alter the plans of Leszek. As a result, Leszek, as prince of Kraków renounced his possession over lands between the rivers Wieprz and the Bug, in return for Daniil supporting Leszek and his brother, Conrad, in their fight with the Prussians. In addition, Daniil received Polish support for his attack against Mstislav in Galicia.[3]

Mstislav's situation was weakened by the defeat of his strongest supporters. The Cumans and the forces of the southern principalities of the Rus' were overcome by the Mongols in spring 1223 by the River Kalka. We can surmise too that the defeat would have decreased the personal prestige of Mstislav among the *boyars* of Galicia, and that is why Andrew II's proposal, to hand over Peremyshl to Prince Andrew, met with their agreement. There is no evidence of military pressure, so the Hungarian king probably managed these negotiations through his envoys; a group within the *boyars* must have favoured the Hungarians again. The beginning of Prince Andrew's rule in Galicia was 1224–25 according to Hrushevsky, 1225 according to Pashuto. It is unlikely Andrew took possession of Peremyshl already after the treaty of 1221, otherwise it is hard to imagine why the Hungarians did not take part in the conflicts between 1221 and 1225. The presence of Prince Andrew in Peremyshl would have required support from the Hungarians against Mstislav.[4]

Based on later events, we can presume that, beside Peremyshl, the locals had offered Prince Andrew the whole of Galicia too and that is why he left Peremyshl and asked for his father's help. Andrew travelled back to Hungary at the end of 1226, and the campaign must have started in early 1227 because, according to Włodarski, Leszek's Poles had raised an army in the spring of 1227. Despite their military successes, Mstislav and Daniil were forced to retreat because the *boyars* turned against them. Włodarski argued that Mstislav originally resigned from power in favour of Daniil.[5] Sudislav, one of the supporters of Hungarian rule, was also involved in these machinations, and he went to Torchesk, Mstislav's seat, and gained hold of Halych from Mstislav.

Leszek the White (Biały) fell victim to a conspiracy on November 23, 1227,[6] Mstislav Udaloy died in 1228,[7] and after these events Daniil was left as the sole opponent of the Hungarians in the region. Vladimir Rurikovich from Kiev and Mikhail Vsevolodich from

---

3 PSRL, 2:746; *Kronika halicko-wołyńska*, 102–7.

4 PSRL, 2:740–45, 2:747–48; *Kronika halicko-wołyńska*, 112–18; Hrushevsky, "Khronologia podij," 19–20; Pashuto, *Ocherki po istorii*, 205; Pashuto, *Vneshniaia politika*, 250; Márta Font, "A Kalka menti csata [The Battle of the Kalka River]," in *Elfeledett háborúk. Középkori csaták és várostromok (6–16. század)*, ed. László Pósán and László Veszprémy (Budapest: Zrínyi, 2016), 45–64.

5 PSRL, 2:748–49; *Kronika halicko-wołyńska*, 118–24; Włodarski, "Polityka ruska Leszka," 312–18 (full citation above); Włodarski, *Polska i Rus*, 87.

6 *Annales Poloniae Maioris*, in *Monumenta Poloniae Historica*, 3:206, 3:485; PSRL, 2:754; Józef Umiński, "Śmierć Leszka Białego [The Death of Leszek Biały]," *Nasza przeszłość* 2 (1947): 3–36; Jerzy Wyrozumski, *Dzieje Polski Piastowskiej (VIII wiek – 1370) [The History of Poland under the Piasts (Eighth Century to 1370)]*, Wielka Historia Polski 2 (Kraków: FOGRA Oficyna Wydawnicza, 1999), 190.

7 PSRL, 2:752; 7:134; *Kronika halicko-wołyńska*, 125.

Chernigov supported Prince Andrew against Daniil thanks to Sudislav's diplomacy. It seems possible that the court of Andrew had some kind of connection with the Cumans of Kötöny (Kotian), or at least the presence of Sudislav in the lower Dniester (the so-called Ponizhie) supports this assumption. Torchesk, where Mstislav had been based and was now held by Sudislav, was also close to Cuman territory.

Let us now address the conflict between Coloman and his younger brother, Andrew, to which only a single piece of evidence refers.[8] It appears that this was caused by their father's decision to transfer the royal title to the younger sibling. An attack by Andrew attack on Coloman's territory is unlikely due its distance and the historical course of events. Andrew was constantly occupied with his own struggle to retain his position in Galicia, and he only travelled to Hungary for help after 1226. If there was a conflict between the brothers at all, it must have happened in this period, but we discount any military element, but instead a metaphorical attack against his "realm."[9]

---

8 *Regesta ducum, ducissarum*, no. 10.

9 Unlike Procházková (Procházková, "Some Notes on the Titles of Coloman," 106) we prefer a tentative conclusion.

PART TWO

COLOMAN, DUKE OF WHOLE SLAVONIA (1226–1241)
GÁBOR BARABÁS

After his ejection from Halych, Coloman moved back to Scepus on the northern border of the kingdom of Hungary where he remained until 1226. At this date he was appointed duke of Slavonia by his father Andrew II. He kept the royal title of king, which he attained in Galicia (despite the loss of that kingdom) and, as a prince in the ruling dynasty, he became responsible for the south-western territories of the so-called Realm of St. Stephen: comprising Slavonia, Croatia, Dalmatia, and several Hungarian counties. As the new Duke of Slavonia, he was subject to his father, and later to his older brother, King Béla IV; nevertheless, within his territory he ruled in the name of the king.

First, we will set Coloman in Scepus after he had left Halych and Galicia, and then his initial years as duke of whole Slavonia, defining how he came to become duke and over which territories he held sway. We will then go on to deal with aspects of this "reign," including the question of Coloman's titles and government within the duchy; his ecclesiastical and secular activities and relations to Bishop Stephen of Zagreb and the papacy; internal governmental affairs, including his treatment of settlers, neighbouring lands, and the management of estates; his campaign in Bosnia, and finally, his involvement in the Hungarian defence during the Mongol invasion in 1241.

Chapter 7

COLOMAN AND SCEPUS, BEFORE 1226

COLOMAN WAS APPROXIMATELY thirteen years old when he and his wife, Salomea, were forced to leave the city of Halych and cease his reign in Galicia. After first returning to Hungary, they then settled in the Scepus region (Szepesség, Spiš), on the estates of the prince. The territory had been given to Coloman probably after the treaty which took place in or around 1214 and it served him—along with Újvár County—as some kind of home base whilst he was in Galicia. Coloman's presence in the region is verified by a charter of Queen Elizabeth of Hungary from 1279. We should resist ideas of some coherent territory, such as a *duchy*, since the estates of the prince in Scepus were scattered, even though he owned several castles and their property. This was not territorial power over the whole Scepus region, unlike Coloman's later situation in Slavonia.[1]

Coloman's estates might not have been the sole reason why the young royal couple was based in Scepus. Presumably the prince had not completely given up his hopes for Galicia, or maybe his father had not come to a conclusive decision concerning which son would be prominent in Galicia. Still, a letter in 1222 from Pope Honorius III indicates that Andrew II intended to transfer Coloman's royal title to his younger son, Prince Andrew. However, the pope rejected this on the grounds that a papal enthronement cannot lose its validity, which meant Coloman keeping his royal title until his death. The Hungarian king had to explore another way to support the Galician claims of his youngest son. His hesitation is reflected in his request to the pope to release him from his earlier promise given to Mstislav, which petition also was rejected by Honorius III.[2]

So it is not inconceivable that Coloman could imagine returning to Galicia, justifying staying in Scepus for several years. Other historians argue that the prince was linked to the district through his mother, Gertrude, who along with her brothers, Berthold, Eckbert, and Heinrich, organized the settlement of *hospes* communities in Scepus. Yet this assumption seems unrealistic, since Scepus was mostly uninhabited at the start of the thirteenth century, and the formation of the royal county was just starting.[3] It is also unlikely that a circle of barons was forming around Coloman to oppose King Andrew II, as occurred with his elder brother, Béla, so it is premature to talk of a formation of a ducal court in Scepus.

---

1 "[Q]ui dum adhuc viveret, terram Scypus possederat usque vitam suam" (*Regesta ducum, ducissarum*, no. 118). Hollý, "Princess Salomea and Hungarian–Polish Relations," 25–26; Feld, "Az erdőispánságok várai az Árpád-kori," 376; Zsoldos, "Szepes megye kialakulása," 25, 28–29, 32–34; Zsoldos, *Családi ügy*, 24; Csákó, "A Magyar–lengyel Krónika," 315; Procházková, "Koloman Haličský na Spiši," 246; Procházková, "Some Notes on the Titles of Coloman," 105.

2 *Regesta Pontificum Romanorum*, no. 6777, *Regesti del Pontefice Onorii papae III*, no. 3764. Cf. Font, *Árpád-házi királyok*, 213–14.

3 See Zsoldos, "Szepes megye kialakulása"; Kanyó, "Kálmán herczeg," 416. Cf. Procházková, "Koloman Haličský na Spiši," 244–45; Font, *Árpád-házi királyok*, 213–14; Labanc, *Spišskí prepošti*, 67.

We know of Coloman's time spent in the Scepus from several sources. Surprisingly, however, no charters by the prince regarding his estates seem to have been issued earlier than 1229, when he was already living in Slavonia. Certain historians even conclude that Coloman was in charge of the southern, Slavonian, provinces only from that date onwards.[4]

We contend that Coloman did hold Scepus prior to 1229. The geographical proximity to Galicia and the role of Denis, *magister* of the treasury, confidant of Andrew II, and count (*comes*) of the Scepus (and Újvár) in 1216, in our opinion, confirm the fact that the young prince did already possess the territory in 1216. It is probably significant too that the nearby Premonstratensian provostry of Jasov (Jászó) in Újvár County was probably founded by Coloman. Furthermore, it seems probable that the prince had jurisdiction also over Sáros (Šariš), Aba, Torna, and Gömör (Gemer) counties. Martin Homza even stated that Coloman established his first duchy in the Scepus, and he uses the title *Dux Scepusiae* for Coloman, even though this term cannot be found in any sources by that date. Géza Kanyó had used this title in 1895 in his study about Coloman, along with the title *count of Scepus* (a title that was in fact in use, but much later). Both titles should be avoided for the early thirteenth century; if Coloman ever used the title *dux* before 1226 it could only refer to his place in the royal family, and not for a territorial power of any kind.[5]

Other scholars have presumed that his estates in Scepus were some kind of power base even after 1226 when he ruled Dalmatia, Croatia, and Slavonia. This is an overstatement, but the importance of the territory in the later life of the prince is clear, according to the aforementioned charters from 1229, so he must have retained his influence in the Scepus as duke of Slavonia.[6]

Slovak researchers credit Coloman's presence for this being the period when the area developed. The beginnings of the building of Spiš castle (*Spišský hrad*), the nearby St. Martin's collegial chapter (*Spišská Kapitula*), and the foundation of a Cistercian monastery (Savnik / Spišský Štiavnik) support this notion. Admittedly, Coloman's father already had made donations to St. Martin's church at the end of the twelfth century, and we have also acknowledged the possible role of settlements in Scepus organized by Coloman's mother, since any colonization of the district would have made an impact

---

4 *Regesta ducum, ducissarum*, no. 4, *Codex diplomaticus et epistolaris Slovaciae*, 1:256 ; *Codex diplomaticus Arpadianus*, 6:477; DF 716 09; *Regesta ducum, ducissarum*, no. 3 ; *Codex diplomaticus Arpadianus*, 2:151. Prince Béla confirmed it through a charter issued in the same year. *Regesta regum stirpis Arpadianae*, no. 587, DF 263 117 (*Codex diplomaticus Hungariae*, 3/2:196), of which the chapter of Spiš made a transcript in 1407. See Zsoldos, "Hercegek és hercegnők," 17.

5 *Regesta ducum, ducissarum*, no. 24, 1255: *Codex diplomaticus et epistolaris Slovaciae*, 2:344; 1256: *Codex diplomaticus et epistolaris Slovaciae*, 2:369. Cf. Kristó, *A feudális széttagolódás Magyarországon*, 44–48; Procházková, "Postavenie haličského kráľa," 71; Procházková, "Koloman Haličský na Spiši," 246–47; Procházková, "Some Notes on the Titles of Coloman," 107; Zsoldos, "Szepes megye kialakulása," 26, 28–29, 31–35; Zsoldos, *Magyarország világi archontológiája*, 205, 217; Zsoldos, "Hercegek és hercegnők," 12–13 ; Kiss, *Királyi egyházak*, 70; Romhányi, *Kolostorok és társaskáptalanok*, entry for "Jászó"; Kanyó, "Kálmán herczeg," 415; Homza, "Včasnostredoveké dejiny Spiša," 1:148.

6 Procházková, "Postavenie haličského kráľa," 71; Homza, "Včasnostredoveké dejiny Spiša," 1:148; Kanyó, "Kálmán herczeg," 415–16; Csákó, "A Magyar-lengyel Krónika," 315. Cf. Hollý, "Princess Salomea and Hungarian–Polish Relations," 26.

Figure 6. Spiš Castle in 2016 (with kind permission of Márta Font).

on the local architecture too. Coloman's Polish connections from his marriage and the geographical proximity of Kraków may have affected building construction in the region too, according to several scholars. For instance, recent archaeological research places the first phase of the building of the local collegial chapter to the 1220s and 1230s, while others state that by the time of Coloman's relocation to Slavonia in 1226 almost the whole building had been finished. It is notable, furthermore, that Béla IV, Coloman's older brother, and Queen Elizabeth, the widow of Stephen V (1270–72), both requested the chapter to pray for the souls of Coloman and his mother, Gertrude.[7]

Spiš castle was finished probably only after the Mongol invasion. Yet its several halls are dated to Coloman's time, so the beginning of its construction can be associated with him, or at least to his influence. Spiš castle was not his only castle: the building of Medvedgrad near Zagreb began in the 1230s, according to certain Slovak and Croatian his-

---

[7] Procházková, "Postavenie haličského kráľa," 70–71; Procházková, "Koloman Haličský na Spiši," 243; Romhányi, *Kolostorok és társaskáptalanok*, entries for "Savnik" and "Szepeshely"; Janovská, "Building Activities in Spiš in the Thirteenth Century," 269–72; Vida, "A ciszterci rend," 463; Labanc, *Spišskí prepošti*, 67; Kristóf Keglevich, "A szepesi apátság története az Árpád- és Anjou-korban (1223–1387) [History of the Abbey of Spiš in the Árpádian and Angevin Era (1223–1387)]," *Fons* 14 (2007): 3–58 at 5; Marosi, *A romanika Magyarországon*, 133. For Hungarian architecture in the twelfth and thirteenth centuries, see Marosi, *Die Anfänge der Gotik in Ungarn*, and Marosi, *A romanika Magyarországon*.

torians, arguing (with no evidence) that this was connected to Coloman's plan to extend his royal title.[8]

The construction of the church of *Spišské Vlachy* started probably also during the prince's residence in the region. The influence of Italian architecture on the church's style seems certain. A later charter of Béla IV states that Coloman himself granted the privileges of the—probably Italian or French—settlements of *Spišské Vlachy*.[9]

It is also hightly likely that Coloman was the founder of the Cistercian monastery in the Scepus region (Spišský Štiavnik / Savnik), and may have been a joint undertaking with his father to cherish and save the soul and memory of his late mother.[10] Dissenting views argue that the monastery was founded by Denis, son of Ampud, the Hungarian master of the treasury (*magister tavernicorum regalium*), who was the count of Scepus in 1216 and later a confidante of Coloman.[11] The role of Coloman is acknowledged later in Abbot Albert's charter from 1260, in which he asked the Hungarian king, Béla IV, to confirm the rights of his abbey. In the king's answer Coloman's role is mentioned, but, somewhat surprisingly, Béla referred to himself as the founder. Kristóf Keglovich argues for a posterior reinterpretation; if a charter was issued by the time of the foundation in the royal chancery at all, the founder must have been Coloman, perhaps with the support of Denis. The royal confirmation of 1260 also mentions a former charter of Béla IV, which had fallen victim to fire and in which text Coloman's foundation had been approved.[12] Perhaps Béla IV had supported the monastery since at least 1241, but his younger brother had initiated the foundation.

There was certainly some connection between Coloman's years in Scepus and the foundation of theis Cistercian monastery. On the basis of a statute of the general chapter of Cîteaux the abbots of the Polish monasteries of Sulejów and Koprzywnica were sent to examine the petition of Denis regarding the plan for a new monastery. They must have found suitable conditions in Scepus, given their decision to grant the right to Denis to bring monks there from another Polish monastery, Wąchock. Among the medieval Cistercian monasteries in Hungary this one was unique, since the other foundations in this period were daughters of French or Austrian houses (Clairvaux, Pontigny, or Heiligenkreutz). Only three other abbeys belonged to the so-called "Morimond group" besides the monastery in the Scepus: Cikádor, Borsmonostor, and Zagreb. Even though the role

---

8 Procházková, "Koloman Haličský na Spiši," 247; Goss, "Slovak and Croatian Art in the Thirteenth Century," 265–66; Janovská, "Building Activities in Spiš in the Thirteenth Century," 279–89.

9 *Regesta regum stirpis Arpadianae*, no. 742. Procházková, "Postavenie haličského kráľa," 71; Procházková, "Koloman Haličský na Spiši," 246; Janovská, "Building Activities in Spiš in the Thirteenth Century," 271–73.

10 For a detailed introduction on this topic see Vida, "A ciszterci rend," 462. Cf. Beatrix F. Romhányi, "The Role of the Cistercians in Medieval Hungary: Political Activity or Internal Colonization?," *Annual of Medieval Studies at CEU* 1 (1994): 180–204 at 194; Romhányi, *Kolostorok és társaskáptalanok*, entry for "Savnik".

11 Keglevich, "A szepesi apátság," 5–11.

12 *Regesta regum stirpis Arpadianae*, nos. 711b and 1239; Procházková, "Postavenie haličského kráľa," 70; Procházková, "Koloman Haličský na Spiši," 245; Keglevich, "A szepesi apátság," 5–11; Vida, "A ciszterci rend," 462–63.

A JÁSZÓI PREMONTREI MONOSTOR
BÖKEZŰ JÓTEVŐJE

Figure 7. Coloman's Plaque on his Statue in Gödöllő
(with kind permission of Péter Terejánszky).

of Polish monasteries can be explained by the geographical proximity or migraton, the presence of Coloman in the Scepus by the time of the foundation (1223) allows us to take his Polish contacts into consideration as one of the reasons for these monasteries' involvement. Prof. Homza once argued that the idea of the foundation came from Salomea herself, which is why Polish involvement was needed, although he later modified this view.[13] It imay be significant that when we come to Coloman's ecclesiastical affairs in Slavonia we then find no Polish involvement.

Finally, in summarizing Coloman's involvement in ecclesiastical foundations, let us recall his supposed connection to the beginnings of the Premonstratensian provostry of Jasov. The foundation charter is lost, so it can only be assumed that the church, consecrated to John the Baptist, was established at the very end of the twelfth or the beginning of the thirteenth century. Was it a royal foundation from the start, or did Coloman simply support the new provostry and it was placed under the patronage of the Hungarian kings subsequently? Later documents confirm that the prince indeed made donations to the church, whilst Pope Boniface VIII's charter of March 1297 talks of a joint foundation by Béla and Coloman.[14]

---

[13] László Koszta, "Die Gründung von Zisterzienserklöstern in Ungarn 1142–1270," *Ungarn-Jahrbuch* 23 (1997): 65–80 at 66–68, 76; Keglevich, "A szepesi apátság," 5, 10–11; Romhányi, *Kolostorok és társaskáptalanok*, entry for "Savnik"; Romhányi, "The Role of the Cistercians in Medieval Hungary," 190; For Homza's position, see Martin Homza, "Vztahy Spiša a Malopolska v rokoch 1138-1241 [Relations between Scepusia and Little Poland from 1138 to 1241]," in *Zborník príspevkov k slovenským dejinám. K životnému jubileu univ. prof. PhDr. Richarda Marsinu, DrSc*, ed. Vincent Sedlák (Bratislava: Slovenský historický ústav Matice slovenskej, 1998), 89–112 at 106 and 111; Procházková, "Koloman Haličský na Spiši," 245; Vida, "A ciszterci rend," 462.

[14] *Regesta regum stirpis Arpadianae*, nos. 1094 and 1062; *Regesta ducum, ducissarum*, no. 24;

Regesta Pontificum Romanorum, no. 24485 ; Procházková, "Postavenie haličského kráľa," 71; Tamás Körmendi, "A premontrei rend megtelepedése az Árpád-kori Magyarországon: A rend korai hazai története a kezdetektől az 1235-i Catalogus Ninivensisig. II [The Establishment of the Premonstratensian Order in Árpádian Hungary. The Early History of the Order in Hungary from the Beginnings to the Catalogus Ninivensis in 1235, II]," *Turul* 75 (2002): 45–55 at 45; Romhányi, *Kolostorok és társaskáptalanok*, entry for "Jászó"; Kiss, *Királyi egyházak*, 70.

Chapter 8

COLOMAN AS DUKE OF WHOLE SLAVONIA FROM 1226

IN 1226 COLOMAN became ruler of a whole swathe of territory, far from Scepus on the border of today's Poland, at the opposite end of the Hungarian kingdom, more than 500 km to the south of Spiš castle, over what we knew till recently as Yugoslavia. From that point we know nothing of any involvement by Coloman and his wife in Scepus.

Coloman became ruler when his father, Andrew II, placed him at the head of the provinces of Dalmatia and Croatia, replacing his elder brother, Béla, who was simultaneously then transferred to Transylvania. Of course, we cannot speak of fully-fledged territories of these royal princes, and even the titles used were somewhat vague. From the second half of the twelfth century in the kingdom of the Árpáds it happened several times that a member of the family was entrusted with the governance of these southern territories (like King Emeric from 1194 to 1196), so he could acquire the necessary skills while governing the area in the name of the king.[1] There was, however, no solid framework of how this operated, and the practice was still fluid in the early thirteenth century.

This transfer to Slavonia marked a significant change in Coloman's life, since the first charters under the prince's own name derive from 1226. Coloman travelled to the Dalmatian coastal cities that same year and his power, newly granted from his father, was proclaimed in the form of solemn entries into these towns.[2]

The Question of Coloman's Residence in Scepus or Slavonia

Coloman stated in one of his charters—albeit, of questionable authenticity—that he became the duke of Croatia and Dalmatia thanks to his father's generosity. It is certain that the prince had visited his new territories by 1226. It seems doubtful if he moved south permanently, and lack of sources makes this impossible to answer. There is a three-year hiatus between Coloman's first extant charters (dealing with southern affairs) and a new batch in 1229. Matters dealt with in these charters are significant: two of them concerned donations in the Scepus region (*Kecerovský Lipovec* and *Spišské Tomášovce*). So, several years after his rise to the dukedom, Coloman was still concerned about the conditions of his estates and the circumstances of his supporters in Scepus. His first ordinance concerning Dalmatian affairs was also formulated in 1229. We might conclude, based on these records, that Coloman still relied on his possessions in Scepus

---

1 Cf. Kanyó, "Kálmán herczeg," 416. See Györffy, "Szlavónia kialakulásának oklevélkritikai," 232; Gál, "Az Árpád-házi királyok," 63; Procházková, "Postavenie haličského kráľa," 71; Hollý, "Princess Salomea and Hungarian–Polish Relations," 26; *Korai magyar történeti*, 282–83 (entry by Ferenc Makk); Basić, "O pokušaju ujedinjenja," 33 ; Zsoldos, "Hercegek és hercegnők," 11–12.

2 *Regesta ducum, ducissarum*, nos. 1 and 2; *Thomae archidiaconi Spalatensis Historia Salonitanorum*, 196–98. See Gál, "Az Árpád-házi királyok," 63, 69–70, 72–74.

after his assignment to Croatia and Dalmatia, and that the situation changed fundamentally only after 1229. Other sources confirm this picture, since from this year onwards the prince seems concerned almost exclusively with the affairs of his southern dukedom. According to certain scholars, the residual interest in Scepus to 1229 can be explained by Coloman's plans concerning Galicia, since his estates were important to him as a base for future aspirations eastward. This dual focus may have changed only after the duke's conflict with his younger brother in 1232,[3] at least according to one argument that we find not persuasive. Coloman's estates in Scepus did not border Galicia directly but Lesser Poland, so this base was less ideal for his presumed plans than has previously been assumed by scholars.

Not only is the nature of the period between 1226 and 1229 hard to decipher, but it is similarly difficult to decide where the residence of Coloman was located in Slavonia, if one can speak in his case of a solid seat at all. Probably Coloman initially followed the example of the Hungarian kings, and while travelling across the duchy, he occupied his own estates as well as those of others. The need for a permanent residency might have emerged in the 1230s, and certain signs point to this conclusion. Zagreb is a likely, but inconclusive, candidate, for instance, because from 1237 Provost File of Zagreb performed the role of ducal chancellor. Furthermore, constructing Medvedgrad castle in the mountains above Zagreb might be related to Coloman's goal. Vladimir Goss even pronounced—although without a reference—that Coloman "had his seat in the capital, Zagreb." The foundation of the collegial chapter of Čazma (Csázma) in 1232 and the development of the settlement offers another possibility: that Coloman's choice of Čazma in Croatia as his permanent seat was done in unison with Bishop Stephen of Zagreb. The plan to merge the bishopric of Zagreb with the archdiocese of Split (Spalato) might create a scenario whereby Zagreb could have been an ecclesiastical, while Čazma a secular, centre for the duchy, yet this is a theory with no evidence to support it.[4]

Coloman's Activity between 1226 and 1229

From surviving sources on Coloman's life, his solemn entries (*adventi*) to certain Dalmatian towns leap out. Among the cities he visited, Split was definitely the most important. We know of this splendid event thanks to the work of Archdeacon Thomas of Split (*Historia Salonitanorum atque Spalateninorum pontificum*). Recently, Judit Gál ana-

---

3 *Regesta ducum, ducissarum*, nos. 1–3 and 6; *Regesta regum stirpis Arpadianae*, no. 587. See Kanyó, "Kálmán herczeg," 416; Kristó, *A feudális széttagolódás Magyarországon*, 54; Gál, "Az Árpád-házi királyok," 63, 69–74; Gábor Thoroczkay, "A messziről jött királyné prépostsága. A hajszentlőrinci társaskáptalan korai története (1342-ig) [The Provostry of the Queen from Far Away: The Early History of the Collegial Chapter of Hajszentlőrinc]," in *Arcana tabularii. Tanulmányok Solymosi László tiszteletére*, ed. Attila Bárány, Gábor Dreska, and Kornél Szovák (Budapest: MTA-DE-ELTE BTK-PPKE, 2014), 321–35 at 321–22; Procházková, "Postavenie haličského kráľa," 71ff.

4 Procházková, "Postavenie haličského kráľa," 71; Goss, "Bishop Stjepan II," 212; Cepetić and Goss, "A Note on the Rose Window in Čazma," 185; Csaba Juhász, "A csázmai társaskáptalan 1232. évi alapítólevelének arengája [The Arenga of the Foundation Charter of Čazma from 1232]," *Magyar Könyvszemle* 133 (2017): 1–12 at 1–4.

lyzed the description here of a donation given by Coloman to the bishop of Trogir (Trau) in August 1226 and confirmed that the event did actually take place. Previous Hungarian kings used to visit the area and would present themselves at these solemn *adventi* pageants. Coloman probably followed their example in Dalmatia.[5]

We can probably assume that Archbishop Guncel of Split was to be found at the duke's side not only in Split, but elsewhere in this perambulation across his new territory. The donation that Judit Gál examined indicates that, beside the local archbishop, Bishop Treguan of Trogir, and the prelates of Knin and Skradin (Scardona) were all present in Split. It seems Prince Coloman tried to establish good contacts with the ecclesiastical elite of Dalmatia from his very first visit, and he reinforced this by his donations. His father's confirmation of these donations in 1227 probably intended to support the duke's prestige with these prelates. Alternatively, we might interpret the need for confirmation as an existing practice whereby donations from Hungarian princes became valid only after royal confirmation. We see this concern for royal ratification when Bishop Treguan asked Béla IV for, and was granted, a new confirmation in 1242 after Coloman's death.[6]

Another charter of Coloman from 1226 also concerns ecclesiastical affairs. The duke and his father, Andrew II, jointly made grants to the collegial chapter of Hajszentlőrinc. It made good an earlier petition of the late Queen Gertrude, the prince's mother, who wanted this house supported "for the sake of the salvation of her soul." The reason behind the donation appears in both charters.[7]

Among affairs handled by the duke, as we find them in charters, we find one case relating back to Scepus in 1229, yet most of them concern his southern territories. One document is known from later mention, and it informs us about Coloman's role in the revision of earlier grants of Andrew II. The king's oldest son, Prince Béla, started to investigate his father's earlier policy regarding gifts from the royal estates under the authorization given by Pope Honorius III's papal bull *Intellecto iam dudum*. The pope's intention was to strengthen royal power in Hungary; in the pope's eyes it had been weakened by the dramatic loss of the king's estates. In Honorius III's view, this situation was harmful for the Hungarian church too which is why he decided to intervene, using the royal heir to do his business for him.[8] Coloman's earlier grants did not belong directly to this investigation, but there was a connection. Coloman had delivered a judgement concerning the social status of several men in Zala County, and they were freed from having to

---

[5] *Regesta ducum, ducissarum*, nos. 1 and 2; *Thomae archidiaconi Spalatensis Historia Salonitanorum*, 196–99; Gál, "Az Árpád-házi királyok," 63, 69–70, 72–74.

[6] *Thomae archidiaconi Spalatensis Historia Salonitanorum*, 196–98. The formulations of the ducal and royal charters indicate that this may be a forgery. *Regesta ducum, ducissarum*, no. 1; *Regesta regum stirpis Arpadianae*, nos. 438 and 716; *Codex diplomaticus Arpadianus*, 7:130. Cf. Gál, "The Social Context of Hungarian Royal Grants to the Church in Dalmatia," 55; Gál, "Az Árpád-házi királyok," 63, 69–70, 73; Kanyó, "Kálmán herczeg," 417. For the practice of royal confirmation of ducal charters see Zsoldos, "Hercegek és hercegnők," 17.

[7] *Regesta ducum, ducissarum*, nos. 1 and 2; *Regesta regum stirpis Arpadianae*, no. 438; Thoroczkay, "A messziről jött," 321–22 (full citation above); Zsoldos, "Hercegek és hercegnők," 16.

[8] Cf. James Ross Sweeney, "The Decretal *Intellecto* and the Hungarian Golden Bull of 1222," in *Album Elemér Mályusz* (Bruxelles: Libr. encyclopédique, 1976), 89–96.

serve the royal castle as its warriors (*iobagiones castri*). Coloman's legal activity is also represented in several more records, including a judgement on an estate of a castle warrior (*iobagio castri*). The decision was not favourable for Tersa, and he could not regain possession because the Cistercian abbey of Topusko claimed rights on the disputed land. Viceban Neemilus and the bishop of Senj investigated the matter and in 1230 verified the judgement, so the monastery could keep the estate.[9]

In another ducal charter the burgers and the count of Split were called upon to send their ships and men to help the duke in his fight against a certain Domald, former count of Split, Zadar (Zára), and Šibenik (he was called an enemy of the king). The order did not specify the reason behind the conflict, but it was probably the increasingly prevalent piracy, attracting papal and royal actions in the early 1220s. The duke himself joined in this struggle later in the decade, although he focused more on Bosnia. Piracy is not the only possible reason for Coloman's order to Split; it is thought that Domald was the leader of the "party" of the Croatian nobility, who opposed the new duke. Others think Domald was a member of the Kačići family, who competed with the Šubićis over town of Split, and the rivalry continued even under Hungarian rule.[10]

The Relationship between Coloman and Prince Béla

Coloman succeeded his elder brother, Béla, as head of the southern provinces of Dalmatia and Croatia. General scholarly opinion about this switch is that the Hungarian king, Andrew II, wanted to instil confrontation between his children, so that they would not join forces against their father. It seems to have failed since most researchers think that Coloman and Béla remained constantly close until Coloman's death in 1241. By contrast, the duke of Slavonia did have a serious conflict with his younger brother, Andrew.[11] Another theory states that the Hungarian king intended to remove Coloman from the vicinity of Galicia to ease the youngest son's situation in the principality of the Rus'. There is no evidence to support this, and we have already argued that Scepus and Galicia were not as close as scholars think. Rather, there is a lot of evidence for the close

---

9 *Regesta ducum, ducissarum*, nos. 3–5 and 7; *Codex diplomaticus et epistolaris Slovaciae*, 1:256; *Codex diplomaticus Arpadianus*, 6:477; DF 716 09; *Regesta regum stirpis Arpadianae*, no. 587; *Codex diplomaticus regni Croatiae*, 3:335. See Procházková, "Postavenie haličského kráľa," 71; Zsoldos, "Az ifjabb király országa," 244; Zsoldos, *Magyarország világi archontológiája*, 44, 228.

10 *Regesta ducum, ducissarum*, no. 6, DL 361 54; *Regesta regum stirpis Arpadianae*, nos. 256, 341, 376, 402; *Thomae archidiaconi Spalatensis Historia Salonitanorum*, 168–69, 180–81, 194–97, 212–13. See Fine, *The Late Medieval Balkans*, 143–44, 149–51; Sokcsevits, *Horvátország*, 125–26; Gál, "The Social Context of Hungarian Royal Grants to the Church in Dalmatia," 55; Kanyó, "Kálmán herczeg," 425–26; Procházková, "Postavenie haličského kráľa," 72; Basić, "O pokušaju ujedinjenja," 34; Majnarić, "Some Cases of Robbing the Papal Representatives," 499–502; Hollý, "Princess Salomea and Hungarian–Polish Relations," 26.

11 Recently Attila Zsoldos compared two princes of the Árpád dynasty, Álmos and Coloman. He stated that almost as many sources remain regarding Álmos from the late eleventh and early twelfth century, as remain concerning Prince Coloman over a century later. The reason for this may be found perhaps in the conflict of Álmos with his brother King Coloman the Learned. See also Zsoldos, "Hercegek és hercegnők," 14.

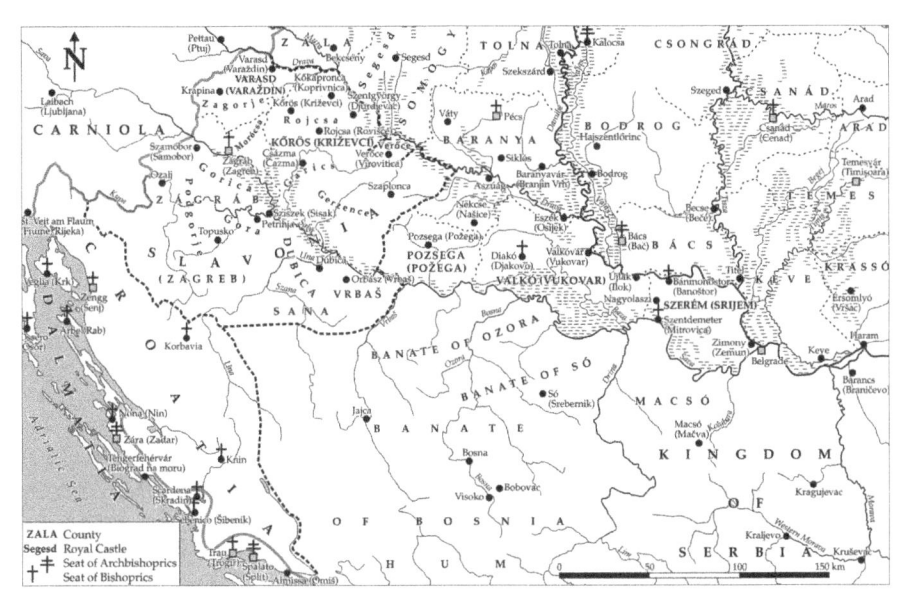

Map 9. Slavonia, Croatia, and Neighbouring Territories in the 1230s.

bonds between the older siblings. For instance, Béla continued the work to restore royal estates in Slavonia even after his relocation to Transylvania, and his charters contain references to Coloman's contribution. Fraternal harmony also presented itself in the phrasing of their charters; according to one from Coloman in 1237, their cooperation was unbroken even after the coronation of Béla.[12]

The brothers' relationship was indeed extraordinary in the history of the Árpád dynasty, especially if we think of all the other serious conflicts within the family (for instance, Emeric and Andrew, Andrew II and Béla, Béla IV and his son, Stephen), but it is also remarkable in comparison with neighbouring countries, particularly Poland. Of course, there could be minor tensions, as Karol Hollý has pointed out. For instance, Béla led a campaign against Galicia from Transylvania, even though Coloman probably had not given up his claim on the Rus'ian principality. This action, according to Hollý, caused Coloman's opposition both to his father and to his brothers.[13] The possible claims of the Slavonian duke will be analyzed later, but this campaign probably influenced only the relations

---

[12] *Regesta ducum, ducissarum*, no. 15. Nataša Procházková has also stated that the duke of Slavonia could also rely—beside Béla—on Archbishop Guncel of Split on matters affecting the duchy. *Regesta ducum, ducissarum*, no. 15. See Font, *Árpád-házi királyok*, 240–42; Procházková, "Postavenie haličského kráľa," 71–72; Procházková, "Koloman Haličský," 247; Basić, "O pokušaju ujedinjenja," 33–34; Barabás, "The Titles of the Hungarian Royal Family," 37–44.

[13] Goss, "The Battle of Cathedrals," 146; Goss, "Bishop Stjepan II," 212; Senga, "Béla királyfi bolgár," 37–40; Hollý, "Princess Salomea and Hungarian–Polish Relations," 27; Zsoldos, "Hercegek és hercegnők," 9.

of the duke to Andrew II and Prince Andrew and not with Béla. Prince Béla took part due to his father's order and desire (*de mandato et voluntate patris*), as Márta Font has shown.

If we return to the possible motives of Andrew II for transferring Béla to Transylvania, it may be that the switch in the siblings' realms may have had a different source. The relationship of the Hungarian king with his first-born son was tense from 1214 onwards. Initially, opponents of Andrew II used the child Béla to put pressure on the king by forcing him to crown his heir in 1214. A letter of Honorius III from July 1222 sent to the Hungarian prelates confirms this picture and informs us of the king's former complaint. By the time of the so-called Hungarian Golden Bull in 1222, Béla could have already been a figure within the social unrest, so the origin of the conflict must be searched there. The tension came into the open in 1224, when Andrew II tried to force his son to reject his fiancée, Maria, the daughter of the Greek emperor of Nicea, Theodore I Laskaris (1204-22), in order to support his new plans for possible new alliances. Béla was forced to flee the country to Austria because he refused to let Maria go. Thanks to papal mediation, father and son finally reconciled and Honorius III authorized Béla with his decretal *Intellecto iam dudum* in 1225 to start a procedure to examine his father's earlier gifts and to take back the ones that were not rightful or those which may have weakened royal power in Hungary. Certainly, the prince's new task could appear as another act of disobedience,[14] so Béla might have been right, therefore, to think of his transfer to Transylvania as an act of ill-will, even if we see no sign of resistance to his father's decision.

The royal decision should also be seen in the light of the theory that Slavonia could, already in the thirteenth century, have been considered as the estate of the current heir to the throne. Attila Zsoldos has emphasized the extraordinary nature of Coloman's becoming duke of Slavonia and states that Béla must have had realized its significance, since later on he returned to this very measure when he got into conflict with his first-born son, Stephen. In that case, the oldest male offspring was also transferred from Slavonia to Transylvania, while the southern duchy was given to the younger son, Béla. As Zsoldos stated, the case of Coloman shows that one did not automatically become the heir by virtue of being duke of Slavonia. Unlike him, Béla would face no challenges in succeeding to the throne after his father's death. On the contrary, his younger brother supported him and even symbolically represented his own subjection at the coronation ceremony, by holding the new king's sword. Then again, maybe the close bond between the two had prevented Coloman using his title as duke of Slavonia to pursue a claim to the throne. Coloman's death in 1241 prevented any possibility of a quarrel between Béla IV and the duke of Slavonia.[15]

---

14 *Regesta Pontificum Romanorum*, no. 6870; Attila Zsoldos, "'Igaz szolgálattal szerzett birtok' ['An Estate Received for True Service']," in *"Múltunk építőkövei..."*, ed. József Csurgai Horváth and Eleonóra Kovács (Székesfehérvár: Székesfehérvár Megyei Jogú Város Levéltára, 2001), 73-83 at 76; Attila Zsoldos, "Karászi Sándor bán és utódai (Megjegyzések a narratiok eredetéről és szerepéről) [Ban Alexander Karászi and his Descendants (Remarks on the Origin and Role of the Charters' Narrationes]," *Századok* 135 (2001): 385-407 at 401-402; Zsoldos, "II. András Aranybullája," 6, 8-10, 24, 37; Zsoldos, "Hercegek és hercegnők," 10.

15 Zsoldos, "Az ifjabb király országa," 235-36. Cf. Procházková, "Postavenie haličského kráľa," 71; Sokcsevits, *Horvátország*, 116-17.

Coloman's Role in the Attempted Restitution of the Former Royal Benefactions

The fact that Coloman still had a good relationship with his older brother after 1226 is reflected in his participation in Béla's investigations regarding the former royal benefactions. The Hungarian king's heir, as mentioned above, was entrusted by the papal bull *Intellecto iam dudum* to examine the legality of former alienations of royal estates. The cooperation of the brothers is clear in several royal and ducal documents, with Coloman himself issuing charters on this matter. A diploma of Béla from 1231 talks of the duke of Slavonia's role as do certain documents written by Thomas, the former Croatian *ban*. Probably Coloman's assistance was needed because of the subject of the investigation. A royal charter from 1231 informs us of the duke's decision concerning the sons of a certain Fabian, initially taking several properties of land from them, but changing this upon request of both his brother and his father, thereby confirming Fabian's possessions. This cooperation continued even after Béla's coronation, and Coloman's support in investigating former grants was expressed in several royal charters. A later royal diploma shows apparent similarities in this business between Coloman's activity in Slavonia and his brother's in the Hungarian kingdom.[16]

The Extent of "Whole Slavonia" in Coloman's Time

Let us now clarify exactly which lands Coloman controlled, either territorially or administratively, since this is a crucial distinction.[17] First, therefore, we have to answer the question: what did the term "whole Slavonia" (*totius Sclavonia*) actually mean and which territories belonged to it?

From the practice of Hungarian princes in their use of titles at this period it is unclear if we are talking about territories ruled by members of the royal family or whether they were simply titles that they bore. At the start of the thirteenth century we do not see a revival of the eleventh-century duchy (*ducatus*): landholdings were diverse and earlier the power of the dukes was centred on the territories of Nyitra (Nitra) and Bihar (Bihor), whereas by our period Transylvania and Slavonia were the core ducal provinces. Importantly, in Transylvania and Slavonia the main royal officials were under ducal power. In the case of Transylvania, the *voivode* was a local royal officer, while in Slavonia the jurisdiction of the Croatian *bans* covered the territory. According to Prof. Zsoldos, the formation of both provinces was due to the activity of Prince Béla.

For Slavonia we should remember that its dukes ruled Croatia and Dalmatia too; these two provinces belonged to Hungary as a result of conquest. A direct antecedent of the southern duchy might have been the rule of Emeric between 1194 and 1196, although it is presumed that his father, King Béla III, also acted as duke of Croatia and

---

16 *Regesta regum stirpis Arpadianae*, nos. 480, 596, 690 and 1039, "de baronum nostroroum consilio reuocare fecissiumus et idem carissimus frater noster feliis memorie rex Colomanus, dux tocius Sclauonie, fecisset in ducatu Sclauonie" (*Codex diplomaticus regni Croatiae*, 4:594).

17 Attila Zsoldos, "Egész Szlavónia bánja [Ban of Whole Slavonia]," in *Tanulmányok a középkorról. Analecta mediaevalia I*, ed. Tibor Neumann (Budapest: Argumentum, 2001), 269–81 at 279.

Dalmatia previously. Prior to Emeric's role, Bishop Calan of Pécs was appointed by Béla III as governor (*gubernator*) of the provinces (1190–94). The prelate was the first Hungarian office-holder who made decisions on the affairs of Slavonia while ruling Croatia and Dalmatia at the same time. The unusual title of governor can refer to this development, since his jurisdiction was separate from the *bans*'. The title "Duke of Slavonia" (*dux Sclavonie*) appears in the famous list of sources of revenue for King Béla III. This inventory, in a French codex, was made probably in preparation for the marriage of the king with Margaret, daughter of King Louis VII of France or even possibly the marriage of Prince Emeric with Constance of Aragon. The precise amounts listed in the inventory are somewhat inflated, according to recent research, yet the scale of revenue is generally authentic, so we can be certain the title "Duke of Slavonia" existed at the end of the twelfth century. Prince Andrew's role is important too, because he was the king who placed first his eldest (Béla) and then his second son (Coloman) to rule the southern provinces. It is less significant, then, whether or not Andrew inherited Croatia and Dalmatia from his father, or—the more likely—he took them by force after Béla III's death.[18]

Hungarian and Croatian historians differ greatly on the territorial status and the expansion of Slavonia in the eleventh to twelfth centuries.[19] Hungarian scholars have insisted that Slavonia was an integral part of kingdom of the Árpáds from its very beginnings. The Croatian Nada Klaić advanced the opinion in the 1970s that the supremacy of the Croatian kingdom spread as far as the river Drava from the tenth century; this is today's boundary between Croatia and the south-western limits of Hungary. According to the Hungarian György Györffy, the expression *totius Sclavonie* described the territory between the Adriatic Sea and the Drava–Sava rivers, both running west to east, with the Sava about one hundred kilometres south of the Drava, both major tributaries of the Danube. On the contrary, Gyula Kristó rejected the theory that the name Slavonia could have referred to Adriatic Croatia. In his view, it first appeared in the early thirteenth century in Hungary and it spread out from the territory between the Drava and Sava rivers to Croatia and Dalmatia. Zsoldos confirmed the term's appearance in the thirteenth century and searched for the reasons for its spread. Like Györffy, he assumed that the territory called Slavonia belonged to Hungary from the time of St. Stephen. He argues that the geographical term *Sclavonia* acquired administrative meaning and spread beyond, to Croatia and Dalmatia, when the counts (*comites/ispáns*) of Zala and Somogy performed the functions of *ban* of Croatia. The administration of these counties reverted later to the river Drava and the authority over them was given to the *ban*. The name of this new district (*totius Sclavoniae*) refers to the common administration of Croatia and

---

18 Kristó, *A feudális széttagolódás Magyarországon*, 45–48, 84–94; *Korai magyar történeti*, 261 (entry by Ferenc Makk); Zsoldos, "Egész Szlavónia bánja," 276, 279–80; Gábor Szeberényi, "Domonkos zágrábi püspök politikai szerepe a 12–13. század fordulóján [The Political Role of Bishop Dominic of Zagreb at the Turn of the Twelfth and Thirteenth Centuries]," in *Középkortörténeti tanulmányok, 3. A III. Medievisztikai PhD-konferencia (Szeged, 2003. május 8–9.) előadásai*, ed. Boglárka Weisz (Szeged: Szegedi Középkorász Műhely, 2003), 159–68 at 161–62; Sokcsevits, *Horvátország*, 116; Barabás, "The Titles of the Hungarian Royal Family," 32–33.

19 The sources were reexamined recently by Tamás Körmendi and he thinks Slavonia was part of the Hungarian kingdom by 1091. Körmendi, "Szlavónia korai hovatartozása," 372–87.

the Drava–Sava territory. Recently, Gábor Szeberényi focused on the question of the latitude of the southern counties of Hungarian "Transdanubia" beyond the Drava and concluded that the river was in fact the border between Hungary and Slavonia.[20] Prof. Fine has underlined the importance of Hungarian rule, with the Croatian territory divided up, according to him, in the 1220s with the appearance of two *bans*. Croatia was more autonomous in his eyes, whereas Slavonia formed more or less a part of the Hungarian administrative system.

Countering these opinions, for instance, Ivan Basić, stated that Slavonia is to be identified with the territory between the Drava and the Gvozd Mountain, Vrbas, and Bosnia. The authors of a volume on medieval customary law of Croatia and Slavonia stated in 2013 that Slavonia was originally Croatian territory, which became an integral part of Hungary only in the late eleventh century as the result of Hungarian conquest, whilst preserving some features of autonomy.

Despite lying between the Drava and Sava rivers but towards the east of this region, we believe that the Hungarian counties (*comitati*) of Baranya, Srem (Syrmium, Szerém), Požega (Pozsega), and Valkó did not belong to Slavonia in the Middle Ages.[21] We also need to emphasize, along with Prof. Zsoldos, the importance of the counts of Somogy and Zala counties (both just north of the Drava river), as they often acted as the *bans* of Croatia. Their rule and the reign of Coloman all held significance concerning the formation of the territory and the appearance of the term *whole Slavonia*.

---

20 Nada Klaić, *Povijest Hrvata u ranom srednjem vijeku [History of the Croats in the Early Middle Ages]* (Zagreb: Školska knjiga, 1971), 278–79, 288; Körmendi, "Szlavónia korai hovatartozása," 370; Györffy, "Szlavónia kialakulásának oklevélkritikai," 226–30, 233–39; Kristó, *A feudális széttagolódás Magyarországon*, 89–94; Zsoldos, "Egész Szlavónia bánja," 271–72, 276–81; Weisz and Zsoldos, "A báni joghatóság Szlavóniában," 478–80; Csákó, "A Magyar-lengyel Krónika," 312; Gábor Szeberényi, "Szlavónia határai a 13–14. században. Megjegyzések a Dráva és a Gvozd határszerepének megítéléséhez [The Boundaries of Sclavonia in the Thirteenth to Fourteenth Centuries: Remarks on the Roles of the River Drava and Mount Gvozd as Borders]," in *Középkortörténeti tanulmányok, 8. A VIII. Medievisztikai PhD-konferencia (Szeged, 2013. június 17–19.) előadásai*, ed. Márta Tóber and Ágnes Maléth (Szeged: Szegedi Középkorász Műhely, 2015), 215–25 at 215–19; Gábor Szeberényi, "Zala és Somogy megye a Dráván túl. Megjegyzések a szlavóniai igazgatástörténet Árpád-kori rekonstrukciójának néhány kérdéséhez [The Counties of Zala and Somogy Across the River Drava. Some Remarks on the Reconstruction of the History of Slavonian Government]," in *Középkortörténeti tanulmányok, 9. A IX. Medievisztikai PhD-konferencia (Szeged, 2015.) előadásai*, ed. Brigitta Szanka et al. (Szeged: Szegedi Középkorász Műhely, 2017), 319–35.

21 Jenő Szűcs, *Az utolsó Árpádok [The Last Árpáds]*, História Könyvtár Monográfiák 1 (Budapest: MTA TTI, 1993), 80–81; Fine, *When Ethnicity Did Not Matter in the Balkans*, 70–94; Basić, "O pokušaju ujedinjenja," 33; Gábor Szeberényi, "A zágrábi püspökség Szlavónia megszervezésében játszott szerepének egyházszervezeti vonatkozásai [Ecclesiastical Aspects of the Role Played by the Bishopric of Zagreb in the Establishment of Slavonia]," in *Az Illyés Gyula Pedagógiai Főiskola Társadalomtudományi Tanszékének Közleményei 1*, ed. György Bebesi (Szekszárd: Illyés Gyula Pedagógiai Főiskola, 1999), 39–51 at 39n2; Szeberényi, "Szlavónia határai," 219–22; Damir Karbić and Marija Karbić, *The Laws and Customs of Medieval Croatia and Slavonia: A Guide to the Extant Sources*, ed. Martyn Rady, Studies in Russia and Eastern Europe (London: UCL School of Slavonic and East European Studies, 2013), <http://discovery.ucl.ac.uk/1469335/1/The%20Laws%20 of%20Croatia.pdf>3; Körmendi, "Szlavónia korai hovatartozása," 369–70.

Regarding the previous question about the territories ruled by Coloman, there is another issue besides the lack of clarity over the definition of Slavonia. Namely, even if a territory was controlled by Coloman that did not automatically mean that it was a part of Slavonia. An especially good example is Virovitica (Verőce), a county that was probably no part of Slavonia then, but undoubtedly belonged to Coloman's duchy. Hungarian princes had control from time to time over several Transdanubian counties. Andrew II held jurisdiction over the counties of Zala and Požega, while his son, Béla, handled the affairs of the Međimurje (Muraköz) region. Coloman's control covered the counties of Zala, Somogy, Baranya, Požega, Valkó, and Varaždin (Varasd), whereas several fortresses belonged to him as personal property (for instance, Segesd and Virovitica). Coloman also ruled over Croatia and Dalmatia, although these two provinces did not appear in each charter under the title *duke of whole Slavonia*; they are mentioned in several other documents, while there are examples in which Slavonia is not even mentioned.[22]

The accurate interpretation of Coloman's territorial control is even more complicated than his father's and brothers', largely due to his royal title from his time in Galicia. This will now be the subject of our next discussion.

---

[22] *Regesta regum stirpis Arpadianae*, no. 823; Györffy, "Szlavónia kialakulásának oklevélkritikai," 129; Zsoldos, "Az ifjabb király országa," 243–44; Zsoldos, *Családi ügy*, 24–25; Weisz and Zsoldos, "A báni joghatóság Szlavóniában," 475–77.

Chapter 9

COLOMAN'S STATUS AND THE INNER WORKINGS OF THE DUCHY

IN THIS CHAPTER we will examine Coloman's titles and what they say about the territory over which he ruled, before going on to examine the structures of government: the court, chancery, treasury, and

Coloman's Titles

To understand the various titles used in historical documents to describe Coloman, let us first turn to the letters written by his father and older brother and the formulations used in them, and then turn to the duke's own charters and papal diplomas.

In the first record, a charter of Andrew II sent to Pope Innocent III in 1214,[1] Coloman is mentioned only as the son of the Hungarian king. But after his coronation in Halych, he was referred to as king in every single case.[2] We know, however—as with Béla too[3]—of examples in which, beside the royal title, the title of Coloman as *the duke of Dalmatia and Croatia* (a title acquired from his father), was emphasized.[4] This is perhaps not so surprising since in this case Andrew II was confirming his son's donation to the bishop of Trogir on the Dalmatian coast. In other records—beside his title as king—Coloman was referred to simply as the *duke of whole Slavonia*.[5] This may be important in the light of the papal letters, as we will see later.

Let us also recall a donation of Andrew II in 1234 in which Coloman—as with the practice of the Holy See—was mentioned as *illustris rex*.[6] In princely or royal charters issued by Béla, written by Béla concerning the support from his brother during the investigations into the royal grants, besides clearly expressing their fraternal connection, Coloman was named *illustrious king* in royal and papal letters alike.[7] The title *duke*

---

1 "[...] ut filium nostrum Colomanum ipsis in regem preficeremus, in unitate et obedientia Sancte Romane ecclesie perseveraturis in posterum" from *Codex diplomaticus Hungariae*, 3/1:163, *Regesta regum stirpis Arpadianae*, no. 294.

2 Even if Coloman was only mentioned in passing: "Prefatus itaque B. rex habito consilio dilecti fratris sui et omnium principum regni, fratris dico, Colomani regis" (*Codex diplomaticus Hungariae*, 3/2:205, *Regesta regum stirpis Arpadianae*, no. 461).

3 See Barabás, "The Titles of the Hungarian Royal Family," 33–36.

4 "Quia enim illustris filius noster Colomanus, Dei gratia, Ruthenorum rex, et liberalitate nostra dux Dalmatie, atque Croatie [...]" (*Codex diplomaticus Hungariae*, 3/2:103, *Regesta regum stirpis Arpadianae*, no. 438; *Regesta ducum, ducissarum*, no. 1).

5 "Carissimus filius noster Colomanus rex et dux tocius Sclavonie" (*Hazai oklevéltár, 1234–1536: néhai gr. Dessewffy Lajos hazafias áldozatával*, ed. Imre Nagy et al. (Budapest: Magyar Történelmi Társulat, 1879), 4:14, *Regesta regum stirpis Arpadianae*, no. 512).

6 *Regesta regum stirpis Arpadianae*, no. 529.

7 "de consensu fratris nostri illustris Cholomani regis" (*Codex diplomaticus Arpadianus*, 6:485,

of whole Slavonia appeared too, and it was so frequent that after the beginning of Béla's rule the expression *beloved brother, King Coloman, the duke of whole Slavonia* came into general use.[8]

The first known charter by Coloman was issued in 1226, and it is remarkable in itself, since we find a relatively complex *intitulatio*, perhaps influenced by the aforementioned inscription of Andrew II. In it, Coloman is called *the king of the Ruthenians by the grace of God and the duke of Dalmatia and Croatia by the grace of his father*.[9] This expression presents the situation of the prince accurately: on the one hand, his coronation could not be rescinded, although by this time his prospects in Galicia were gone, as his younger brother Andrew represented the Hungarian interests there. Maybe that is the reason why he used the term *Ruthenian* as a supplement to his royal title, referring to the eastern Slavic, Rus' population living there. On the other hand, the reference to Dalmatia and Croatia is eloquent, since Andrew II had given this territory to Coloman instead of Béla, ending thereby his "political inactivity" away in Scepus.

Later examples from the charters are less informative: *King of Ruthenia and even duke of Dalmatia and Croatia*, or: *by the grace of God king of Galicia and the duke of Slavonia*.[10] In one case the royal title is missing; this can be explained by the specific cicrumstance, since Coloman was addressing his letter to the count—and people—of the Dalmatian town of Split.[11] Before 1229 Coloman was called only *duke of Dalmatia and Croatia* and not of Slavonia, but the exact reason for this is unclear. It may be a result of the developing sense of "whole Slavonia," though it was established in 1230 if we follow a charter of the cathedral chapter of Zagreb from this year, in which Coloman's dukedom of whole Slavonia is mentioned.[12] The royal title is missing from this diploma, yet it is found in a charter of the viceban and *comes* of Zagreb from 1234 in

---

Regesta regum stirpis Arpadianae, no. 593 and cf. Kristó, *A feudális széttagolódás Magyarországon*, 76).

8 "carissimus frater noster rex Colomanus et dux tocius Sclavonie" (*Codex diplomaticus Arpadianus*, 11:306, *Regesta regum stirpis Arpadianae*, no. 665). Cf. Basić, "O pokušaju ujedinjenja," 34.

9 "nos Colomannus, Dei gratia Ruthenorum rex, et largitate gloriosi patris nostri Andree, Hungarorum regis, dux Dalmatie atque Croatie" (*Codex diplomaticus Hungariae*, 3/2:90–91, *Regesta ducum, ducissarum*, no. 1). Cf. Kristó, *A feudális széttagolódás Magyarországon*, 54.

10 "C. dei gratia rex Ruthenie, nec non Croacie, Dalmacieque dux" (*Codex diplomaticus Hungariae*, 6/2:363, DF 280 230, *Regesta ducum, ducissarum*, no. 2). "Colomanus Dei gracia Halicie rex ac dux Sclavonie" (*Codex diplomaticus Arpadianus*, 6:477, *Regesta ducum, ducissarum*, no. 4).

11 "C. Dei gracia dux Crohatie et Dalmatie" (*Codex diplomaticus Arpadianus*, 6:482, *Regesta ducum, ducissarum*, no. 6).

12 "Andrea magno rege existente, Bela filius eius regnum Hungarie gubernante, Colomano tocius Sclauonie ducatum tenente, Stephano secundo episcopo Zagrabiensi presidente, Mathia preposito, Pugrino cantore, Gabriele custode, Symeone decano et ceteris canonis in ecclesia Zagrabiensi feliciter residentibus" (*Codex diplomaticus regni Croatiae*, 3:336). We cannot speak about any consistent practice though, since a charter of the chapter of Zagreb from 1236 does not mention Coloman: "Secundo Stephano episcopo Zagrabiensi existente, Fila preposito, Pangracio cantore, Johanne lectore, Gregorio custode, Petro decano et al.s multis" (*Codex diplomaticus regni Croatiae*, 4:20–21). Cf. Kristó, *A feudális széttagolódás Magyarországon*, 92; *Thomae archidiaconi Spalatensis Historia Salonitanorum*, 196n4.

which Archbishop Guncel of Split had simply called Coloman *king and duke of Slavonia* in 1229.[13]

In the 1230s the practice became more stable, maybe reflecting greater institutionalization of the ducal chancery, and the following *intitulatio* was the most frequent in the prince's charters:[14] "*Nos Colomanus, Dei gratia rex, et dux totius Sclavonie.*"[15] The title *duke of whole Slavonia* can be seen as a *novum*, although Béla had used it once before.[16] But this *intitulatio* should not be read as any form of claim byColoman on lands outside his duchy, such as Bosnia, or any land of the Hungarian Kingdom inhabited by Slavic peoples.[17]

We can see that in the overwhelming majority of the examples the royal title was not linked to any territorial belongings for Coloman. Only the expression *king of Galicia* can be found occasionally. By contrast Slavonia—sometimes with Dalmatia and Croatia appended—emerged exclusively as an adjunct to the title of *dux*. The phrase *king by the grace of God and duke of whole Slavonia* (*Dei gratia rex, et dux totius Sclavonie*) can hardly be interpreted as the king of Slavonia. At least, it would have been unusual to link multiple titles to a single territory; the opposite was normal. Therefore, we cannot speak about a Kingdom of the Slavic people or similar formations, even if we acknowledge the importance that Scepus played in the life of Coloman. Most particularly, this was the exact period when the authority of the Croatian-Dalmatian *bans* spread over the territory between the Drava and Sava rivers, and it was in connection with this that the title *banus totius Sclavonie* evolved. Finally, let us reemphasize that the coronation of

---

[13] "Acta sunt haec anno MCCXXXIIII, domino Colomano rege et duce Sclavoniae, et Jula bano existentibus" (*Codex diplomaticus Arpadianus*, 12:681). Cf. Zsoldos, *Magyarország világi archontológiája*, 229. "[...] Quia cum nuper in curia domini Colomani regis et Jule bani eiusdem multa controuersia super [...]" (*Codex diplomaticus regni Croatiae*, 3:315–16).

[14] For the possible consolidation of Coloman's chancery, in which process his later chancellor, provost Phyla of Zagreb, could have played an important role, see Zsoldos, *Magyarország világi archontológiája*, 118. Procházková, "Some Notes on the Titles of Coloman," 108.

[15] For example, DF 283 328, *Codex diplomaticus Arpadianus*, 11:268, *Regesta ducum, ducissarum*, no. 12. The supplement *Rutenorum* did not disappear completely, as a charter of 1240 still includes it: "Colomanus Dei gracia rex Ruthenorum et dux tocius Sclavonie" (*Codex diplomaticus Arpadianus*, 11:313, *Regesta ducum, ducissarum*, no. 20. Cf. Zsoldos, *Magyarország világi archontológiája*, 118; Procházková, "Some Notes on the Titles of Coloman," 108. The royal title was also used outside the ducal chancery, as the charter of the collegial chapter of Pécs demonstrates: "[...] illustri regi Colomano duci totius Sclauonie [...]" (*Codex diplomaticus regni Croatiae*, 4:74, DL 337 01).

[16] We can read in two notarial charters from Dalmatia, issued in 1239, about the dukedom of Andrew in Slavonia, but it might have projected the present situation back into the past: "quo dominus Andreas bone recordationis quondam rex Ungarie erat dux Sclauonie" (*Codex diplomaticus regni Croatiae*, 4:91). See Zsoldos, "Egész Szlavónia bánja," 280; Kristó, *A feudális széttagolódás Magyarországon*, 92; Attila Zsoldos considered the possibility that the consolidation of special territorial rules in Slavonia and Transylvania was completed by Prince Béla (Zsoldos, "Egész Szlavónia bánja," 280).

[17] György Györffy was referring to this possibility, and recently Nataša Procházková expressed a similar view. Györffy, "Szlavónia kialakulásának oklevélkritikai," 234; Procházková, "Some Notes on the Titles of Coloman," 107–8.

Coloman approved by the papacy concerned Galicia alone, even though such a kingdom only existed in theory.

There is no extant evidence either to support any hypothesis that Coloman, after his return to Hungary, might have used the title "Duke of Scepus" (*dux Scepusiae*) or started the later tradition of the lords of this region, *"dominus terrae Scepusiensis*.[18]

Moving from the charters issued in the name of the prince to the papal charters, we see a slightly different picture. In 1231, Pope Gregory IX called Coloman *the illustrious king of the Ruthenians and the duke of Slavonia* when he gave a mandate to Bishop Bartholomew of Pécs, regarding litigation between the prince and the Templars of Slavonia. The first papal letter sent directly to Coloman named him—following the formulas of the Chancery of the Apostolic See and Hungarian practice—*beloved son in Christ and illustrious king*.[19] Yet in two papal mandates issued in the same year, 1233 (December 23),[20] he was called *the king of Slavonia* (*Sclavonie*). This phrase has led to some wild interpretations, such as the idea that behind this *inscriptio* a reference to the Slavic kingdom of Svatopluk can be seen, while others have talked of Coloman's goal of creating an autonomous political entity within the Hungarian kingdom.[21] In our opinion, these presumptions are highly improbable since here the royal title was linked to a territory not an ethnicity (unlike the later term *sclavorum*). Later examples suggest that the peculiarities of these charters can be traced back to the operations of the papal chancery, where the term Slavonia was in use in a different sense than in Hungary.[22] It is also possible that the nature of the mandates—papal protections of two Polish widowed duchesses, Grzymisława of Sandomierz and Viola of Opole—had some influence on the address of Coloman, which is why it never appeared again. There are other records from 1234 in which the prince was named king without any territorial indicators. The sense that the use of "king" in the cases above were an error is further indicated by the fact that Pope Gregory IX wrote about the Slavonian duchy of Coloman in his letter to the duke con-

---

[18] See the use further: "haličským kráľom, chorvátsko-slavónslcym i spišským vojvodom" in Homza, *Uhorsko polska kronika*, 25; Zsoldos, "Szepes megye kialakulása," 25; Bagi, "Sclavonia a Magyar–lengyel krónikában," 46; Dąbrowski, *Daniel Romanowicz, biografia polityczna*, 361–64; Zsoldos, "Egész Szlavónia bánja," 276–78; Font, *Árpád-házi királyok*, 206–10; Procházková, "Postavenie haličského kráľa," 70–71; Procházková, "Koloman Haličský na Spiši," 246; Procházková, "Some Notes on the Titles of Coloman," 105–9; Kanyó, "Kálmán herczeg," 415.

[19] "carissimi in Christo filii nostri Colomani, Regis Ruthenorum illustris, et Ducis Sclavonie" (*Codex diplomaticus Hungariae*, 3/2:112, *Regesta Pontificum Romanorum*, no. 8776). Also "carissimo in Christo filio nostro, Colomano, regi illustri" in *Vetera monumenta historica Hungariam*, 1, no. 201, *Regesta Pontificum Romanorum*, no. 9305, *Registres de Grégoire IX*, no. 1522 (October 10, 1233).

[20] In this, Coloman was entrusted to be a lay protector of the widowed polish duchesses. See Barabás, "Prinz Koloman," 2–6.

[21] "Carissimo in Christo filio, C. illustri regi Sclavonie" (*Vetera monumenta historica Hungariam*, 1, no. 204; *Regesta Pontificum Romanorum*, no. 9352; *Registres de Grégoire IX*, no. 1649). See furthermore *Regesta Pontificum Romanorum*, no. 9349. Cf. Procházková, "Some Notes on the Titles of Coloman," 108–9; Goss, "Bishop Stjepan II," 212; Goss, "Slovak and Croatian Art in the Thirteenth Century," 261.

[22] Fine, *When Ethnicity Did Not Matter in the Balkans*, 106–9.

cerning the planned union of the bishopric of Zagreb with the archbishopric of Zagreb in June 1240.[23]

Only one single passage in Coloman's charters exists in which the duke referred to his territory as a *regnum*. One such case does not justify the assumption that Coloman thought of his rule in Hungary in terms of a kingdom, since it seems to be a curious usage of the word in connection to his royal title. It is just one instance, questionable wording, and the charter itself is only known due to a later transcrip.[24]

One other record—although of questionable authenticity—at first sight might support the theory of Coloman planning to establish an independent kingdom in Slavonia. Bishop Stephen of Zagreb addressed himself, according to the text, as *general vicar of the Slavonian kingdom*,[25] but the authenticity of this charter is highly doubtful, and the phrase is found nowhere else in other diplomas of the prelate, or anywhere else for that matter.

Conceivably Coloman might have intended to connect his royal dignity with territorial rule in Slavonia, but no documentation can back this up. A charter of King Béla IV from September 1241 may appear to support the interpretation, since Béla referred to Slavonia after his brother's death explicitly as a duchy.[26] But it is contradicted by another royal diploma. Béla IV confirmed the privileges, borders, and estates of the Dalmatian town, Trogir, in March 1242, while he took refuge there from the Mongol threat. In it a passage mentions the Mongol attack against *the kingdom of Hungary and Slavonia*.[27] Nevertheless, the word "kingdom" was used in its singular form, so there is no reason to read it as if Béla IV were acknowledging assumed earlier intentions of his brother. Finally, Coloman was called the king of Hungary in the annals of the Cistercian abbey of Heiligenkreutz in Austria, while reporting his death. Yet there is no reason to give any credit to this reference, and it must have been the mistake of the author.[28] The

---

23 Barabás, "Prinz Koloman," 2-6. Cf. Dąbrowski, "Slovak and Southern Slavic Threads in the Genealogy of the Piast and Rurikid Dynasties," 113-16; Procházková, "Some Notes on the Titles of Coloman," 108. "carissimo in Christo filio nostro illustri regi Colomanno" in *Vetera monumenta historica Hungariam*, 1, no. 218, *Regesta Pontificum Romanorum*, no. 9726, *Registres de Grégoire IX*, no. 2128. See furthermore *Regesta Pontificum Romanorum*, nos. 9728 and 9735. In the letter sent to Coloman's wife Andrew II was mentioned too: "Salomee regine, uxori Colomanni regis, nati [...] illustris regis Ungarie" (*Registres de Grégoire IX*, no. 2126). And "[...] ducatum tuum Sclavonie" in *Vetera monumenta historica Hungariam*, 1, no. 322, *Regesta Pontificum Romanorum*, no. 10890, *Registres de Grégoire IX*, no. 5216.

24 *Regesta ducum, ducissarum*, no. 10. Cf. Basić, "O pokušaju ujedinjenja," 34; Kristó, *A feudális széttagolódás Magyarországon*, 67, 93.

25 "Nos Stephanus diuina prouidencia episcopus Zagrabiensis et regni Sclauonie vicarius generalis" (*Codex diplomaticus Arpadianus*, 7:74).

26 "[...] contra quendam potentem de Theotonia nomine comitem Albrihum de Myho confinia ducatus Sclavonie sepius invadentem dimicando viriliter exercuit [...]" (*Codex diplomaticus regni Croatiae*, 4:136, *Regesta regum stirpis Arpadianae*, no. 709).

27 "[...] nostrum dominium reuerentes, qui eciam nos tam honorifice supectos in suis munitionibus simul cum nostris pluribus, qui de regno Vngarie et Sclauonie fatie (!) Tartarorum affugerant" (*Codex diplomaticus Croatiae*, 4:146, *Regesta regum stirpis Arpadianae*, no. 715).

28 "Cholomannus rex Ungarie obiit" in the *Continuatio Sancrucensis II* (*Catalogus fontium historiae*

same can be stated regarding the formulation of the *Chronicon Poloniae* of Godysław Baszko, which refers to Béla and Coloman as *kings of the Hungarians*.[29]

Compared to those exceptional, probably mistaken, formulas, a royal charter of 1255 shows the general practice in the 1230s (*king and duke of Slavonia*), a charter describing Coloman's participation in the investigations on the former royal benefactions.[30] Likewise, Coloman appears in the works of Thomas of Split also as duke, and not once as king of Slavonia.[31]

Parallel to the Hungarian situation, there is one example in which Coloman was called *noble man and duke of Slavonia*, neglecting his royal title. This can be explained by the nature of the case (litigation concerning several possessions) and perhaps by the fact that the charter was issued in a case under papal jurisdiction. But in a papal letter of 1235—but still under the reign of Andrew II—Pope Gregory IX addressed Coloman as *king and the son of his father*, presumably not independently of the fact that he was confirming Andrew's donation to prince Coloman. Later on, we do observe members of the papal chancery using the title *duke of Slavonia* and his rank as king differentially and separately.[32] This is a clear contrast to the consolidation of the royal and ducal titles within Coloman's own charters.

Let us conclude with a few remaining exceptional charters. Coloman was called *illustrious king and the duke of the Slavs* in two papal charters, issued in April and December 1238, concerning the affairs of Bosnia. This was repeated on June 6, 1240, when Gregory IX wrote to the duke about the planned union of the archbishopric of Split with the dio-

---

Hungaricae, no. 1782) cited by Gábor Bradács, "A tatárjárás osztrák elbeszélő forrásainak kritikája [Critique of the Austrian Narrative Sources of the Mongol Invasion]," *Hadtörténeti Közlemények* 127 (2014): 3–22 at 16.

29 "[...] occurrerunt ei Bela et Colomanus fratres, reges Hungarorum" (*Chronicon Poloniae* of Godysław Baszko in the *Catalogus fontium historiae Hungaricae*, no. 2569).

30 "[...] carissimus frater noster felicis memorie rex Colomanus, dux tocius Sclauonie, fecisset in ducatu Sclauonie" (*Codex diplomaticus regni Croatiae*, 4:59, *Regesta regum stirpis Arpadianae*, no. 1039).

31 "Post hec vero Colomannus filius Andree regis, dux Sclavonie, cum magno principum comitatu ad mare descendit at a Spalatensibus multum honorifice susceptus est" (*Thomae archidiaconi Spalatensis Historia Salonitanorum*, 196–98).

32 "carissimo in Christo filio Colomano illustri regi Ruthenorum ac duci Sclavonie" in *Vetera monumenta historica Hungariam*, 1, no. 253, *Regesta Pontificum Romanorum*, no. 10086, *Registres de Grégoire IX*, no. 2920. See: *Regesta Pontificum Romanorum*, nos. 10671, 10688, 10822, 10890 and *Registres de Grégoire IX*, no. 5774, 6058. "Dei dilecto filio nobili viro Colomanno duci Sclavon" (DF 206 949, *Regesta Pontificum Romanorum*, 9848. Vagy csak mint Szlavónia hercege). "Cum ex litteris Colomani, **ducis Sclavonie, intelleximus** [...]" in *Vetera monumenta historica Hungariam*, 1, no. 312, *Regesta Pontificum Romanorum*, no. 10823, *Registres de Grégoire IX*, no. 4992 (my emphasis). See also "carissimo in Christo filio, illustri regi Colomano, nato carissimi in Christo filii nostri A. illustris regis Ungarie" in *Vetera monumenta historica Hungariam*, 1, no. 229, *Regesta Pontificum Romanorum*, no. 9986, *Registres de Grégoire IX*, no. 2726. And "carissimo in Christo filio Colomano illustri regi Ruthenorum ac duci Sclavonie" in *Vetera monumenta historica Hungariam*, 1, no. 253, *Regesta Pontificum Romanorum*, no. 10086, *Registres de Grégoire IX*, no. 2920. Cf. Bárány, "II. András balkáni külpolitikája," 158–59.

cese of Zagreb and called him again *king and the duke of the Slavs*. In our opinion, these exceptions should not be overstated; the genitive case is not referring to the royal title but to the ducal one alone, and so we cannot deduce that Coloman was king of some territorial entity. The nature of each case is relevant for the peculiar formulations, since dealing with the affairs of Bosnia and Dalmatia (Split) could explain the need to mention ethnicity.[33] It seems us to be clear that consistent and unambiguous separation of the titles of prince and king exists and can be observed both in the Hungarian and the papal documentary records.

Two remaining formulas for Coloman's titles now need to be dismissed. Prof. Homza has used the term *duke of Scepus* and has also written about Coloman's *Croatian–Slavonian kingdom*. Meanwhile, Prof. Goss has used the formulation of *viceroy*. Neither of these terms exist in the extant charters and should be avoided.[34]

Finally, let us examine a special group of sources, the charters issued in 1233 by Andrew II, Béla, and Coloman. In this year Jacob of Pecorari, the papal legate in Hungary, finally achieved his goal and managed to sign a concordat with the Hungarian king, the so-called Oath of Bereg. Consistent with this pact, Andrew and his sons took an oath to abide by the agreement, and moreover they even issued their own charters about this oath. Admittedly, the letters of the king and Béla were released by the staff of the papal legate and show typical features of the *stilus curiae*. Yet Coloman's charter is written consistent with the practices and form of conventional princely documents. The *intitulationes* corroborate these observations as well. Andrew II was only mentioned by legate Jacob, and even there with an unusually short formula. Later the charter was transcribed, with the later version showing more standardized elements, although the list of the territories ruled is still absent. In Béla's charter, we cannot speak of significant variations, though these can all be linked to the personnel of the legate.[35] The *intitulatio* of Coloman, however, resembles the traditional formulas from the 1230s. The reason for this difference may lie in the priorities of Legate Jacob, since the assurance of the king and his heir could have been more important for him, whereas that of the duke of Slavonia was only subsidiary.

---

33 "carissimus in Christo filius noster, Colomanus rex et dux Sclavorum illustris" in *Vetera monumenta historica Hungariam*, 1, no. 289, *Regesta Pontificum Romanorum*, no. 10585, *Registres de Grégoire IX*, no. 4286. To the abbot of Pécsvárad: "carissimi in Christo filii nostri Colomanni, regis illustris. ducis Sclavorum" in *Vetera monumenta historica Hungariam*, 1, no. 304, *Regesta Pontificum Romanorum*, no. 10690, *Registres de Grégoire IX*, no. 4696. And "carissimo in Christo filio Colomano, illustri regi et duci Sclavorum" in *Vetera monumenta historica Hungariam*, 1, no. 322, *Regesta Pontificum Romanorum*, no. 10890, *Registres de Grégoire IX*, no. 5216; Györffy, "Szlavónia kialakulásának oklevélkritikai," 234; Basić, "O pokušaju ujedinjenja."

34 "haličským kráľom, chorvátsko-slavónslcym i spišským vojvodom" (Homza, *Uhorsko polska kronika*, 25); "królestwo chorwacko-slawońskie" (Homza, "Včasnostredoveké dejiny Spiša," 148). See further, Goss, "Bishop Stjepan II," 211.

35 *Regesta ducum, ducissarum*, no. 11 ; *Regesta regum stirpis Arpadianae*, nos. 500, 501, 599. Béla's charter of 1234: *Regesta regum stirpis Arpadianae*, no. 604. "Constitutionem sigillorum domini Andree, illustris regis, et filiorum suorum, scil. domini Bele, et domini Colomani regum munimine roboratam" (*Codex diplomaticus Hungariae*, 3/2:312). Cf. Almási, "Egy ciszterci bíboros," 135–38.

In summary, with regard to the *intitulationes* in the charters, the only aspect of heterogeneity occurs when Coloman, by virtue of being the son of Andrew II, became the duke of Slavonia whilst retaining his previous royal title as well. In papal sources, by contrast, the mixed use of the titles is far more apparent. We can observe a trend towards unification—which led to a more consistent practice of issuing charters in both cases—and this trend was reinforced as Coloman's rule was consolidated. The matter of forms of titles in charters has gained a special importance because they have often been examined out of context and without a critical eye, leading to sold wild conclusions. Our more systematic analysis of the complete corpus, however, can reveal which expressions are probably false formulations and can show the kind of processes underlying the practice of linking the regal and ducal titles.

The Ducal Court, Officers, and Chancery

We know far more about the court of Duke Coloman (*aula ducis*) than where it was. The ducal court probably included, beside the Slavonian and Croatian *bans* and Croatian-Dalmatian lords, the royal officials, and the *ispáns* (counts) of the relevant Hungarian counties. Of these the counts of Zala, Somogy, Valkó, and Baranya appear at Coloman's court, whilst his master of the stewards was the count of Bodrog County. Additional officials comprised a treasurer (*camerarius*), master of the horses (*magister agazonum*), and master of the cupbearers (*magister pincernarum*).[36] Indeed the duke frequently referred to the consensus of his barons regarding his measures, and even the agreement of the lords of Béla IV have been mentioned, if we believe the relevant records.[37]

One of the most important developments in the first half of the thirteenth century was a change in the jurisdiction of the Croatian *ban*, which by then took in Slavonia too, and so the title was changed to *ban of whole Slavonia*, the highest title after the duke's own. The office of *viceban* also appears in documents frequently at that period, and this title was held by the counts of Zagreb. In most cases the *bans* and their deputies did not refer to Duke Coloman in their documents,[38] although this can be explained by the purpose of their charters, which were meant to guarantee certain judgements and agreements.

---

[36] *Regesta ducum, ducissarum*, nos. 9 and 19; *Regesta regum stirpis Arpadianae*, no. 529; cf. Györffy, "Szlavónia kialakulásának oklevélkritikai," 129; Kristó, *A feudális széttagolódás Magyarországon*, 60–61, 69, 84–94; Zsoldos, "Az ifjabb király országa," 243–44; Zsoldos, *Magyarország világi archontológiája*, 71, 73–74; Sokcsevits, *Horvátország*, 116–17; Zsoldos, "Hercegek és hercegnők," 18–19.

[37] *Regesta ducum, ducissarum*, nos. 13 and 15. Cf. Kristó, *A feudális széttagolódás Magyarországon*, 60–61.

[38] For example, *Codex diplomaticus Arpadianus*, 9:216; *Hazai okmánytár—Codex Diplomaticus Patrius*, ed. Imre Nagy et al., 8 vols. (Győr and Budapest, 1865–91), 8:37; *Codex diplomaticus regni Croatiae*, 4:122. See Zsoldos, *Magyarország világi archontológiája*, 41, 44–46, 48; Angelika Herucová, "Dionýz de Türje – priateľ a spolubojovník Bela IV [Denis Türje—Friend and Colleague of Béla IV]," in *Vojenské konflikty v dejinách Európy*, ed. Nikoleta Dzurikaninová, Stretnutie mladých historikov 5 (Košice: Univerzita Pavla Jozefa Šafárika v Košiciach, 2016), 36–48.

Last but not least, was Bishop Stephen of Zagreb, probably the most important person in Slavonia beside the duke. His relevance is reflected among other things in the intended union of the bishopric of Zagreb with the archbishopric of Split, in Dalmatia, to which we will return later because of its quite extraordinary nature. The peace and alliance between the Dalmatian cities of Split and Trogir in 1239 shows Coloman's success, according to extant documents, at the furthest flung quarter of his territory.[39]

Surviving ducal charters offer insights into Coloman's chancery. After a short period of time the provost of Zagreb bore the position of the chancellor, similar to the previous practice under Prince Béla. This was a position of trust, so it is not very surprising that the duke repeatedly promoted Provost File from the Miskolc kindred. The reputation of the office is reflected in a charter of the provostry of Pécs, where his position as chancellor of Coloman was added to File's name alongside his *magister*-title.[40]

We know nothing about the intellectual life of the ducal court, although the so-called *Hungarian–Polish Chronicle* offers some information. The author of the chronicle is unknown, but some claim it was presumably written in Slavonia in Coloman's court in the first half of the thirteenth century. Homza even talks of an intellectual circle around the duke and his brother, Béla, to justify the origin of the chronicle.[41] But this remains conjecture.

Coloman and the *Hungarian–Polish Chronicle*

Let us now examine the possible circumstance for the creation of the *Hungarian–Polish Chronicle* (*Chronicon mixtum*, *Chronicon Hungarico–Polonicum*), to know more about Coloman's court, but we will neglect the stories themselves, since most of the narrative is generally considered not authentic. The remaining exemplars exist in at least four different manuscripts, all now in Poland. Scholars have tended to look for a Polish author, partly because the chronicle was known in Poland, partly because of its influence on Polish medieval historiography.

Ryszard Grzesik first formulated a theory of a Hungarian origin. His assumed nominee was bishop Calan of Pécs, but he later changed his opinion due to the importance of Slavonia and the presence of Croatian traditions in the history. In Grzesik's view, the chronicle was written in the court of Coloman a few years after the death of the bishop of Pécs. Others beside Grzesik emphasized the possible role of Coloman based on the Southern-Slavic and Dalmatian elements of the chronicle, whilst the duke's wife, Salomea, and her entourage gained attention too. Adrien Quéret-Podesta argues that the fictional work was intended as a present for the ducal couple and the widowed Salomea

---

39 *Codex diplomaticus Hungariae*, 7/4:88.

40 *Codex diplomaticus regni Croatiae*, 4:74. Coloman's chancellor was Provost Paska of Eger in 1231–1232, while Matthias, provost of Zagreb, acted as Prince Béla's chancellor since 1224. See Györffy, "Szlavónia kialakulásának oklevélkritikai," 129–30; Zsoldos, *Magyarország világi archontológiája*, 118.

41 Kristó, *A feudális széttagolódás Magyarországon*, 75; Homza, *Uhorsko polska kronika*, 37, 189, 193–94.

brought it with herself back to Poland after Coloman's death. It is also conceivable that Béla IV's daughter, Kunigunda, carried an example of the chronicle to Kraków, when she married Bolesław V the Chaste, Salomea's younger brother in 1239. Karol Hollý believes, based on the chronicle's narrative of the Hungarian campaigns in the Rus', that the main reason for creating the stories was Coloman's goal to find a way to legitimate his rule in Galicia. Grzesik also sees the chronicle as the manifestation of Hungarian claims over Galicia, and so places the chronicle's creation to the Galician years of Coloman's brother, Prince Andrew.[42]

Recently Martin Homza came up with an idea which diverged from the Slavonian theory. In his view, the chronicle can be linked to Coloman's environment, but instead of the southern provinces he has suggested Scepus. He even offers a particular candidate for author: the chronicle being written by Provost Adolf of Scepus in the 1220s or 1230s. According to Homza, Adolf could have been even the tutor of Coloman. He uses one particular scene to make this connection, the request by the first Hungarian king, St. Stephen, for a crown from the Holy See. In the chronicle, the pope made contemptuous comments on the barbaric Hungarians while granting the requested diadem to Stephen. According to Homza, a native Hungarian could not have written this part. He, like many other scholars, thinks that the work was meant to support Coloman's claims for Galicia; in his opinion, the Ruthenian conquests of King Ladislaus mirrored the Slavonian duke's plans. Homza also attacks the idea that the chronicle originated in *Sclavonia* since the term, he argues, was used generally for any area populated by Slavic inhabitants, and not to a specific district within the Kingdom of Hungary. Dániel Bagi, conversely, argued that the *Sclavonia*-concept mentioned in the chronicle can be identified, unquestionably, with the region of Slavonia.[43]

Recently, Judit Csákó, has dedicated a study to the questionable nature of the chronicle and reflected on the theories concerning the date and place of its writing. She does not think that the southern elements of the *Hungarian–Polish Chronicle* are conclusive,

---

42 Ryszard Grzesik, *Kronika węgiersko-polska. Z dziejów polsko-węgierskich kontaktów kulturalnych w średniowieczu [The Hungarian–Polish Chronicle and Medieval Polish-Hungarian Cultural Relations]* (Poznań: Wydawnictwo Poznańskiego Towarzystwa Przyjaciół Nauk, 1999), 210, 216; Ryszard Grzesik, "Sources of a Story About the Murdered Croatian King in the Hungarian-Polish Chronicle," *Povijesni prilozi* 4 (2003): 97–104 at 98; Bagi, "Sclavonia a Magyar–lengyel krónikában," 45; Martin Homza, "Pokus o interpretáciu úlohy kňažnej Adelaidy v Uhorsko-pol'skiej kronike [An Attempt to Interpret the Role of Duchess Adelaide in the *Hungarian-Polish Chronicle*]," in Martin Homza, *Mulieres suadentes. Presviedčajúce ženy* (Bratislava: Lúč, 2002), 110–43 at 142–43; Tóth, "A lengyel–magyar," 223–24; Hollý, "Princess Salomea and Hungarian–Polish Relations," 28, 33–34; Adrien Quéret-Podesta, "Vom Ungarn der Árpáden zum Polen der Piasten. Zur Entstehung und zum Schicksal der sogenannten Ungarisch-polnischen Chronik," in *Mittelalterliche Eliten und Kulturtransfer östlich der Elbe. Interdisziplinäre Beiträge zu Archäologie und Geschichte im mittelalterlichen Ostmitteleuropa*, ed. Anne Klammt and Sébastien Rossignol (Göttingen: Universitätsverlag Göttingen, 2009), 70–79 at 73–75; Csákó, "A Magyar–lengyel Krónika," 307–9.

43 Homza, *Uhorsko polska kronika*, 22–27, 58–59, 83–85, 191; Procházková, "Koloman Haličský na Spiši," 248; Csákó, "A Magyar–lengyel Krónika," 312–13; Bagi, "Sclavonia a Magyar–lengyel krónikában," 45. For Adolf see also *Regesta regum stirpis Arpadianae*, no. 243 and Labanc, *Spišskí prepošti*, 66–70.

and, even so, this does not link the work to Coloman, since his elder brother, Béla, was duke of Slavonia before him, so information could have derived just as well from Béla's court. Csákó went further and even argued that the chronicle was not necessarily written in Hungary (either in Slavonia or in the Scepus), and that a Polish place of origin cannot be ruled out. The milieu of Salomea, or even Princess Kunigunda, daughter of king Béla IV, and her younger sister, Princess Jolanta, the wife of Bolesław the Pious, duke of Greater Poland, could offer the perfect opportunity for the author of the chronicle to gather the necessary information and stories. According to her, any presumed role of Coloman needs re-evaluation, as too any theories concerning Slavonia or Scepus.[44]

Notwithstanding, we cannot rule out the chronicle having been written in Coloman's environment, even if the exact place is hard to find. Were this the case, we might conclude that a semi-historical work was written in the ducal court, perhaps imitating royal models. Serious factual errors might be explained, however, by the desire for narrative strength and the lack of knowledge of the Hungarian dynastic tradition. The author tried to fill the holes with his own interpretations, so it is unlikely that the chronicle was written in Coloman's environment, or, indeed, anywhere in Hungary.

Coloman's Revenues and Treasury

Coloman received income from many sources and extant documentations can tell us about taxes, though we know nothing about any minting of money in the duchy under his rule. The number of territories over which he ruled complicates our analysis, since one has to include ducal incomes from Slavonia, Croatia, Dalmatia, and several Hungarian counties as well. In Slavonia the dukes received two-thirds of the special tax for the province, the so-called *marturina* (literarily, the tax of the leather of the marten; see the name of the Croatian currency, the *kuna*, or marten). This tax was paid in coins by peasants since the time of King Coloman the Learned, equivalent first to twenty-four, later forty-two, Friesach pennies per household (*mansio*) at the beginning of the thirteenth century. The nobility, the inhabitants of the royal castles, and the clergy were exempt from the *marturina*. Coloman indeed expected this type of tax, and even donated it to several existing territories on numerous occasions, even if this led to disputes, as his litigation with the Templars of Slavonia proves.

Among other regular income for Coloman can be included the ducal *descensus*, the free pennies (*denarii*), the *pondus*, and several tolls. The duke's treasury probably received extraordinary taxes too, although no sources can vouch for this assumption.[45]

---

44 Csákó, "A Magyar–lengyel Krónika," 308–13, 315.

45 *Regesta regum stirpis Arpadianae*, no. 719; Boglárka Weisz, "Királyi adók Szlavóniában a középkor első felében (11–14. század) [Royal Taxes in Slavonia in the First Half of the Middle Ages (Eleventh to Fourteenth Centuries)]," in *Aktualitások a magyar középkorkutatásban. In memoriam Gyula Kristó (1939–2004)*, ed. Tamás Fedeles et al. (Pécs: PTE BTK TTI Középkori és Koraújkori Történeti Tanszék, 2010), 125–40; Boglárka Weisz, "Királyi adók Szlavóniában az Árpád-kortól az Anjou-kor első feléig [Royal Taxes In Slavonia from the Árpádian Age Until the First Half of the Angevin Era]," in *A horvát–magyar együttélés fordulópontjai. Intézmények, társadalom, gazdaság, kultúra*, ed. Pál Fodor et al. (Budapest: MTA Bölcsészettudományi Kutatóközpont Történettudományi

There is a special charter though, which deserves attention. Béla IV confirmed several estates and incomes of the Templars due to the request of their *magister*, Rambald, in 1238. According to the king's ordinance, the knights were obliged to hand over one-fifth of any estates to Coloman, in case they happened to find gold there. After the eventual closure of the mine, they could repossess these territories, according to the royal charter, whilst two-thirds of the remaining taxes from the land should by custom go to the royal treasury.[46] Despite evidence of local taxes going to Hungarian royal coffers, it seems that Coloman's brother kept his eye on the duke's interests and secured him necessary incomes while investigating the former royal benefactions.

Having examined the territories over which Coloman ruled and the structures of government at his command, let us now explore how he governed, starting with some key episodes with major ecclesiastical and secular figures.

Intézet, Horvát Történettudományi Intézet, 2015), 233–41. Cf. Sokcsevits, *Horvátország*, 118. Regarding coinage in Slavonia see: Tamás Körmendi, "A magyar királyok kettőskeresztes címerének kialakulása [The Development of the Hungarian King's Coat of Arms with the Double Cross]," *Turul* 84 (2011): 73–83 at 74, 79–82.

46 *Regesta regum stirpis Arpadianae*, no. 637; Boglárka Weisz, "II. András jövedelmei: régi és új elemek [Incomes of Andrew II: Old and New Elements]," in *II. András és Székesfehérvár / King Andrrw II and Székesfehérvár*, ed. Terézia Kerny and András Smohay (Székesfehérvár: Székesfehérvári Egyházmegyei Múzeum, 2012), 49–80 at 58.

Chapter 10

COLOMAN'S ECCLESIASTICAL AND SECULAR ACTITIVITIES IN SLAVONIA

WE KNOW ABOUT several interactions with ecclesiastical and secular lords which cast light on Coloman's rule. In turn we will discuss his conflict with the Knights Templar, his relationship with Bishop Stephen of Zagreb, major constructions of castles and religious buildings, and then the ambitious union of the bishopric of Zagreb with the archdiocese of Split.

Litigation with the Knights Templar of Slavonia

The Templars of Slavonia approached the court of the Apostolic See to litigate against Coloman. The papal procedure was initiated due to a complaint from the order who claimed that the duke had taken hold of certain possessions and had restricted their privileges. The Templars instigated proceedings in July 1231, and in a letter to the duke the pope admonished Coloman to respect the order's privileges and to restore their estates.[1]

This letter was, however, not the first step in the procedure. The duke's actions had already led to papal authorization of the bishops of Pécs and Zagreb, and the archbishop of Kalocsa who were delegated to engage in ecclesiastical censure of Coloman and his advisers, if necessary. It is remarkable that the Templars would work with the bishop of Zagreb, with whom they had previously been in litigation over a particular estate; the procedure started at the Slavonian duke's court, whereas later the agreement was made with the help of Archbishop Ugrin of Kalocsa.[2] The pope had to authorize new delegates because of the duke's refusal to cooperate, so the bishop and the provost of Pécs, and the Benedictine abbot of Pécsvárad were mandated instead in July 1231. They were, however, not empowered to excommunicate Coloman, even though the duke finally accepted the terms of Gregory IX and granted immunity to the Slavonian, Croatian, and Dalmatian provinces of the Templars and freed their estates from all taxes (*marturina*, *collecta*, *pondus*, and so forth) and from tolls.[3] Nevertheless, a later papal letter makes it clear

---

1 *Regesta ducum, ducissarum*, no. 8; Kanyó, "Kálmán herczeg," 421–23; Weisz and Zsoldos, "A báni joghatóság Szlavóniában," 471. Nataša Procházková dates the opposition back to 1227 and states that the privilege of 1231 is a result of it. Procházková, "Postavenie haličského kráľa," 72. For the local Templars see Zsolt Hunyadi, "The Formation of the Territorial Structure of the Templars and Hospitallers in the Medieval Kingdom of Hungary," in *Die geistlichen Ritterorden in Mitteleuropa: Mittelalter*, ed. Karl Borchardt and Jan Libor (Brno: Matice moravská für Das Forschungszentrum für die Geschichte Mitteleuropas, 2011), 183–200 at 184–86.

2 *Codex diplomaticus regni Croatiae*, 3:331–32.

3 *Regesta ducum, ducissarum*, no. 8; *Regesta Pontificum Romanorum*, no. 8762, *Registres de Grégoire IX*, no. 679; *Regesta Pontificum Romanorum*, no. 10216, *Registres de Grégoire IX*, no. 3255. See Koszta, "Egy francia származású," 30; Weisz and Zsoldos, "A báni joghatóság Szlavóniában," 471; Weisz, "Királyi adók Szlavóniában a középkor," 131, 134.

that the duke did not comply with his own promises. Gregory IX admonished Coloman's actions again in January 1236, as he took hold of several estates from the order. Tension must have been high, since several Hungarian clerics received a papal mandate in 1236, and they were authorized to end the conflict.[4]

The first known agreement took three years, however, in 1239, when Bishop Bartholomew of Pécs issued a charter jointly with the local cathedral chapter over a settlement between the duke and the order. This measure did not exclusively treat the conflict between Coloman and the Templars, but the duke's donation to the bishop was secured, as too the tithe of Našice (Nekcse) in Baranya County for the knights. This seems the show that the conflict was passed by then. A later event also points in this direction, as the *magister* of the Hungarian province of the order, Rambald de Carumb, fought along with Coloman against the Mongols in the battle of Muhi in 1241, where he even lost his life.[5]

Coloman's Relation to Bishop Stephen of Zagreb

One of the key figures in Coloman's rule of Slavonia was the senior prelate in the area. The duke's relation to Bishop Stephen of Zagreb was very close, and not only because of the partial overlap of Slavonia and the diocese of Zagreb.[6] Stephen gained his bishopric only a few years before Coloman's rule started, and they cooperated effectively from then onwards, if we follow what the sources say.

Stephen belonged, according to certain scholars, to the Croatian Babonić family, although others think he was Hungarian, possibly of the Hahót-Buzád or the Atyusz kindred. It is unquestionable, however, that beside his ecclesiastical dignities he also held an important secular office as provost of Arad. He was additionally royal chancellor for Andrew II in 1224 and was elected bishop of Zagreb the following year. He had also been a papal subdeacon, which must have had an impact on his career in the Church. His election is interesting because Stephen's predecessor, who bore the same name, was complained about by Primogenitus, another papal subdeacon, to Pope Honorius III. The procedure against Stephen (I) is unclear but seems to involve two papal clerics. By 1225 Stephen (II) was now the elected bishop of Zagreb in 1225.[7]

The prelate had a good relationship with the papacy according to the letters of Gregory IX from July 1227. The pope confirmed earlier donations to the bishopric of Zagreb

---

[4] *Regesta Pontificum Romanorum*, no. 10086, *Registres de Grégoire IX*, nos. 2920 and 2921; *Regesta Pontificum Romanorum*, no. 10216, *Registres de Grégoire IX*, nos. 3255 and 3256. See Györffy, "Szlavónia kialakulásának oklevélkritikai," 232; Koszta, "Egy francia származású," 30.

[5] *Codex diplomaticus Hungariae*, 4/1:172, DF 280 267. See Györffy, "Szlavónia kialakulásának oklevélkritikai," 235; Zsoldos, "Az ifjabb király országa," 244; Szabó, *A tatárjárás. A mongol hódítás*, 135–38.

[6] Cf. Györffy, "Szlavónia kialakulásának oklevélkritikai," 230.

[7] Basić, "O pokušaju ujedinjenja," 34; Procházková, "Some Notes on the Titles of Coloman,"; Zsoldos, *Magyarország világi archontológiája*, 108; Dujmović and Jukić, "The 'Koloman Renaissance'," 174; Goss, "Battle of Cathedrals," 146; Goss, "Bishop Stjepan II," 212; Goss, "Slovak and Croatian Art in the Thirteenth Century," 261; Körmendi, "Szlavónia korai hovatartozása," 379; Juhász, "A csázmai társaskáptalan," 1–3 (full citation above).

by King Emeric and Andrew II in one of his first charters ever issued on Hungarian matters. This confirms a royal charter of 1217 which seems to be an impressive forgery. Its quality is reflected not only in its confirmation by Gregory IX but also by subsequent royal confirmations. Tamás Körmendi, even stated that it was Bishop Stephen himself who as former royal chancellor performed the forgery.[8]

We might assume that the relation of Coloman to the bishop of Zagreb was influenced by the fact that they appeared in Slavonia shortly after each other. Certain scholars even think that this situation was the result of Andrew II's "political masterplan," although the theory has no supporting evidence. Thomas of Split characterized Bishop Stephen in his *Historia Salonitanorum* as a man who "had great wealth in gold and silver and was endowed with other riches as well and who lavished in worldly pomp."[9] Modern Croatian historians see Stephen, on the contrary, as essentially positive: a talented administrator, a skilled and educated man, and the supporter of the dynasty, as someone who revived the tradition of learning in Zagreb. Some even call the era of Coloman and Stephen, quite hyperbolically, as a "little renaissance."[10]

One of the most ambitious manifestations of the cooperation between duke and prelate was the plan to unite the bishopric of Zagreb with the archbishopric of Split.[11] Before we analyze this topic, let us investigate another aspect of Coloman's relation to Bishop Stephen and their possible impact on the architecture of Slavonia.

Slavonia's Architectural Remains

Two major Slavonian constructions can be—hypothetically—linked to the pairing of the duke and the bishop in the first half of the thirteenth century: Medvedgrad castle near Zagreb and the St. Mary Magdalene church and its monasteries of Čazma (which in turn demonstrates the influence of the cathedral of Esztergom, perhaps thanks to the role of Coloman). Some scholars believe that Čazma was meant to be the future seat of the Slavonian duke, and certain constructions in the town also show ambitions for urbanization in the area.[12]

The castle of Medvedgrad also reflects the influence of Hungarian architecture. At least a window in its chapel seems to be related to that of the Cistercian abbey of Kerc (Cârța)

---

8 *Regesta Pontificum Romanorum*, nos. 7959–60, *Registres de Grégoire IX*, nos. 148–49; *Regesta regum stirpis Arpadianae*, no. 323. See Györffy, "Szlavónia kialakulásának oklevélkritikai," 230–34. See Körmendi, "Szlavónia korai hovatartozása," 374–80.

9 *Thomae archidiaconi Spalatensis Historia Salonitanorum*, 306–7.

10 See Goss, "Battle of Cathedrals," 146; Goss, "Bishop Stjepan II," 212; Cepetić and Goss, "A Note on the Rose Window in Čazma," 184; Goss, "Slovak and Croatian Art in the Thirteenth Century," 261; Dujmović and Jukić, "The 'Koloman Renaissance'," 174.

11 Cf. Goss, "Bishop Stjepan II," 212. Stephen became elected archbishop of Split in 1242, but he never received the necessary papal confirmation. He died in 1247. See Goss, "Battle of Cathedrals," 150–52.

12 See Dujmović and Jukić, "The 'Koloman Renaissance'," 174–76; Cepetić and Goss, "A Note on the Rose Window in Čazma," 184–87; Goss, "Slovak and Croatian Art in the Thirteenth Century," 263–64.

Figure 8. The Castle of Medvedgrad (with kind permission of Gábor Barabás).

in Transylvania. Medvedgrad is traditionally thought to be built after the Mongol invasion on the command of Bishop Philip of Zagreb, later archbishop of Esztergom. Based on the mention of the castle in a papal charter of 1252 and on the analysis of its architectural features, it is quite possible that the construction had already begun in the time of Coloman. For instance, the gate of Medvedgrad can be linked to the previously discussed gates of Halych, Gyulafehérvár (Alba Iulia), and even the church of Ják, while the pillars in the castle show similar characteristics to the St. Martin church in Spišská Kapitula and Spiš castle.[13]

If we take a look beyond the strict limits of Slavonia, both the building and the window in the St. Peter chapel in Novo Mesto Zelinsko (near Zagreb) could possibly be related to the architecture and style of Coloman and Stephen's era. Equally, though the Cistercian monastery of Topusko cannot be linked to the duke directly, it is one of the best Slavonian examples of Gothic style in the early thirteenth century.[14]

The period under Coloman has been called "The Slavonian Renaissance" by certain scholars, and they suspect that the duke and Bishop Stephen observed Hungarian prosperity at the turn of the twelfth to thirteenth centuries and tried to transmit the influence of the royal architecture of the time of Béla III, Emeric, and Andrew II into Slavonia. The importance of the St. Adalbert cathedral of Esztergom and the church of Ják sup-

---

13 *Regesta Pontificum Romanorum*, no. 14513; Goss, "Battle of Cathedrals," 147–48; Goss, "Bishop Stjepan II," 214–17; Goss, "Slovak and Croatian Art in the Thirteenth Century," 264–66; Cepetić and Goss, "A Note on the Rose Window in Čazma," 187; Procházková, "Koloman Haličský na Spiši," 247. For Hungarian architecture in the twelfth to thirteenth centuries, see Marosi, *Die Anfänge der Gotik in Ungarn*, and Marosi, *A romanika Magyarországon*.

14 Goss, "Bishop Stjepan II," 213–14; Maja Cepetić and Danko Dujmović, "St Peter at Novo Mesto Zelinsko: New Iconography for Claiming Political Continuity," *Ikon* 5 (2012): 323–30 at 323; Goss, "Slovak and Croatian Art in the Thirteenth Century," 267.

Figure 9. The Church of Čazma (with kind permission of Gergely Kiss).

port this notion, as too a presumed contribution by a builder from Bamberg. Perhaps Andrew II supported his son and his former chancellor and he himself sent craftsmen. Goss stated that the cooperation of Coloman and Stephen imitated, as a *regnum* and *sacerdotium* pairing, the former relation between Béla III and Archbishop Job of Esztergom, although this is perhaps best treated as a hypothesis.[15]

---

[15] Cepetić and Goss, "A Note on the Rose Window in Čazma," 184–87, 189; Goss, "Bishop Stjepan II," 212–14; Goss, "Slovak and Croatian Art in the Thirteenth Century," 266. Regarding Esztergom see Marosi, *Die Anfänge der Gotik in Ungarn*, 53–89; Marosi, *A romanika Magyarországon*, 85–91.

It is worth, furthermore, comparing these Slavonian phenomena with the situation in Scepus, even if any parallels are only theoretical. Coloman's character can be seen, with this argument, as the link between the territories. His influence can be found in the effect of Hungarian architecture in Slavonia. The castles of Medvedgrad and Scepus show resemblances, particularly the towers, so the duke might have had a role in their establishment. The churches of Spišská Kapitula and Čazma suggest that Hungarian royal architecture made an impact even outside of Slavonia. The town of Split offers excellent examples in Dalmatia too.[16]

The Intended Union of the Bishopric of Zagreb and the Archbishopric of Split

To understand the relation between Coloman and Bishop Stephen, we just have to focus on their most ambitious plan, namely, the union of Zagreb and Split, which would have led to the unification of the ecclesiastical system across Croatia, Dalmatia, and Slavonia. The origin of the idea is hard to trace, but scholars agree that the duo of duke and bishop lies behind it. For instance, György Györffy emphasized that by this point there was an added link between Coloman and Stephen, since the provost of Zagreb, File, was the chancellor of the duke. It also could be relevant that Thomas, the later historian, was archdeacon in Split by this time. In his work, the *Historia Salonitanorum atque Spalatinorum pontificum*, he emphasizes his approval of Coloman, making his perhaps one of the duke's supporters, perhaps a silent one, even if he never wrote of the planned union.[17]

The planned union would have concerned territories controlled by Coloman but which ecclesiastically belonged to separate archbishoprics. The diocese of Zagreb was established in the late eleventh century under the Hungarian church and became the suffragan of the archbishop of Kalocsa in the second half of the twelfth century. The new construct of whole Slavonia only partially covered the diocese of Zagreb,[18] which might

---

For the church of Ják: Marosi, *A romanika Magyarországon*, 95–102. For the royal architecture of the era: Marosi, *Die Anfänge der Gotik in Ungarn*, 169–80; Marosi, *A romanika Magyarországon*, 121–32.

16 Dujmović and Jukić, "The 'Koloman Renaissance'," 174; Goss, "Bishop Stjepan II," 215–20; Goss, "Battle of Cathedrals," 151; Goss, "Slovak and Croatian Art in the Thirteenth Century," 261–67; Janovská, "Building Activities in Spiš in the Thirteenth Century," 274–77; Procházková, "Some Notes on the Titles of Coloman," 106.

17 *Thomae archidiaconi Spalatensis Historia Salonitanorum*, 198. See Györffy, "Szlavónia kialakulásának oklevélkritikai," 234; Goss, "Battle of Cathedrals," 146; Goss, "Bishop Stjepan II," 212; Körmendi, "Szlavónia korai hovatartozása," 381.

18 Györffy, "Szlavónia kialakulásának oklevélkritikai," 230; *Korai magyar történeti*, 78 (by Tibor Almási); Basić, "O pokušaju ujedinjenja," 33, 35; Goss, "Battle of Cathedrals," 146; Goss, "Bishop Stjepan II," 212; Tamás Körmendi, "A zágrábi püspökség alapítási éve [The Year of Foundation of the Bishopric of Zagreb]," in *"Köztes-Európa" vonzásában: Ünnepi tanulmányok Font Márta tiszteletére*, ed. Dániel Bagi and Tamás Fedeles and Gergely Kiss (Pécs: Kronosz, 2012), 329–41 at 340–41; Szeberényi, "A zágrábi püspökség Szlavónia megszervezésében," 43; László Koszta, "State Power and Ecclesiastical System in Eleventh Century Hungary," in *"In my Spirit and Thought I Remained a European of Hungarian Origin": Medieval Historical Studies in Memory of Zoltan J. Kosztolnyik*, ed.

have been the reason why Duke Coloman wanted to implement this change, so that his province would have been unified in an ecclesiastical sense. Goss stated that beside Slavonia, Dalmatia, Croatia, even Bosnia could have belonged to this conglomerate, forging a new realm that theoretically still would have belonged to the kingdom of St. Stephen. According to certain scholars, the essence of the planned union was the elevation of the bishopric of Zagreb into a new archbishopric that could have been extracted from the Hungarian church hierarchy. This would have met the ambitions of Bishop Stephen too.[19] Nevertheless, extant document could equally well argue for the possible aim of Coloman being to attach the churches of Dalmatia to the Hungarian ecclesiastical system. Both possibilities remain hypothetical for now.

Coloman might, however, have been following a previous pattern of making suggestions concerning the church of Split, since the Hungarian kings had certainly not been afraid to do so earlier. The change would have been favourable for the duke, since the entire ecclesiastical organization of his duchy would have belonged to Zagreb, instead of distant Split, and would have meant promotion for Bishop Stephen. Some scholars have argued that Coloman even intended to revive his claim for Galicia by initiating this change. This way Bishop Stephen could have been the ecclesiastical and—according to this theory—the secular leader of all of the duke's territories at once, whilst Coloman, as king of Galicia, could focus on the affairs of his former kingdom, perhaps based from his estates in the Scepus. Coloman died in 1241, so it cannot be proven, yet it seems rather unlikely because of the contemporary situation in Galicia and the inactivity of the Hungarian royals after 1235. This theory seems unlikely at best.[20]

Changing any existing ecclesiastical framework was, of course, impossible without papal consent, so Coloman sought permission from Pope Gregory IX. The pope responded to what must have been a request in writing in which Coloman seems to have emphasized the devastation of the archbishopric of Split and the desperate situation of Archbishop Guncel. It is remarkable that Coloman could convince Guncel, who was of Hungarian origin, to support the idea of the union. In the Dalmatian town, however, not everyone must have been enthusiastic about the notion, as has been mentioned above, and Thomas of Split, the archdeacon of the town, ignored the plan in his history.[21]

The pope did not reject the proposal, but nor did he give it his blessing. He let Coloman know in June 1240 that the consensus of the Archbishop of Kalocsa, the bishop of Zagreb, and their cathedral chapters were also needed for approval. We might sus-

---

István Petrovics, Sándor László Tóth, and Eleanor A. Congdon, Capitulum 6 (Szeged: JATE Press, 2010), 67–78 at 71–73; Koszta, *A kalocsai érseki*, 85, 98–103.

19 Goss, "Battle of Cathedrals," 146; Goss, "Bishop Stjepan II," 212, 221.

20 Györffy, "Szlavónia kialakulásának oklevélkritikai," 234; Zsoldos, "Egész Szlavónia bánja," 270; Font, *Árpád-házi királyok*, 238–42; Basić, "O pokušaju ujedinjenja," 35; Goss, "Bishop Stjepan II," 212, 221; Goss, "Battle of Cathedrals," 146; Dujmović and Jukić, "The 'Koloman Renaissance'," 177.

21 *Thomae archidiaconi Spalatensis Historia Salonitanorum*; *Regesta Pontificum Romanorum*, no. 10890, *Registres de Grégoire IX*, no. 5216. See Kristó, *A feudális széttagolódás Magyarországon*, 91; Basić, "O pokušaju ujedinjenja," 35; Goss, "Battle of Cathedrals," 150; Goss, "Bishop Stjepan II," 218; Dujmović and Jukić, "The 'Koloman Renaissance'," 177; Herbers, *Geschichte des Papsttums*, 172–210.

pect then that Archbishop Ugrin disapproved. The motives of Gregory IX are obscure; he probably did not want to jeopardize his good relations with Coloman in a period when the pope felt under threat from, and needful of support against, Emperor Friedrich II.[22]

The affair completely lost its relevance because of Coloman's death in 1241, and the pope died in a besieged Rome a few months later too. Who knows what could have happened if Gregory IX had survived, but it is indeed imaginable that the plan, or as Goss formulated it "the battle of the Cathedrals," could have ended differently. Bishop Stephen was left alone in 1241, the new pope, Celestine IV, died that year too, and the following *sedes vacantia* was yet again adverse for Stephen. Innocent IV was elected only in 1243 but his relationship with Bishop Stephen can be characterized as ambivalent, as his denial of the confirmation of Stephen as elected archbishop of Split demonstrates. It seems that the bishop sought another way to reach his goal of becoming an archbishop after Coloman's death. Both Hungarian archiepiscopal seats became vacant after the Mongol attack, so Stephen could have turned there, instead, but he decided on the Dalmatian archbishopric. The details of his election are known from his successor, Thomas of Split, whose history describes secular political influence and neglect of canonical regulations. Thomas's personal involvement cannot be forgotten; so his report has to be handled delicately, especially, if he were one of the opponents of the planned union before 1241, so he would not have been fond of the idea of Stephen's election. Stephen was eventually forced to resign from the title of the archbishop and return to Zagreb, where he focused on recovery after the Mongol devastation. After his death in 1247 he was buried in Čazma, near to Duke Coloman's remains.[23]

---

[22] *Regesta Pontificum Romanorum*, no. 10890, *Registres de Grégoire IX*, no. 5216. See Basić, "O pokušaju ujedinjenja," 32–33, 35–36; Kristó, *A feudális széttagolódás Magyarországon*, 91; Goss, "Battle of Cathedrals," 151; Dujmović and Jukić, "The 'Koloman Renaissance'," 178; Herbers, *Geschichte des Papsttums*, 180–85.

[23] *Thomae archidiaconi Spalatensis Historia Salonitanorum*, 306–7, 322–23. See Basić, "O pokušaju ujedinjenja," 38–41; Goss, "Battle of Cathedrals," 150–52; Goss, "Bishop Stjepan II," 219; Dujmović and Jukić, "The 'Koloman Renaissance'," 178; Zsoldos Zsoldos, *Magyarország világi archontológiája*, 81, 84; Herbers, *Geschichte des Papsttums*, 185; Judit Gál, "The Roles and Loyalties of the Bishops and Archbishops of Dalmatia (1102–1301)," *Hungarian Historical Review* 3 (2014): 471–93 at 477.

Chapter 11

COLOMAN'S RULE IN SLAVONIA

WE CAN GET a good insight into Coloman's internal policy in Slavonia from two charters from 1229, though we can also see that occasionally his actions involved neighbouring lands. The first such action concerning a former donation, the second an order to the count of Split regarding actions against pirates off the Dalmatian coast.[1] It is remarkable that the duke was involved in an issue outside Slavonia, but this was not a single incident since he also delivered a judgement in a law-suit concerning the social status of certain royal men in Zala County that same year. We learn about this case because the duke issued a charter confirming an agreement between the Cistercian abbey of Topusko and certain laymen in September 1234. The litigants were required to pay a fine to Coloman, if they failed to follow the settlement.[2] Two diplomas of 1239 offer further details on the ducal adjudication. Both charters of Arnold, count of Zala, contain references to the role of the *pristaldus* of King and Duke Coloman. The Latin term refers to an obsolete practice in Hungarian law, linked to oral testimony, the *pristaldi* being in effect both summoners and official witnesses at the same time.[3] The duke was being represented, it seems, beyond the core territory of Slavonia by his agents. One of his own charters from 1229 also seems to confirm this practice.[4]

A 1231 disposition from Coloman shows his attitude towards western European settlers in his duchy, as he regulated the privileges and duties of these "guests" (*hospites*) in Vukovar; they were given safety on an estate of the castle. This ordinance shows not only ducal policy, but reveals the nationality of the settlers: Germans, Hungarians, and Slavs were included, though we should be cautious about any such ethnic statements. King Béla IV confirmed his brother's disposition in May 1244, as did his son, the younger king Stephen, in 1263.[5]

Coloman was involved in a similar affair in 1234. He determined the privileges and the required services of the *hospites* in the villages of Virovitica (Verőce). They were given the right to transfer property to their heirs and to select the judges and jurymen of their

---

[1] *Regesta ducum, ducissarum*, nos. 3 and 6. Cf. Zsoldos, *Magyarország világi archontológiája*, 181.

[2] *Regesta ducum, ducissarum*, nos. 5 and 12, *Regesta regum stirpis Arpadianae*, nos. 461, 480, 593, and 596. Gyula Kristó stated that Coloman, like his brother in comparable situations, generally decided against people who intended to gain a higher social status. Kristó, *A feudális széttagolódás Magyarországon*, 7.

[3] *Korai magyar történeti*, 552 (entry by Attila Zsoldos).

[4] *Codex diplomaticus Arpadianus*, 7:86, 7:88. and *Regesta ducum, ducissarum*, no. 4. For the legal activity of Coloman in another case see *Az Árpád-kori nádorok és helyetteseik okleveleinek kritikai jegyzéke. Regesta palatinorum et vices gerentium tempore regum stirpis Arpadianae criticodiplomatica*, ed. Tibor Szőcs. A Magyar Országos Levéltár Kiadványai 2, Forráskiadványok 51 (Budapest: Magyar Országos Levéltár, 2012), no. 43.

[5] *Regesta ducum, ducissarum*, no. 9; *Regesta regum stirpis Arpadianae*, no. 65; DL 536, *Regesta regum stirpis Arpadianae*, no. 1813. Cf. Fine, *When Ethnicity Did Not Matter in the Balkans*, 73–74.

own will. The settlers were freed from a particular type of tax, the *descensus* paid to the local *ban*, whilst the characteristic tax of Slavonia (*marturina*) was raised to a maximum amount for them. Foreign settlers were clearly liable to the *marturina* under the rule of Coloman, even if they were later freed from it. The provision of 1234 was presumably intended to settle existing practice.[6] The status of the *hospites* of Petrinja (Petrinya) was regulated in 1240, and they received a ducal charter concerning their estates, their legal rights, and ecclesiastical privileges, whereas they must be paid if the *ban* wanted to make use of his right to accommodation (*descensus*), and required food for himself and his animals. Béla IV confirmed this measure in August 1242.[7] It is known, thanks to another royal charter of the same year, that Coloman guaranteed the same rights for the settlers of Samobor as the inhabitants of Petrinja.[8] A royal charter of 1242 reveals information about the situation in Varaždin where settlers received a ducal guarantee of their privileges and their duties towards Coloman. Foreign settlers of Slavonia were especially motivated to obtain royal confirmations of their privileges right after the Mongol attack and Coloman's death in 1242. This endeavour manifested itself again in 1271, when King Stephen V renewed his father's confirmation for the settlers of Petrinja.[9]

Duke Coloman did not simply offer guarantees to settler communities; the guests of Dubica, for instance, were ordered to allow an eremitical reiligous community (possibly Paulines) to settle on their estates. From the charter of the inhabitants of Dubica, we can see that they received the estate in question from Coloman himself.[10]

Privileges of various kinds were not exclusively given to *hospes* communities, as a royal charter of 1242 demonstrates. Coloman made an agreement with the inhabitants of Zadar, according to a later diploma of Béla IV, whereby he undertook to help build the town's walls, while the royal taxes of Zadar were assigned to them in return.[11]

A charter of Coloman from 1232 allows us to take a look at another aspect of ducal policy. The duke granted Rovišće castle (Rojcsa) to certain serfs, Dragan and his son, who had served him loyally when Coloman was attacked by his brother, Prince Andrew. It appears that the duke, besides the gift of the estate, also regulated the status of all men

---

[6] *Regesta ducum, ducissarum*, no. 13. See Weisz and Zsoldos, "A báni joghatóság Szlavóniában," 472; Weisz, "Királyi adók Szlavóniában a középkor," 125, 128–29, 132–33, 135, 140; Dujmović and Jukić, "The 'Koloman Renaissance'," 176.

[7] *Regesta ducum, ducissarum*, no. 20, *Regesta regum stirpis Arpadianae*, no. 721. See Weisz and Zsoldos, "A báni joghatóság Szlavóniában," 471. Cf. Fine, *When Ethnicity Did Not Matter in the Balkans*, 77; Dujmović and Jukić, "The 'Koloman Renaissance'," 176; Zsolt Hunyadi, *The Hospitallers in the Medieval Kingdom of Hungary c. 1150–1387*, METEM Könyvek 70 / CEU Medievalia 13 (Budapest: CEU Press and METEM, 2010), 292.

[8] *Regesta ducum, ducissarum*, no. 21; *Regesta regum stirpis Arpadianae*, no. 725. See also on urbanization: Fine, *The Late Medieval Balkans*, 152; Sokcsevits, *Horvátország*, 119 (though Fine did not mention Coloman's role).

[9] *Regesta regum stirpis Arpadianae*, nos. 728 and 2111.

[10] *Regesta ducum, ducissarum*, no. 26; *Codex diplomaticus regni Croatiae*, 4:264. See Kristó, *A feudális széttagolódás Magyarországon*, 78.

[11] *Regesta regum stirpis Arpadianae*, no. 719. Cf. Kanyó, "Kálmán herczeg," 444; Kiss, *Dél-Magyarországtól Itáliáig*, 20.

belonging to the castle; for instance, he limited the amount of the *descensus* they had to pay the *ban*. We know this from a charter of Ban Stephen of the Gutkeled kindred from 1255, which confirmed the donation of the castle of Rovišće to the serfs, and Coloman's role. The possessions, which the free men (*liberos homines*) among the serfs received from the Slavonian duke earlier that year, were confirmed.[12]

Another Coloman charter, this time from February 1240, reports a gift to Demeter of the Aba kindred, count of Bodrog County, and master of the stewards in the ducal court at the time. The duke referred to the services Demeter provided him while he was in Galicia as a child and ever since, which is why Coloman gave him the estate of Našice in Baranya County and also the *marturina* attached to it; moreover, he was freed from the *ban's descensus* and jurisdiction too. Našice had previously belonged to Jula (Gyula) of the Kán kindred, until Béla IV seized it from him, so Coloman had gained possession of it as a result of the restitutions of former royal grants.

The support of the duke was evident not only in the form of donations or confirmations but in practical support. A charter of Andrew II from 1233 shows Coloman helping certain inhabitants of the castle of Bakony in a legal dispute with Count Andrew. Details are obscure, and we only know the location of the disputed lands thanks to a charter of the bishop of Veszprém. Yet we know, from a royal charter of 1241, that Coloman freed several men of the castle of Zala from the jurisdiction of the local counts and they were now solely under his control.[13]

A ducal charter from 1237 contains details of another type of business, intended to secure the exchange of estates between Coloman and his chancellor, File, the provost of Zagreb, and his relative, Count Thomas. The agreement dealt with the new disposal of previously exchanged possessions, later confirmed by the chapter of Pécs in October 1240 and King Béla IV four years later. Coloman made another transfer in 1237: the former land of Count Abraham from the Tétény kindred was given to Chancellor File, as a charter of the cathedral chapter of Pécs from 1239 states, intending to secure the matter. Béla IV dealt with this affair in several charters, stating that he had supported Coloman's decision concerning the donation during his lifetime. File's brothers retained the king's favour even after the provost of Zagreb died, since Béla IV assured them of every former possession of File, specifically those he received from the duke as a reward for his services. The siblings, Thomas and Peter, even used the old charter of Coloman successfully as evidence in a law-suit in November 1252.[14]

---

[12] *Regesta ducum, ducissarum*, no. 10; *Codex diplomaticus regni Croatiae*, 4:596 and 4:613. See Gábor Szeberényi, "A rojcsai prediálisok a 13–14. században [Nobles, Castle Warriors, and Praediales of Rovišće in the Thirteenth to Fourteenth Centuries]," in *Középkortörténeti tanulmányok, 7. A VII. Medievisztikai PhD-konferencia (Szeged, 2011. június 1–3.) előadásai*, ed. Attila Kiss P. et al. (Szeged: Szegedi Középkorász Műhely, 2012), 291–312 at 293–95.

[13] *Regesta ducum, ducissarum*, nos. 19 and 22; *Regesta regum stirpis Arpadianae*, nos. 512 and 711. Cf. Kristó, *A feudális széttagolódás Magyarországon*, 59; Weisz and Zsoldos, "A báni joghatóság Szlavóniában," 473; Zsoldos, "Hercegek és hercegnők," 17.

[14] *Regesta ducum, ducissarum*, nos. 14, 15, and 16; DL 222; *Regesta regum stirpis Arpadianae*, no. 787. Cf. *Regesta regum stirpis Arpadianae*, no. 634, DL 337 01; *Regesta regum stirpis Arpadianae*, nos. 722, 900, and 981.

It seems that Duke Coloman engaged in several similar measures in the 1230s. A royal charter from November 1239 was meant to confirm another donation regarding changes of ownership; this time it concerned an estate neighbouring the ducal possession in Virovitica. Coloman seized an additional piece of land bordering his own, this time in Segesd, and in return he gave the previous owner several other estates with certain rights, according to a royal charter. The diplomas of Béla IV indicate several similar ducal donations.[15]

Ecclesiastical Arrangements

Coloman donated several churches during his years in the Scepus and the foundation of the Cistercian monastery in Spišský Štiavnik and the Premonstratensian provostry of Jasov might be directly related to his name. As duke of Slavonia he continued these donations inside and outside of his territory, as his position demanded. His benefactions to the bishop of Trogir and to the collegial chapter of Hajszentlőrinc have already been touched upon,[16] but Coloman also might have supported a monastery beyond the Kingdom of Hungary. Prince Béla might have donated in 1230 the Cistercian abbey of Heiligenkreutz with the consent of his father and his younger brother, as a probably forged charter states. It is certain that Andrew II had given donations to the monastery prior to this date, whether or not Coloman in fact was involved has to remain unclear.[17]

Coloman also took great interest in the bishopric of Bosnia, probably as part of his policy for the Balkans. Béla IV's charter from June 1244 reports that the duke freed several estates of the bishopric (e.g that of Đakovo) from the jurisdiction of the Slavonian *ban* and placed them under the bishop's control. All the estate tax of the estates reverted to the prelate too. The bishop of Pécs received, due to his role in the litigation between the duke and the Templars, a similar donation from Coloman, namely the tithe from the *marturina* of Valkó and Baranya counties. It has also been assumed that the duke—along with his uncle, Patriarch Berthold of Aquileia—was the founder of the collegial chapter of Požega, but this is *prima facie* contradicted by the fact that the provostry was first mentioned back in 1217. Therefore, László Koszta and Gergely Kiss assumed Bishop Calan of Pécs to be the founder.[18] The establishment of the Dominican cloister of Čazma,

---

15 *Regesta regum stirpis Arpadianae*, nos. 665, 762, and 763; *Codex diplomaticus Hungariae*, 4/1:338; *Regesta ducum, ducissarum*, nos. 25, 27. See Györffy, "Szlavónia kialakulásának oklevélkritikai," 129; Weisz and Zsoldos, "A báni joghatóság Szlavóniában," 472, 477; Zsoldos, "Az ifjabb király országa," 243–44; Zsoldos, *Családi ügy*, 24–25; Kiss, *Királyi egyházak*, 11. For the *marturina* tax of Slavonia see Weisz, "Királyi adók Szlavóniában a középkor," 125–36.

16 *Regesta ducum, ducissarum*, nos. 1 and 2.

17 *Regesta regum stirpis Arpadianae*, nos. 333 and 594.

18 *Regesta regum stirpis Arpadianae*, no. 771 ; Györffy, "Szlavónia kialakulásának oklevélkritikai," 235; Fine, *The Late Medieval Balkans*, 144–45; Weisz and Zsoldos, "A báni joghatóság Szlavóniában," 470; Bálint Ternovácz, "A boszniai latin püspökség története 1344-ig [History of the Latin Bishopric of Bosnia to 1344]," in *Micae Mediaevales V. Fiatal történészek dolgozatai a középkori Magyarországról és Európáról*, ed. Laura Fábián et al. (Budapest: ELTE BTK Történelemtudományok

which later on became his burial place, can be probably linked to Coloman's rule too, whilst the settlement of the hermits around the St. Dominic church in Dubica was also initiated by the duke.[19]

Coloman's relation to the church is reflected in more than just foundations, donations, and privileges. A judgement of Archbishop Guncel of Split and his fellow judges from 1229 states that they had undertaken their adjudication in the court of the duke of Slavonia. Coloman's milieu served, it seems, as a place for mediating conflicts, as a charter of Archbishop Ugrin of Kalocsa from 1230 also confirms. The litigation between Bishop Stephen of Zagreb and the Templars was first handled in the ducal court before the parties came to an agreement before the archbishop. A charter of the papal legate, Jacob of Pecorari, informs us about Coloman's involvement in a dispute: the settlement of the provostry of Székesfehérvár and the Benedictine abbey of Pannonhalma were meant to have been confirmed with the seals of Prince Béla and Coloman in 1234, although we cannot say if that was the limit to the duke's role in the affair.[20]

Coloman's involvement with Pope Gregory IX manifested itself in a personal privilege given to the duke and his wife, Salomea. The royal couple received a licence from the pope in October 1234 to attend masses despite the fact that the aforementioned papal legate, Jacob of Pecorari, had laid the whole realm under interdict. This is just one example characterizing the excellent relationship between Coloman and the pope, and there are countless other affairs that support this appearance. Karol Hollý even formulated the opinion that this mutual alliance was a defining characteristic of Coloman's rule. This makes sense to us, since the pope not only contacted the duke in major cases, such as issues relating to heretics, papal protections, or privileges, but the Slavonian duke was asked to support the abbey of Pannonhalma, which fell into Coloman's personal territory, to help them to collect their rightful tithes in Somogy County.[21]

These ecclesiastical arrangements will be crucial when we discuss below Coloman's involvement in the Bosnian church, his crusade against heretics, and then in how he dealt with the Mongol invasion.

Doktori Iskola, 2016), 215–28; Šuljak, "Bosansko-humski krstjani," 442–44; Slišković, "Dominikanci i bosansko-humski krstjani," 492.

19 *Regesta ducum, ducissarum*, no. 26.

20 *Codex diplomaticus regni Croatiae*, 3:315–16 and 3:331–32; DF 206 936, *Codex diplomaticus Hungariae*, 7/1:240.

21 *Regesta Pontificum Romanorum*, no. 9728, *Registres de Grégoire IX*, nos. 2125–26; DF 206 949, *Regesta Pontificum Romanorum*, no. 9848. See Almási, "Egy ciszterci bíboros," 136; Hollý, "Princess Salomea and Hungarian–Polish Relations," 29; Procházková, "Postavenie haličského kráľa," 72; Brković, "Bosansko-humski kršćani," 139–40.

Chapter 12

POLITICS AND DYNASTIC AFFAIRS

BÉLA WAS ABLE to occupy the Hungarian throne after his father, Andrew II, died, as no one challenged him. This state of affairs was unique in the history of the Árpád family, since any living relative, especially a brother, meant almost every time a threat to the rightful heir, as happened between Béla's and Coloman's father and his older brother, King Emeric. On this occasion, the duke of Slavonia did not challenge his brother's claim and even actively supported the new king in many ways.[1] This assertion is not made simply through the lack of countervailing evidence but in the circumstances of Béla's enthronement.

Let us first consider the background of the coronation, since it is assumed that Coloman's wife, Salomea, had a role in the preparations of the ceremony. According to the narrative in the *Fourteenth Century Chronicle-Composition* (particularly the text of the *Hungarian Illuminated Chronicle / Chronicon Pictum*), Prince Daniil also took part in the enthronement ceremony. Hollý suspects that the ruler from the Rus' intended to approach the Hungarian royal family after the death of his rival, Prince Andrew, who was epresentative of the Hungarian claims in Galicia. It is perhaps not inconceivable that Daniil turned to Salomea's mother, the widow of Leszek the White, and therefore the mother-in-law of Coloman, who was of Rus'ian origin herself. Maybe the duchess of Sandomierz made use of her family ties and mediated between Daniil and Coloman, and finally King Béla IV. Whatever the background, the Galician duke was present at the coronation; he even had a role in the ceremony. According to the *Illuminated Chronicle*, Coloman held his brother's sword, whilst Daniil led the new ruler's horse, in which act he symbolically acknowledged Béla's superior status and also placed himself below Coloman hierarchically in this quasi-feudal custom. Daniil's intention was probably to secure himself Hungarian support. It is remarkable to see the Hungarian king, the prince with the royal title connected to Galicia, and the *de facto* Galician ruler all three cooperating, which implies prior mediation, whether or not Grzymisława or Salomea were involved or not.[2]

---

[1] According to Gyula Kristó, Béla allowed his brother to remain at the head of Slavonia even after his own coronation (Kristó, *A feudális széttagolódás Magyarországon*, 48).

[2] *Scriptores rerum Hungaricarum*, 1:467, 2:42. See Font, *Árpád-házi királyok*, 233–36; Hollý, "Princess Salomea and Hungarian–Polish Relations," 30–31; Procházková, "Koloman Haličský na Spiši," 247–48; Radek: *Das Ungarnbild*, 146; Procházková, "Some Notes on the Titles of Coloman," 107; Dąbrowski, *Daniel Romanowicz, biografia polityczna*, 188. Cf. Мирослав Волощук, "Вассальная зависимость Даниила Романовича от Белы IV в 1235–1245 гг.: актуальные вопросы реконструкции русско-венгерских отношений второй четверти века [Vassal Dependence of Daniil Romanovych on Béla IV. between 1235 and 1245: Recent Questions for a Reconstruction of Russian–Hungarian Ties in the Second Quarter of the Thirteenth Century]," *Specimina Nova, Pars Prima: Sectio Medievalis* 3 (2005): 83–115.

The siblings continued their cooperation beyond 1235, as the wording of several royal charters show, with Béla IV frequently referrig to his younger brother's support, will, and consent. The case of Jula of the Kán kindred is a significant case where the king emphasized Coloman's role in his judgement against the former *ban* of Slavonia.[3]

The brothers' good relations are reflected in ecclesiastical matters such as the election dispute in Esztergom after the death of Archbishop Robert in 1239. Several papal letters from March 1239 present difficulties around the confirmation of the new archbishop, since Gregory IX at first rejected the election of Matthias, former bishop of Vác. The pope suspected irregularities in canon law processes during the election. Though Gregory IX changed his mind as a result of several ecclesiastical and secular office holders' statements, the king and Coloman expressed their support as well. As a result, the pallium was sent to Archbishop Matthias.[4]

Coloman also appears in connection with another affair, in which he again supported his elder brother. The royal siblings turned to the papacy because of the desperate situation of their uncle, Berthold, patriarch of Aquileia in 1239, excommunicated due to his ties to Emperor Friedrich II. The former Archbishop of Kalocsa had taken the side of the Staufer emperor in his conflict with Gregory IX in the late 1230s, which is why the ecclesiastical censure was placed upon him. Béla and Coloman requested the pope to absolve Berthold from the excommunication. Gregory IX could not refuse the petition of what he described as "*among the Christian rulers especially kind kings*", though he had one condition, namely, that the patriarch should appear before him personally. Their request was due to kinship: Berthold becoming archbishop of Kalocsa through the support of Andrew II, his brother-in-law, and he remained archbishop there until 1219. The death of his sister in 1213 weakened his position in Hungary, but he managed to become the patriarch of Aquileia, which is why he left for Italy. It seems likely that Béla and Coloman were close to their maternal uncle from childhood, or perhaps held good memories of him.[5]

---

3 "[..] pro manifesto infidelitatis crimine per nostram, nec non karissimi fratris nostri Colomani regis et ducis tocius Sclauonie illustris, hac omnium baronum nostrorum sentenciam fuisset condempnatus" (*Codex diplomaticus Arpadianus*, 7:100), *Regesta regum stirpis Arpadianae*, no. 691 (and 690), DL 246. Cf. Procházková, "Postavenie haličského kráľa," 74. References to the royal accord are to be found in several charters of Coloman. See also Zsoldos, "Hercegek és hercegnők," 17.

4 *Regesta Pontificum Romanorum*, no. 10850, *Registres de Grégoire IX*, no. 5082; *Regesta Pontificum Romanorum*, no. 10851, *Registres de Grégoire IX*, no. 5085. See Klaus Ganzer, *Papsttum und Bistumbesetzungen in der Zeit von Gregor IX. bis Bonifaz VIII. Ein Beitrag zur Geschichte der päpstlichen Reservationen* (Köln: Böhlau, 1968), 129; *Esztergomi érsekek 1001–2003 [Archbishops of Esztergom. 1000-2003]*, ed. Margit Beke (Budapest: Szent István Társulat, 2003), 102, 104.

5 *Regesta Pontificum Romanorum*, no, 10830, *Registres de Grégoire IX*, no. 4998; *Catalogus fontium historiae Hungaricae*, no. 2597. See Edmund Oefele, "Bertold, Patriarch von Aquileja," in *Allgemeine deutsche Biographie*, vol. 2 (Leipzig, 1875), 516–18; Jonathan R. Lyon, "Die Andechs-Meranier und das Bistum Bamberg," in *Das Bistum Bamberg in der Welt des Mittelalters*, ed. Christine von Eickels and Klaus von Eickels, Bamberger interdisziplinäre Mittelalterstudien: Vorlesungen und Vorträge 1 (Bamberg: University of Bamberg Press, 2007), 247–62 at 259; Zsoldos, *Magyarország világi archontológiája*, 84; Koszta, *A kalocsai érseki*, 110–11; Gergely Kiss, "Meránia és Aquileia között. Berthold kalocsai érsek pályafutásának egyházkormányzati tanulságai [Between Merania and Aquileia: Lessons of the Career of Archbishop Berthold of Kalocsa in the Circles of the Ecclesiastical

The affair of Berthold did not come to a rapid conclusion, despite the first papal letter. Gregory IX mandated his subdeacon, Gregorius de Montelongo, to absolve the patriarch as early as January 1241. This new papal document refers to the earlier request of the Hungarian royal brothers, though it may simply be extracted from the former petition, so we should not read too much into this fact.[6]

Coloman appears along with his brother in yet another papal charter. Gregory IX invited, among other European rulers, Béla and Coloman to a proposed ecumenical council to deal with Emperor Friedrich II's threat, though it never took place due to the pope's desperate straits.[7]

Coloman and Andrew, his Younger Brother

The duke of Slavonia did not have as good relationship with every member of his family as he had with Béla; his younger brother, Andrew, was his adversary. A likely reason is their shared interest in Galicia. After Coloman was forced to leave the principality, it was his younger brother who represented the Hungarian claims in the region, especially, because due to the agreement between his father and Prince Mstislav Udaloy he was engaged to the daughter of the Novgorodian ruler. It has been assumed that Coloman did not completely give up his claims on Galicia, which is why he and his wife, Salomea, moved to Scepus after they were expelled from their kingdom. The duke retained his royal title to that land and maybe retained desings on it even while ruler in Slavonia.[8]

Some historians even believe it was Andrew II's intention to remove Coloman from proximity to Galicia, in moving him to the southern provinces. This assumption is supported by the fact that Prince Andrew possessed Peremyshl from 1224, and he had the opportunity to take control over Galicia in the following year.[9] Yet the tension between the brothers did not disappear after 1226, on the contrary, it developed into an armed conflict. The details are, however, completely obscure, and its existence is known from a single reference in a charter of Duke Coloman. According to the diploma, he gave donations to one of his supporters and his son in 1232, as they had loyally fought by Coloman's side against Andrew, who, it says, had attacked the realm of Coloman led by false advisers. The text of the charter deserves closer attention in many aspects. On the one hand, it places and verifies the date of the attack before the year 1232 (*terminus ante quem*); on the other hand, it states that Andrew, in fact, attacked his brother's realm (*reg-*

Government]," in *Egy történelmi gyilkosság margójára. Merániai Gertrúd emlékezete, 1213–2013*, ed. Judit Majorossy (Szentendre: Ferenczy Múzeum, 2014), 87–94.

6 *Regesta Pontificum Romanorum*, no. 10980; *Catalogus fontium historiae Hungaricae*, no. 2598.

7 *Regesta Pontificum Romanorum*, nos. 10926, 10930, 10945, 10952, 10994–95; *Registres de Grégoire IX*, nos. 5550-60, 5773, 5774, 5764–72, 5886–87; *Regesta regum stirpis Arpadianae*, no. 703. Cf. Donald Matthew, *The Norman Kingdom of Sicily* (Cambridge: Cambridge University Press, 1992), 347–54; Herbers, *Geschichte des Papsttums*, 185.

8 Cf. Procházková, "Postavenie haličského kráľa," 73; Procházková, "Koloman Haličský na Spiši," 244–45; Barabás, "The Titles of the Hungarian Royal Family," 37–44.

9 Font, *Árpád-házi királyok*, 214–17. Cf. Procházková, "Koloman Haličský na Spiši," 247.

num). This final phrase complicates our interpretation, since it is not clear if this refers to Slavonia or Galicia. Márta Font presumes Slavonia based on the indistinct formulation of the charter, whereas Nataša Procházková finds it strange that Andrew headed to the distant Slavonia when Coloman's estates in the Scepus were nearby. Maybe it was not a military conflict but a skirmish, since a large-scale war within the royal family would have been identified in other sources. Perhaps the target of the attack was the ducal estate of Rovišće, the home of Coloman's free men. We know simply that Coloman felt attacked by his brother; whether metaphorically or by some actual act of war remains unclear.[10]

The conflict between Coloman and Andrew is not reflected in any other sources, although one episode of the so-called *Hungarian–Polish Chronicle* deserves attention. The story describes the marriage of Ladislaus, grandson of St. Ladislaus, to the daughter of Mstislav, the prince of the Ruthenians, by which he secured himself the throne of Galicia, whilst his brother, Solomon, ruled over Slavonia at this time. Ladislaus later became the king of Hungary and despite the fact that his brother gave his consent, Ladislaus imprisoned his sibling. Aside from the question of the origin of the chronicle, certain elements of the narrative do correlate to known facts. Nevertheless, in our opinion, the similar motives are not enough to conclude that the author of the *Chronicle* intended to reflect on events from the first third of the thirteenth century, on the contrary, it is more likely, based on research, that the story is almost entirely fictional.[11]

If we return now to the historical events, we have to ask whether this fraternal conflict had an impact on Coloman's relation to his father, and if so, to what extent. From extant sources, it does seem that the relationship between Andrew II and Coloman was definitely affected by the events of the 1220s. It was definitely heavy, to say the least, probably caused by the king's decision to support his third son, Andrew, once Coloman was forced to leave Galicia. The youngest brother managed to seize and rule over the principality from 1227, but his position weakened in 1228 with the death of Mstislav Mstislavich, because Daniil Romanovich then took control over Galicia and expelled Andrew. Coloman must have had mixed feelings about this repetitious turn of events, since this could have easily affected his relations with his father, Andrew II. Coloman's feelings toward his older brother, Béla, were clearly friendly, but his younger sibling and especially Béla's involvement in the Hungarian campaign to Galicia may have cast a shadow over their relationship too; Coloman—alone in his family—stayed away from this campaign. The failed action did not have a long-lasting impact on the brothers, but the ten-

---

10 *Regesta ducum, ducissarum*, no. 10. Cf. Procházková, "Postavenie haličského kráľa," 72; Procházková, "Some Notes on the Titles of Coloman," 106; Gábor Szeberényi, "A gorai comitatus a XIII. században. Megjegyzések a 'hat gorai nemzetség' és a Babonič-ok korai történetéhez [The *comitatus* of Gora in the Thirteenth Century. Remarks on the Early History of the 'Six Genera of Gora' and the Baboniči]," in *Középkortörténeti tanulmányok, 6. A VI. Medievisztikai PhD-konferencia (Szeged, 2009. június 4–5.) előadásai*, ed. Péter G. Tóth and Pál Szabó (Szeged: Szegedi Középkorász Műhely, 2010), 233–48 at 233; Szeberényi, "A rojcsai prediálisok," 291–93.

11 Tóth, "A lengyel–magyar," 241–42. Cf. Homza, *Uhorsko polska kronika*, 59–60; Procházková, "Koloman Haličský na Spiši," 248; Procházková, "Some Notes on the Titles of Coloman," 106–7.

sion between Coloman and his father dissolved only after Prince Andrew's death in 1234, when the duke of Slavonia felt no longer threatened by his younger brother's claims.[12]

The Campaigns against Austria

The relationship between the Árpáds and their western neighbours, the Babenberg family, was not a friendly one in the 1230s. Local conflicts along the border of Hungary and Austria to the north-west, and Styria to the west, started probably in 1230, when Duke Friedrich II (1230–46) who ruled both came to power and sent his army into Hungarian territories. Prince Béla was leader of the Hungarian army, when they struck back in 1231 and 1233, but he had to withdraw his troops from Styria. Meanwhile, in Hungary the Austrian army was defeated. Andrew II had intended bringing military help to his youngest son in Galicia in 1233, but he had to change plan because of the threat from the Babenberg ruler. The struggle broke out again in 1235 despite several truces; this time Coloman took part and the Hungarian troops managed to reach Vienna, so Duke Friedrich was forced to sue for peace. Coloman's role is unknown but his involvement in warfare may be interpreted as an overture of his campaign(s) to Bosnia in the following years. The location of the duke's territory might justify his participation, although we might ask why he didn't get involved in resisting Friedrich's first incursion. Maybe he was held back by his resources being split between Scepus and Slavonia. Maybe his strained relationship with father and younger brother at this point held him back before 1235. He certainly wasn't keen on helping the royal army in 1233 when the primary goal was to provide aid to Prince Andrew in Galicia, but Andrew's death in 1234 would have changed his calculation, allowing him to support his father in 1235.[13]

Papal Protection and the Duke of Slavonia

On December 23, 1233 two charters were issued in the papal chancery to the Duke of Slavonia. These letters were meant to secure the protections of the Apostolic See given to Grzymisława of Sandomierz and to Viola of Opole. Responding to their requests, Pope Gregory IX had provided protection to the widowed duchesses and Prince Coloman was one of the secular guardians ordered to protect both duchesses and their children, as well as their belongings and rights.[14]

---

12 Senga, "Béla királyfi bolgár," 37–40; Font, *Árpád-házi királyok*, 213–14, 218–24; Hollý, "Princess Salomea and Hungarian–Polish Relations," 27–28; Kádár, "Az Árpád-házi uralkodók," 92; Dąbrowski, *Daniel Romanowicz, biografia polityczna*, 155–87.

13 Senga, "Béla királyfi bolgár," 40–41, 48, 50; Almási, "Egy ciszterci bíboros," 136–37; Font, *Árpád-házi királyok*, 223–24; Kádár, "Az Árpád-házi uralkodók," 92.

14 *Regesta Pontificum Romanorum*, nos. 9349 and 9352; *Registres de Grégoire IX*, no. 1649. See Fried, *Der päpstliche Schutz*, 264–65, 290, 309–10; Zientara, *Heinrich der Bärtige*, 255, 280–81, 285, 289; Anna Grabowska, "The Church in the Politics of the Duke of Opole Mieszko II Obese (1238–1246) in the Light of Diplomatic Sources," in *Cogito, Scribo, Spero. Auxiliary Historical Sciences in Central Europe at the Outset of the 21st Century*, ed. Martina Bolom-Kotari and Jakub Zouhar (Hradec Králové: Univerzita Hradec Kralové, Filozofická Fakulta, 2012), 192–208 at 193, 198–99;

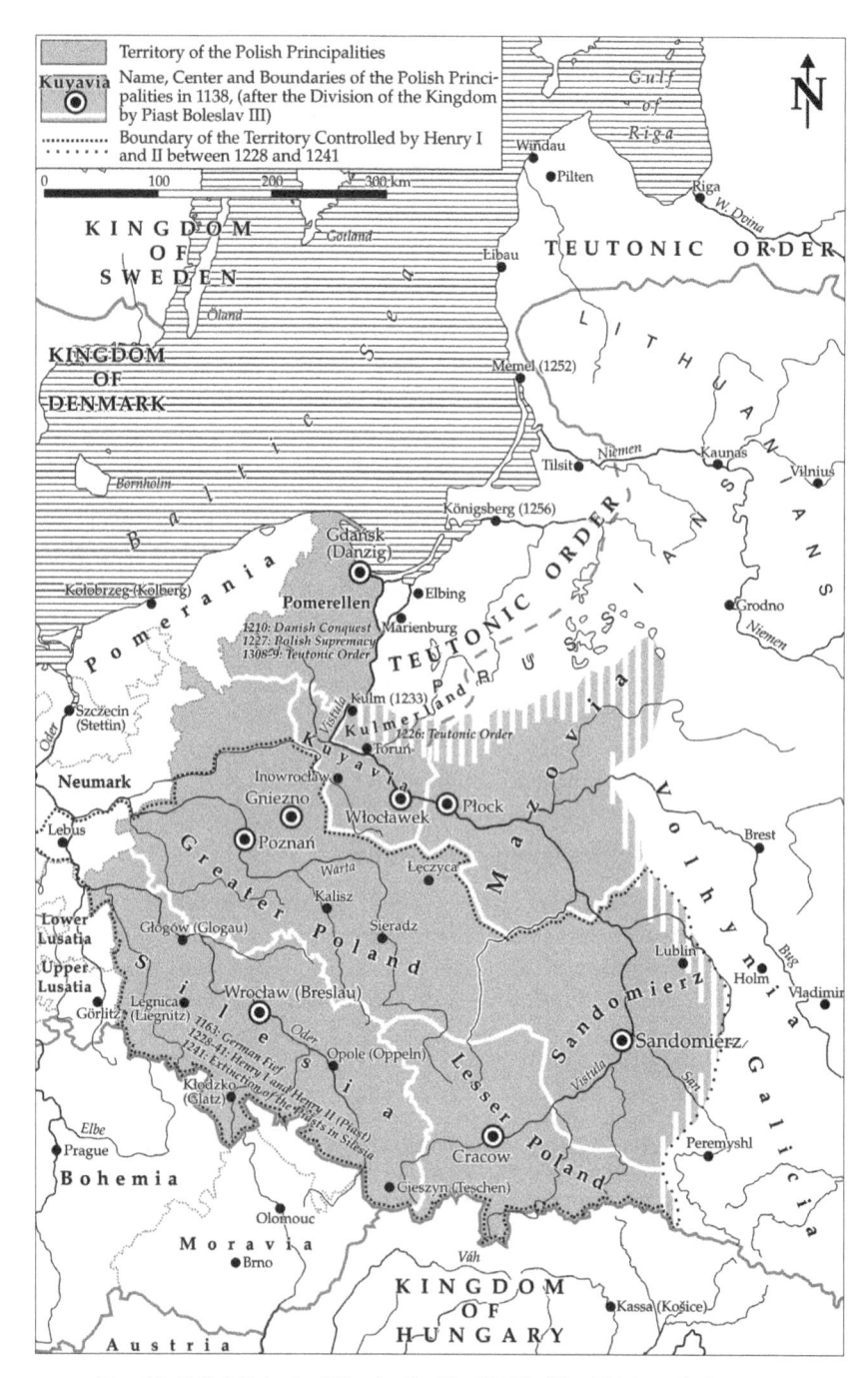

Map 10. Polish Principalities in the First Half of the Thirteenth Century.

Coloman was not the only appointed protector. The archbishop of Gniezno and the bishop of Wrocław were ecclesiastical guardians to them both. For Viola the bishop of Olomouc, and for Grzymisława the bishop of Kraków, were also involved. Besides Coloman, Grzymisława's interests were to be safeguarded by Henry the Bearded, Duke of Silesia, who previously had acted many times on behalf of the duchess and maintained an especially good relationship with the papacy.[15]

The background to these papal mandates and the tasks imposed on Coloman, although similar, were not the same in each case. They go back to the connection of Grzymisława and Viola with the Duke of Slavonia and more broadly to the Hungarian royal family. The case of the duchess of Sandomierz seems to be clearer, so we will examine it first.

Grzymisława, as has been stated several times, was the widow of Leszek the White and mother of Salomea, and therefore mother-in-law of Coloman. Leszek was murdered at the meeting of the Polish dukes in Gąsawa on November 27, 1227. As a result, Władysław III Laskonogi, ruler of Greater Poland, and Conrad of Mazovia, Leszek's brother, fought for the throne of Kraków. Leszek's widow renounced the rights of her son in favour of Władysław in 1228 and received the territory of Sandomierz in return. After the death of Laskonogi, Henry the Bearded became the primary supporter of mother and her son, Bolesław, against Conrad of Mazovia. The duke of Silesia helped Grzymisława in contacting the Apostolic See; his contribution was essential, since Grzymisława and her son had been captured by Conrad by now.[16]

The papal mandate of Coloman must be related to his close kinship with Grzymisława. Benedykt Zientara shares this opinion too, while Karol Hollý preferred to emphasize the role of Salomea. We know nothing about Colomans' dealings with his mother-in-law, though we may wonder if the distance from Slavonia to Lesser Poland made this a burdensome responsibility, in his eyes or in reality. On the other hand, by the time the papal charter was issued the duchess had already been freed from captivity, while later, thanks to the mediation of the Polish prelates, an agreement was made between Henry and Conrad in which the rights of Grzymisława and son were likewise secured.[17]

The second case is not as simple as the first, since the connection of Viola to Coloman cannot be easily proven. She was the widow of Prince Casimir of Opole, who died in 1230, possibly 1229. After the death of her husband, Viola became the guardian of their sons, Mieszko and Władysław, and she became regent of the Duchy of Opole–Racibórz.

Pavol Hudáček, "The Legal Position of Widows in Medieval Hungary up to 1222 and the Question of Dower," *Historický Časopis* 62 Supplement (2014): 3–39 at 3–12; Barabás, "Prinz Koloman," 1–3.

15 *Ioannis Dlugossii Annales seu Cronicae*, 6:250–52; *Regesta Pontificum Romanorum*, nos. 9337 and 9348, 9350–51, *Registres de Grégoire IX*, nos. 1645–48, 1650. See Zientara, *Heinrich der Bärtige*, 285; Przemysław Wiszewski, *Henryk II Pobożny. Biografia polityczna [Henry II the Pious, a Political Biography]* (Legnica: Muzeum Miedzi w Legniczy, 2011), 28, 124, 235.

16 Zientara, *Heinrich der Bärtige*, 173–76, 247–86; Wiszewski, *Henryk II Pobożny*, 26–27, 229–31; Kozłowski, "The Marriage of Bolesław of the Piasts and Kinga of the Árpáds," 84–85.

17 *Regesta Pontificum Romanorum*, no. 9352, *Registres de Grégoire IX*, no. 1649. See Zientara, *Heinrich der Bärtige*, 285–87; Hollý, "Princess Salomea and Hungarian–Polish Relations," 28–29.

This situation, however, did not last long: in 1231 the aforementioned Silesian duke, Henry the Bearded, as the closest male relative of the young children, claimed guardianship of them, along with rule over Opole. His purpose was probably to secure the resources of the duchy for himself in his struggle for rule over Kraków. Pushing Viola into the background was simply part of the conflict within the Piast dynasty. We should not forget, though, that the Silesian duke's wife was Hedwig (Jadwiga) of Andechs, the sister of Gertrud, Coloman's mother. So, Henry was in fact related to Coloman, and in Grzymisława's case he was on one hand protector of Coloman, whilst on the other hand his rival.[18]

In this situation Duchess Viola turned to the Apostolic See in 1233, trying to secure her and her sons' rights against Henry. Pope Gregory IX granted her request. His charters also mandated a number of ecclesiastical and secular protectors, but it was only partly effective. As we have stated, Henry the Bearded had an especially good relationship with the papacy, so he engineered a compromise whereby he retained guardianship of the underage princes, while recognizing their claims on Opole, and in so doing held on to real power over the duchy. In return, Viola and her sons could take possession of Kalisz and Ruda in Greater Poland, which had just been seized by Henry the Bearded.[19]

We know of no actual practical involvement by Coloman in Viola's case. All we know is from the papal charter, but maybe Viola can shed light on why Coloman was asked to be her protector. There is no evidence of any Hungarian–Polish interaction in the 1220s or after the death of Duke Casimir to explain the involvement of Coloman. Nevertheless, Grzymisława might offer a parallel, so maybe Viola had some family connection to Coloman. Sadly, we know next to nothing about Viola's ancestry, in contrast to her later life, just a single sentence by Jan Długosz in his work *Chronica seu Annales Regni Poloniae* from the fifteenth century. The annalist wrote under 1251 on the death of the princess: "Viola, of the Bulgarian kindred and nation, princess of Opole, died."[20] On the basis of one statement Viola is traditionally considered to be a Bulgarian duchess in Polish historiography. Other historians have argued that Viola could have had Hungarian, Ruthenian, Dalmatian, even Croatian roots.[21] This may open a connection to Coloman, but it remains a puzzle.

---

18 With detailed literature see Barabás, "Prinz Koloman." Cf. Zientara, *Heinrich der Bärtige*, 163, 175, 207–39, 280–81; Dariusz Dąbrowski, "Piasten und Rjurikiden vom 11. bis zur Mitte des 13. Jahrhunderts," in *Fernhändler, Dynasten, Kleriker. Die piastische Herrschaft in kontinentalen Beziehungsgeflechten vom 10. bis zum frühen 13. Jahrhundert*, ed. Dariusz Adamczyk and Norbert Kersken (Wiesbaden: Harrassowitz, 2015), 155–189 at 189; Procházková, "Postavenie haličského kráľa," 70; Hudáček, "The Legal Position," 11.

19 *Regesta Pontificum Romanorum*, nos. 9337 and 9348–49; *Registres de Grégoire IX*, nos. 1645–46. See Zientara, *Heinrich der Bärtige*, 173–76, 289; Grabowska, "The Church," 192–93 (full citation above).

20 "Viola genere et natione Bulgara, Ducissa de Opol, moritur" (*Ioannis Dlugossii Annales seu Cronicae*, 6:327).

21 For detailed bibliography see Barabás, "Prinz Koloman," 11–15. Cf. Gładysz, *Zapomniani krzyżowcy*, 166–67; Dąbrowski, "Slovak and Southern Slavic Threads in the Genealogy of the Piast and Rurikid Dynasties," 113–16; Holly, "Princess Salomea and Hungarian–Polish Relations," 13; Dąbrowski, "Piasten und Rjurikiden," 178.

Unfortunately, as with Grzymisława, we have no information whatsoever about any actions undertaken by Coloman in relation to Viola. We cannot be even sure if Coloman had the intention to help at all. Maybe it is significant that he never again received an authorization of this type in his lifetime.

Coloman's Wife and Further Aspects to Polish–Hungarian Relations

Coloman became, from an early stage, involved in Polish affairs thanks to his engagement to Salomea, the daughter of the duke of Kraków. Their marriage had a great impact on Coloman's life. Salomea's possible role has been mentioned already concerning the Cistercian monastery of Spišský Štiavnik, Grzymisława's papal protection, and the possible negotiations with Daniil Romanovich. Her role must have been significant in the marriage of Béla IV's daughter, Kunigunda (Kinga) to Bolesław V the Chaste, Salomea's younger brother. This evnt features in the legend of St. Kinga (*Vita Sanctae Kyngae Ducissae Cracoviensis*) and claims the new tie between the Piasts and the Árpáds was formed thanks to the mediation of Coloman's wife, who was both the bride's aunt and the groom's sister. The marriage has recently been analyzed by Wojciech Kozłowski, who tried to clarify the traditional view. Traditionally, the main reason behind the matrimony was the Hungarian king's attempt to find support, through dynastic connections, against the growing Mongol menace. Kozłowski argues instead that the main reason was Béla IV's intention to enter into an alliance with Henry II (the Pious), duke of Silesia, since he, not Bolesław, was the leading Polish prince in 1239, and last but not least, because he held Kraków. It must have seemed rather unrealistic to expect that Salomea's brother could take power over the former territories of his father in the near future. We might wonder why Béla did not turn directly to Henry II, especially because he had three sons. But direct marriage between the two families would have been impossible because of their kinship, as Henry and Béla's mothers, Hedwig and Gertrud, were sisters. Nevertheless, Bolesław was the Silesian duke's ally, already tied to the Hungarian royal family as the brother of Salomea and a possible match for Béla IV's daughter. Kozłowski even stated that the Mongols were aware of the existing new alliance which is why they attacked Poland in parallel to Hungary, with Henry II killed at the battle of Legnica. Kozłowski's theory cannot be proven, yet it seems reasonable.[22]

---

22 *Vita b. Kingae* (*Catalogus fontium historiae Hungaricae*, no. 5025). Salomea's role in Polish–Hungarian relations was investigated recently by Karol Hollý (Hollý, "Princess Salomea and Hungarian–Polish Relations," especially pp. 12, 14–15, 31–32). See also Wertner, *Az Árpádok családi története*, 475–79; Kanyó, "Kálmán herczeg," 444–45; Kozłowski, "The Marriage of Bolesław of the Piasts and Kinga of the Árpáds," 80–99; Font, *Árpád-házi királyok*, 233–39; Niezgoda, "Między historią, tradycją i legendą," 243–44.

Chapter 13

CHALLENGES IN THE BALKANS

COLOMAN HAD TO face various severe challenges after 1226 due to the geographical location of his duchy. As duke of Slavonia he had to handle affairs in the Balkans, or more specifically the Hungarian interest there, especially in Bosnia. The issue of the Bosnian heretics and the threat of the Dalmatian pirates were of greater relevance for Coloman; his possible campaign to Bosnia was probably one of the greatest enterprises of his lifetime. But in a wider sense his politics can be seen to be aligned with the traditional tendency of Hungarian expansion southwards since the late eleventh century.[1]

The Bosnian Heresy

The Bosnian heresy, or the so-called *Bosnian Church*, is held traditionally to be a dualistic teaching related to the Bogomils and the Cathars. The complex nature of the situation caused by the presence of the heretics makes it necessary to take a wider, contextual perspective, not focusing alone on Coloman's deeds. We shall not examine here the doctrines of the Bosnian heresy; it is enough to know that scholars now doubt a direct relation between the Bosnian Church and dualist teachings. The influence of the Bogomils or the Cathars cannot be excluded completely, but it was certainly intermixed with Eastern monasticism and popular beliefs.[2]

The fight against the heresy had become central in papal–Hungarian relations by the early thirteenth century; Pope Innocent III was in regular contact with Hungarian rulers due to various plans concerning the matter, whilst the pope was also interested in restoring union of the Eastern, or orthodox, churches with Rome. Coloman had confronted this split in the universal church as king of Galicia, a "schismatic" territory. It is not known whether Innocent III had an underlying plan when he granted permission for Coloman's coronation there, but he was no doubt keen to expand Roman authority into this region. Members of the Hungarian royal family were given key roles in papal policy. Prince Béla actively supported the Dominican mission among the nomadic Cumans and

---

1 Cf. Ferenc Makk, *Magyar külpolitika 896–1196 [Hungarian Foreign Policy, 896–1196]*, Szegedi középkortörténeti könyvtár 2 (Szeged: Szegedi Középkorász Műhely, 1996²), 147–222.

2 For the church and heresy of Bosnia see Runciman, *The Medieval Manichee*, 63–115; Lambert, *The Cathars*, 297–313; Dimiter Angelov, "Ursprung und Wesen des Bogumilentums," in *The Concept of Heresy in the Middle Ages (11–13 C.). Proceedings of the International Conference, Louvain May 13–16, 1973*, ed. W. Lourdaux and D. Verhelst, Mediaevalia Lovaniensia, ser. 1. studia 4 (Leuven: Leuven University Press, 1983), 144–56; Lorenz, "Bogomilen, Katharer und bosnische 'Christen',' 107–21; Bálint Ternovácz, "A bogumil eretnekség a XI. századi Magyar Királyság déli területein [The Bogomil Heresy in the Southern Part of the Hungarian Kingdom in the Eleventh Century]," *Fons* 20 (2013): 501–23 at 502–03; Rabić, "Im toten Winkel der Geschichte," 56–58; Brković, "Bosansko-humski kršćani," 131–32; Margetić, "Neka pitanja abjuracije," 85–90; Slišković, "Dominikanci i bosansko-humski krstjani," 480–84. Cf. Kristó, *A feudális széttagolódás Magyarországon*, 77.

helped the establishment of a missionary bishopric while he was the duke of Transylvania, and Coloman was given responsibility for the Bosnian heresy as duke of Slavonia.[3]

The Bosnian situation was taken seriously from the papal side. Innocent III's successor, Honorius III, sent a legate to Dalmatia and Bosnia in 1221 to act against the pirates and the heretics. The mission of papal chaplain Acontius was not entirely unsuccessful, but a final solution to both problems remained. It is remarkable for Coloman's name to appear alongside the papal legate's in connection with these southern problems. A charter of Andrew II from 1221, perhaps 1222, offers information on the possible involvement of Princes Béla and Coloman against the pirates of Dalmatia. It seems rather unlikely that the Hungarian king indeed intended to send his young sons to war; perhaps he just wanted to appear compliant to the pope, which is why he sent his letter about actions required against the pirates to the leader of the Kačići family.[4]

Actual involvement in the early 1220s seems rather unrealistic, but after 1226 as the duke of Croatia and Dalmatia Coloman did have to face up to the challenge of the Dalmatian pirates and the heretics. One of his charters, from 1229, shows this, ordering the count and people of Split to bring their ships to his aid against the king's enemy, Domald, former count of Split, Zadar, and Šibenik. In the text we cannot find *expressis verbis* that the action against Domald was motivated by his piracy, but other papal and royal actions at this time point in this direction. The piracy issue was probably not connected to the heresy in Bosnia, even if piracy was treated in certain cases as a type of heresy. Others think that Coloman did not face the Dalmatian piracy in 1229, and his rule was rather challenged by a group of Croatian noblemen led by Domald.[5]

If we return to the issue of the Bosnian Church, the role of Archbishop Ugrin of Kalocsa must be emphasized. The prelate was concerned from the early 1220s about the threat the heresy presented. Honorius III praised his efforts to repel the heretics in 1225. We think the papal letter referred to a campaign led by Ugrin in which Coloman could have participated. The source does not give enough information but we can see the prelate spreading his jurisdiction over the Bosnian territories of Usura and Soy.[6]

---

3 *Regesta Pontificum Romanorum*, no. 6777, *Regesti del Pontefice Onorii papae III*, no. 3764. Cf. Szeberényi, "A zágrábi püspökség Szlavónia megszervezésében," 47; Szilvia Kovács, "History of the Cumans to the Mongol Invasion," *Chronica. Annual of the Institute of History. University of Szeged* 13 (2017): 205–10 at 207; Lorenz, "Bogomilen, Katharer und bosnische 'Christen,'" 115–17; Rabić, "Im toten Winkel der Geschichte," 62–69.

4 *Regesta Pontificum Romanorum*, no. 6618; *Regesta regum stirpis Arpadianae*, no. 376; *Codex diplomaticus regni Croatiae*, 3:187–88. See Basić, "O pokušaju ujedinjenja," 34; Hollý, "Princess Salomea and Hungarian–Polish Relations," 26; Majnarić, "Some Cases of Robbing the Papal Representatives," 499–502; Dall'Aglio, "Crusading in a Nearer East," 176; Gábor Barabás, "Heretics, Pirates, and Legates. The Bosnian Heresy, the Hungarian Kingdom, and the Popes in the Early Thirteenth Century," *Specimina Nova, Pars Prima: Sectio Mediaevalis* 9 (2017): 35–58 at 40–44; Majnarić, "Tending the Flock," 445.

5 *Regesta ducum, ducissarum*, no. 6, DL 361 54. See Procházková, "Postavenie haličského kráľa," 72; Basić, "O pokušaju ujedinjenja," 34; Fine, *The Late Medieval Balkans*, 143–44, 149–50; *Thomae archidiaconi Spalatensis Historia Salonitanorum*, 169n4; Sokcsevits, *Horvátország*, 125–26; Gál, "The Social Context of Hungarian Royal Grants to the Church in Dalmatia," 55.

6 *Regesta Pontificum Romanorum*, no. 7407. See Majnarić, "Some Cases of Robbing the Papal

The idea emerged a few years later to establish a new bishopric in Syrmia (Srem), in the vicinity of Bosnia, to help the mission among the heretics, whilst the union of the local orthodox churches with Rome would have been a side-effect of the measure. Archbishop Ugrin's idea was actualized with the help of a papal chaplain, Egidio, in 1229, but we don't know what effect it had. Later, in May 1233, the papal legate in Hungary, Cardinal Jacob of Pecorari, was authorized by the pope to engage in actions because of the desperate situation of the diocese. Jacob performed a change of leadership and placed the Dominican Johannes Teutonicus (Wildeshausen) as head of the diocese.[7]

Prince Coloman appeared in the sources regarding the Bosnian situation in 1233 too, the year when earlier accusations of heresy emerged again towards Bosnia and its ruler. Perhaps the accusations even originated from the Hungarian side. Pope Gregory IX sent letters, besides to Coloman as duke of Slavonia, to Matej Ninoslav, *ban* of Bosnia, and the Dominicans of the area, who were long-time active missionaries in Bosnia. The pope's requests can be found in Ninoslav's negotiations with the papacy. He presented himself, partially in response to Dominican activity, ready to lead the church of his realm into a union with Rome and fight the heretics. Gregory IX reacted to the *ban*'s offer and placed him and his family under papal protection and informed Coloman and the friars of his decision.[8]

Papal good-will towards the *ban* did not last long; in fact, Gregory IX began to organize a crusade against Ninoslav, and he probably intended to give the leadership of the expedition to Coloman, as many papal charters from 1234 show. It is still possible, however, that it was the Hungarian prince himself who again accused the Bosnian ruler, forcing a change in the papal plans.[9] The pope contacted Coloman in October and tried to convince him of the need to attack using arguments of the duties of good Christian rulers, the importance of the faith, and the need to follow Christ's will. The bishop of Bosnia was ordered to preach against the heresy in *Sclavonia* (probably meaning the territories

---

Representatives," especially 499–502; Bárány, "II. András balkáni külpolitikája," 159; Barabás, "Heretics, Pirates, and Legates," 44–45. Cf. Runciman, *The Medieval Manichee*, 105–6.

7 *Regesta Pontificum Romanorum*, no. 9211, *Registres de Grégoire IX*, no. 1375. See Ganzer, *Papsttum*, 132–33 (full citation above); Fine, *The Late Medieval Balkans*, 144; Lambert, *The Cathars*, 299; Lorenz, "Bogomilen, Katharer und bosnische 'Christen'," 115–16; Bárány, "II. András balkáni külpolitikája," 158–59; Barabás, *Das Papsttum*, 261–63; Dall'Aglio, "Crusading in a Nearer East," 176, 179; Rabić, "Im toten Winkel der Geschichte," 59–62; Barabás, "Heretics, Pirates, and Legates," 49–50; Majnarić, "Tending the Flock," 448–49.

8 *Regesta Pontificum Romanorum*, nos. 9303–5, *Registres de Grégoire IX*, nos. 1521–23; *Regesta ducum, ducissarum*, no. 6. See Szeberényi, "A Balkán," 329 (cited at the start of this book); Fried, *Der päpstliche Schutz*, 288; Fine, *The Late Medieval Balkans*, 143–45; Procházková, "Postavenie haličského kráľa," 72–73; Harald Zimmermann, *Der Deutsche Orden im Burzenland. Eine diplomatische Untersuchung* (Köln: Böhlau, 2000), 119; Font, *Árpád–házi királyok*, 220; Koszta, "Egy francia származású," 33–34; Bárány, "II. András balkáni külpolitikája," 158–59; Rabić, "Im toten Winkel der Geschichte," 63–64; Brković, "Bosansko-humski kršćani," 144; Margetić, "Neka pitanja abjuracije," 98–99; Slišković, "Dominikanci i bosansko-humski krstjani," 486–87; Dall'Aglio, "Crusading in a Nearer East," 180.

9 Lorenz, "Bogomilen, Katharer und bosnische 'Christen'," 116–17; Rabić, "Im toten Winkel der Geschichte," 63–67.

inhabited by Slavs), and he was even authorized to employ ecclesiastical censures where necessary. Gregory IX offered papal protection to the possible crusaders in a charter addressed to the warriors. Coloman even received extraordinary protection for himself and his family while leading the campaign, and the bishop of Zagreb was informed about this intention too.[10]

The pope even authorized a legate to act on behalf of the mission against the heretics, as he told the prelates and clergy of Dalmatia, Bosnia, Serbia, and other Slavic territories, while also encouraging them to engage in actions themselves. They should support the legate and convince as many people as possible to join the crusaders. The results of this papal mandate are not known, neither is the activity of the anonymous legate, and whether he even managed to get to the aforementioned provinces at all.[11] Nevertheless, according to certain scholars, we assume a campaign by Coloman in 1233 or perhaps 1234, which brought about the submission of Ninoslav.[12]

Gregory IX's response in August 1235 seems to support this picture, as he confirmed a royal benefaction to Coloman. Andrew II secured several rights for his son, which were subsequently acknowledged from the papal side. It is significant that Andrew supported his son's plans in Bosnia, and accusation of heresy might have even been meant to help Coloman's cause.[13]

Despite papal efforts, we cannot speak of any actual actions against Ninoslav and the heresy in 1235. Coloman did not start a campaign, so further instructions became necessary from the papal side. Gregory IX revived the business in August 1236 and sent out several charters because of the desperate situation of Sibislav, Ninoslav's rival, and son of his predecessor, Stephen. The *ban* had earlier attacked him, which is why Sibislav turned to the Apostolic See for protection. Gregory IX in turn ordered the archbishop and the provost of Esztergom and the bishop of Pécs as ecclesiastical protectors to support Sibislav.[14]

Coloman finally made a decision due to these new situations, and he seems to have led his army to Bosnia in 1236 or 1237. The duke received papal and royal guarantees for his campaign; his brother, Béla IV, affirmed all of his rights to his possessions. The events of Coloman's expedition are not entirely known, but it seems he managed to take control over parts of Bosnia, although he could not crush Ninoslav completely. The military actions lasted till 1239, according to Steven Runciman. Recently, some scholars

---

10 *Regesta Pontificum Romanorum*, nos. 9726, 9733–38; *Registres de Grégoire IX*, nos. 2121–24, 2127–29. See Fine, *When Ethnicity Did Not Matter in the Balkans*, 106–9. Cf. Procházková, "Postavenie haličského kráľa," 73; Basić, "O pokušaju ujedinjenja," 34.

11 *Regesta Pontificum Romanorum*, no. 9402, *Registres de Grégoire IX*, no. 1782. See Szeberényi, "A zágrábi püspökség Szlavónia megszervezésében," 47.

12 Rabić, "Im toten Winkel der Geschichte," 61.

13 *Regesta Pontificum Romanorum*, no. 9986, *Registres de Grégoire IX*, no. 2726. See Lorenz, "Bogomilen, Katharer und bosnische 'Christen'," 115ff; Rabić, "Im toten Winkel der Geschichte," 62ff; Slišković, "Dominikanci i bosansko-humski krstjani," 489.

14 *Regesta Pontificum Romanorum*, nos. 10019, 10223–26; *Registres de Grégoire IX*, nos. 2769, 3272–75. Cf. Pauler, *A magyar nemzet története*, 136; Fried, *Der päpstliche Schutz*, 288; Lambert, *The Cathars*, 299; Koszta, "Egy francia származású"; Rabić, "Im toten Winkel der Geschichte," 65.

have cast doubt whether Coloman, in fact, led his army to Bosnia, or if it was merely rhetoric in the papal letters on the crusader theme. In our view, the measures of King Andrew II and Béla IV in favour of Coloman make it plausible to think that the duke of Slavonia indeed had aspirations over Bosnia, so one or more campaigns are not completely beyond the realm of reality.[15]

The pope ordered the bishop of the Cumans to consecrate the Dominican friar, Ponsa, as the new bishop of Bosnia in April 1238, since the previous prelate, Bishop Johannes Teutonicus, had resigned, presumably in opposition to Coloman's plans in Bosnia.[16]

The new prelate received authorization as a legate on taking office or soon afterwards. His job was to strengthen the structure of his bishopric, for instance, establish a new cathedral and a chapter, whilst the main aim of his duty as legate was to contain heresy. In this endeavour Ponsa was supported by Coloman; he bestowed the town of Đakovo (Diakóvár) in the diocese of Pécs, and it later became the new seat of the bishopric. Besides Coloman, somewhat surprisingly, Ban Ninoslav also donated to the Bosnian bishopric, perhaps trying to win back good-will from the pope to protect himself against the duke of Slavonia. Nevertheless, Coloman himself received a papal letter in 1238, in which Gregory IX encouraged him to continue his fight.[17] The pope repeated these calls in December 1239.[18]

We know no further details of Coloman's activity in Bosnian affairs, but the issue of heresy did not come to an end through the duke's campaign. Ninoslav regained his independence after 1241 and managed to take back previously lost territories. Yet again, he returned to his old methods, and tried to prevent a Hungarian attack by turning to the papacy.[19]

---

15 *Regesta regum stirpis Arpadianae*, nos. 634 and 787. See Runciman, *The Medieval Manichee*, 106; Fine, *The Late Medieval Balkans*, 144–45; Lambert, *The Cathars*, 299; Bárány, "II. András balkáni külpolitikája," 158–59; Procházková, "Postavenie haličského kráľa," 74; Dujmović and Jukić, "The 'Koloman Renaissance,'" 177; Lorenz, "Bogomilen, Katharer und bosnische 'Christen,'" 116; Rabić, "Im toten Winkel der Geschichte," 61–64; Brković, "Bosansko-humski kršćani," 144–48, 163–64; Margetić, "Neka pitanja abjuracije," 100–101; Slišković, "Dominikanci i bosansko-humski krstjani," 487–89; Dall'Aglio, "Crusading in a Nearer East," 180; Majnarić, "Tending the Flock," 450–51.

16 *Regesta Pontificum Romanorum*, nos. 10505 and 10585; *Registres de Grégoire IX*, nos. 4058 and 4286. See Ganzer, *Papsttum*, 132–33 (full citation above); Ternovácz, "A boszniai latin," 220; Rabić, "Im toten Winkel der Geschichte," 65–67; Zsoldos, *Magyarország világi archontológiája*, 92.

17 *Regesta Pontificum Romanorum*, no. 10832; *Registres de Grégoire IX*, nos. 4691–97. See Heinrich Zimmermann, *Die päpstliche Legation in der ersten Hälfte des 13. Jahrhunderts. Vom Regierungsantritt Innozenz' III. bis zum Tode Gregors IX. (1198–1941)* (Paderborn: Schöningh, 1913), 139; Fine, *The Late Medieval Balkans*, 144–45; Procházková, "Postavenie haličského kráľa," 73; Hollý, "Princess Salomea and Hungarian–Polish Relations," 32; Lambert, *The Cathars*, 299; Basić, "O pokušaju ujedinjenja," 34; Dujmović and Jukić, "The 'Koloman Renaissance,'" 177; Lorenz, "Bogomilen, Katharer und bosnische 'Christen,'" 116; Ternovácz, "A boszniai latin," 220ff; Rabić, "Im toten Winkel der Geschichte," 66–67; Brković, "Bosansko-humski kršćani," 164–65; Slišković, "Dominikanci i bosansko-humski krstjani," 491–92.

18 *Regesta ducum, ducissarum*, no. 18; *Regesta Pontificum Romanorum*, nos. 10822–24; *Registres de Grégoire IX*, nos. 4991–93.

19 Runciman, *The Medieval Manichee*, 106–7; Lambert, *The Cathars*, 299–300; Lorenz, "Bogomilen, Katharer und bosnische 'Christen,'" 116.

The Question of the Crusade

The issue of crusading was not limited in Coloman's time simply to the Bosnian Church. Whereas Coloman was active in the Bosnian heretical question he remained inactive in the broader crusading movement. His father, Andrew II, was the first Hungarian ruler to take the cross and led his troops to the Holy Land in 1217–18. Later still, Pope Honorius III tried to convince the king to embark on a new crusade in 1223 and in 1227, but in vain.[20]

The question of the crusade emerged from the desperate state of the *Imperium Romaniae* or Latin Empire in the 1230s, established in 1204 at the expense of Byzantium by Western leaders of the Fourth Crusade. Andrew II had already received requests from Pope Gregory IX, but the situation became more urgent after his death in 1235. The siege of Constantinople by Bulgarian and Greek armies forced the pope to organize a campaign in order to help the empire, making demands for Hungarian contributions in the process.[21]

Prince Coloman was contacted, as well as his elder brother, by the papacy as early as December 1235, and the pope sent letters to several Hungarian prelates repeatedly. The Hungarian royal brothers, despite papal agitation and pressure from a papal legate (Salvi, bishop of Perugia), stayed aloof, while carefully not closing down the future possibility of assistance.[22] Béla IV even requested legatine rights for himself in return for intervention, but the pope declined; Gregory IX argued that a layman could not receive the office of a papal legate. Béla was probably reluctant to get involved and needed an excuse. Coloman was a more peripheral figure for Gregory IX but was still asked to grant safe passage through his territories for Emperor Baldwin II on his return to the Latin Empire in 1238.[23] The duke's reaction is unknown, but we do know that Baldwin travelled through the Hungarian kingdom on his way home in 1239–40. Coloman received no further papal requests, and the planned military campaign faded away. In comparison with the Bosnian heresy, Coloman clearly played a marginal role from a papal point of view in the prospective crusade to support the Latin Empire.

---

20 *Regesta Pontificum Romanorum*, nos. 7131 and 7646, *Regesti del Pontefice Onorii papae III*, no. 4262; *Codex diplomaticus Arpadianus*, 1:224–25; *Catalogus fontium historiae Hungaricae*, 1:764 (*Continuatio Claustroneuburgensis* 3). Cf. Dall'Aglio, "Crusading in a Nearer East," 176.

21 *Regesta Pontificum Romanorum*, nos. 9878, 10028; *Registres de Grégoire IX*, nos. 2511–17, 2745, 2766, 2786–89. See Nikolaos G. Chrissis, "A Diversion That Never Was: Thibaut IV of Champagne, Richard of Cornwall and Pope Gregory IX's Crusading Plans for Constantinople, 1235–1239," *Crusades* 9 (2010): 123–45; Michael Lower, "Negotiating Interfaith Relations in Eastern Christendom: Pope Gregory IX, Bela IV of Hungary, and the Latin Empire," *Essays in Medieval Studies* 21 (2004): 49–62; Dall'Aglio, "Crusading in a Nearer East," 180–81; Barabás, *Das Papsttum*, 195–98.

22 *Regesta Pontificum Romanorum*, nos. 10066, 10165, 10225–26, 10368, 10369, 10385, 10387–89; *Registres de Grégoire IX*, nos. 2872–76, 2911, 3156, 3273, 3275, 3694–96, 3716–20. Cf. Dall'Aglio, "Crusading in a Nearer East," 181–83.

23 *Regesta Pontificum Romanorum*, nos. 10505–8, 10535, 10631, 10632, 10634, 10636–39, 10671; *Registres de Grégoire IX*, no. 4056–64, 4154–57, 4482–86, 4488–90, 4623, 4624; *Regesta regum stirpis Arpadianae*, no. 642; *Vetera monumenta historica Hungariam*, 1:294. See Jenő Szűcs, "A kereszténység belső politikuma a XIII. század derekán. IV. Béla és az egyház [Inner Politics of the Church in the Mid-Thirteenth Century. Béla IV and the Church]," *Történelmi Szemle* 21 (1978): 158–81 at 162–63; Kozłowski, "The Marriage of Bolesław of the Piasts and Kinga of the Árpáds," 87–88; Barabás, *Das Papsttum*, 198–200.

Chapter 14

THE MONGOL ATTACK AND COLOMAN'S DEATH

COLOMAN, AND HIS brother King Béla IV, faced a new menace in 1241, bigger than any other previous threat, the Mongol invasion. They could not ignore it, as they had done in the case of the help requested for the Latin Empire.

The Mongol Invasion and the Papal Reaction

Not only did Coloman start making military provisions for an attack by the nomadic Mongols, but he informed the pope about the situation, perhaps before his brother but after the catastrophe of the battle of Muhi in April 1241. The pope's response[1] for the request for help was the last letter Gregory IX ever sent Coloman. The Hungarian Kingdom received no practical help in its moment of great need, as Béla IV later complained to Pope Innocent IV. Belatedly, Coloman was granted the protection of the Apostolic See and warriors who fought the Mongols were given an indulgence, as was the case for crusaders. Béla was given the same, while the prelates in Hungary were instructed to censure the enemies of the king.[2]

The Glorious Last Battle at Muhi

Coloman maintained loyalty to his brother even in the shadow of the Mongol menace and joined his troops to those of the royal army, marching fatefully forward. We are fortunate to have not one but two contemporary sources reporting the events of 1241 in detail.[3] One was Roger of Apulia, who served as the chaplain of cardinal-legate Jacob of Pecorari in 1232, and later received several ecclesiastical benefices.[4] He lived through the Mongol attack as archdeacon of Várad/Nagyvárad (Oradea), was captured by the nomads, but eventually managed to escape. Roger wrote his *Carmen miserabile*, or *Epistle to the Sorrowful Lament upon the Destruction of the Kingdom of Hungary by the Tatars*, of his experiences and the general state of the Hungarian kingdom from the 1230s to 1243–44 and dedicated it to Cardinal Jacob Pecorari. No medieval manuscript

---

1 For the papal reaction see Fried, *Der päpstliche Schutz*, 288; Felicitas Schmieder, *Europa und die Fremden. Die Mongolen im Urteil des Abendlandes vom 13.-15. Jahrhundert*, Beiträge zur Geschichte und Quellenkunde des Mittelalters 16 (Sigmaringen: Thorbecke, 1994), 73–75.

2 *Regesta regum stirpis Arpadianae*, nos. 706 and 934; *Regesta ducum, ducissarum*, no. 23; *Registres de Grégoire IX*, nos. 6055, 6057–62, 6094; *Regesta Pontificum Romanorum*, nos. 11032–36, 11043. See Fried, *Der päpstliche Schutz*, 263–64; Kiss, *Dél-Magyarországtól Itáliáig*, 22–23.

3 Coloman's participation in the defence of Hungary is mentioned, for instance, in the *Galician-Volhynian Chronicle* and in the *Chronicon Posoniense*. PSRL, 2:786–87; *A tatárjárás emlékezete*, 87; *Tatárjárás*, 36; *Chronicon Posoniense*, chap. 68 (*Scriptores rerum Hungaricarum*, 2:42), and in the *Chronicon Poloniae* of Godysław Baszko (*Catalogus fontium historiae Hungaricae*,, no. 2569).

4 *Korai magyar történeti*, 576–77 (entry by Tibor Almási).

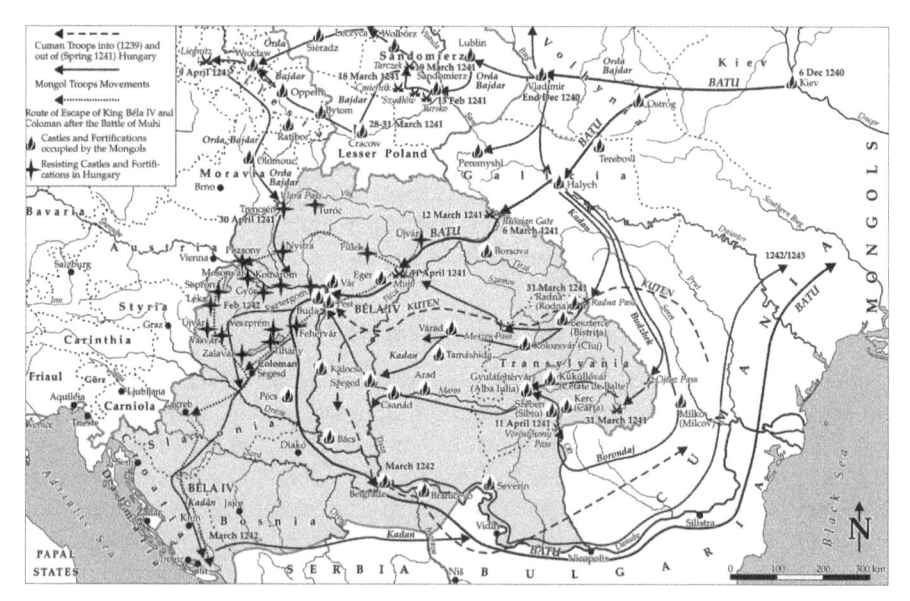

Map 11. The Mongol Invasion of Central Europe in 1241–42.

of the work is extant and is known from Johannes de Thurocz, who edited it as a supplement of his *Chronicle* published in Brno in 1488. The other source has already featured several times concerning Coloman's life. Thomas of Split's *Historia Salonitanorum atque Spalatinorum pontificum* (or *History of the Bishops of Salona and Split*) recorded the Mongol invasion also.[5] Unfortunately much of the information in the two are contradictory, but much good, factual work has been done recently by the military historian, János B. Szabó.

Béla IV convened the Hungarian troops to Pest in March 1241 on receiving news of the Mongol attack. Thomas of Split stated explicitly that Coloman answered the call of his brother, whilst Roger wrote about the arrival of a larger army in the realm. We do not know when the duke of Slavonia exactly arrived; perhaps not when Archbishop Ugrin fell for the stratagem of the Mongol vanguard and almost got killed after deciding to pursue them.[6]

The traditional view of the Hungarian strategy before the battle of Muhi in April is that the king's decision to build up a wagon fort was a poor system of defence. Szabó believes the plan was not doomed, since the king was probably trying to compensate for the loss of the Cuman troops on his side (the Cumans left Hungary after their leaders had been massacred in Pest, after the locals found out that there were Cumans fighting in the Mongol army and believed that the Cumans in Hungary as the king's allies since

---

[5] *Master Roger*; *Thomae archidiaconi Spalatensis Historia Salonitanorum*.

[6] *Master Roger*, 168–69. Cf. *Thomae archidiaconi Spalatensis Historia Salonitanorum*, 256–57; Szabó, *A tatárjárás. A mongol hódítás*, 117–26; Kanyó, "Kálmán herczeg," 437–40.

1239 were enemy spies). The Mongol forces started their attack on the night of April 10 and attacked the camp in three places.

Thomas of Split's description offers the most detailed picture of Coloman's deeds in the battle, so we will follow him, even if his work has to be handled delicately regarding its credibility. Thomas of Split presents the duke of Slavonia as one of the main figures of the combat, the one who, along with Archbishop Ugrin, stopped the Mongols at the bridge over the river Sajó after he learned of the attack from a Ruthenian fugitive. At first sight, this account seems suspicious and it was probably meant to emphasize the importance of the king of Galicia, though there may be some underlying reality. Thomas's charge that the Hungarians were so satisfied after their victory that they went to sleep and forgot to set guards sounds dubious. In his narrative it was again Coloman, along with Archbishop Ugrin and the master of the Templars, Rambald de Carumb, who picked up the fight at dawn. This time they were not able to hold the Mongols back, were forced to retreat to the Hungarian camp, where Archbishop Ugrin could not persuade the Hungarians to continue fighting, so Coloman, Ugrin, and Rambald attacked the Mongols again without their support. According to Thomas of Split, the duke and his companions caused a great deal of casualties on the Mongol forces, but Coloman and the prelate were seriously injured, and the master of the Templars died in the battle. For Thomas this meant the end: his heroes were either dead or unable to continue fighting. As a cleric from a Dalmatian town he emphasized the heroism and gallantry of Coloman and Ugrin, since they had direct connections to the southern territories of the Hungarian Kingdom. In Thomas's eyes they represented quality, while King Béla IV and the Hungarians were poor.[7]

Master Roger's description of the combat is substantially different. In his narrative the battle was fought in broad daylight and the Hungarian army got into a serious situation only in the afternoon. He also mentions the efforts of Archbishop Ugrin, yet Roger presents the prelate fighting alongside Béla IV. In the *Carmen miserabile*, the reader can learn of Coloman's valour and that he spent the whole day fighting the enemy. It is not easy to decide which narrative is more reliable, but Roger was a contemporary of the Mongol invasion and, even if he himself was not present in the battle, his description seems generally more realistic.

His contemporaries clearly valued the heroism Coloman showed in the battle, even if it was not enough to turn around the catastrophic defeat. The outcome of Muhi was devastating for the Kingdom of Hungary: besides many warriors and the aforementioned master of the Templars, Archbishop Matthias of Esztergom, Ugrin of Kalocsa, and the bishops of Győr, Transylvania, and Nyitra also lost their lives on the battlefield. King Béla IV and his small entourage barely escaped the massacre.[8]

---

7 *Thomae archidiaconi Spalatensis Historia Salonitanorum*, 262–69; Szabó, *A tatárjárás. A mongol hódítás*, 135–38. Cf. James R. Sweeney, "'Spurred on by the Fear of Death': Refugees and Displaced Populations during the Mongol Invasion of Hungary," in *Nomadic Diplomacy, Destruction and Religion from the Pacific to the Adriatic*, ed. Michael Gervers and Wayne Schlepp. Toronto Studies in Central and Inner Asia 1 (Toronto: University of Toronto, Central and Inner Asia Seminar, 1994), 34–62.

8 *Master Roger*, 181–91. Cf. Szűcs, "A kereszténység belső," 167; Szabó, *A tatárjárás. A mongol hódítás*, 138–57.

Coloman did manage to escape, perhaps even the Mongols granted him (and the king) passage. He returned to Pest, but the records are contradictory of his actions there. According to Roger, Coloman deserted the inhabitants behind despite their prayers for help, whereas Thomas of Split states that the fugitives ignored the duke's advice to move to fortified areas. Thomas's version seems more articulated, but has the benefit of hindsight, when the author knew of the relevance of castles and fortified churches in defending against attack. Whatever happened in Pest, Coloman continued his escape on to his estate in Segesd, and then to Čazma. His wounds were, however, fatal, and he died at the age of thirty-three in May 1241. The king without a kingdom was dead.[9]

Coloman's death was important news at the time, finding its way into several narratives, mostly in connection with the Mongol attack. In Austrian works his death appears even more frequently than King Béla IV's escape. The duke's final resting place is not completely agreed upon, since the *Chronicon Posoniense* stated that the duke was buried in the nunnery of Kloštar Ivanić, whereas Thomas of Split and other sources state that his corpse lay in the Dominican friary of Čazma. The circumstances of the funeral are also obscure. Thomas of Split stated that his grave was unmarked because of the Mongol threat, whereas some scholars believe his red marble gravestone was in Čazma until the Croatian–Hungarian Settlement in 1868 (which defined Croatia's place within the Austro-Hungarian empire), but since then its location has been unknown.[10]

Coloman's wife, Salomea returned to her homeland, Poland, after her husband's death, first settled in the nunnery of Zawichost (1245–55), later in Skała, near Kraków, where she founded the Poor Clare nunnery. She died as a nun with a saintly reputation in 1268. Salomea's legend was written in the late thirteenth or early fourteenth century, and it focuses on her religious life in Poland, so says little about Coloman. She was beatified by Pope Clement X in May 1673.[11]

Coloman's brother, Béla IV, fled to Austria after his escape from the battlefield, but this turned out to be a mistake, since his former ally, Duke Friedrich II, captured and blackmailed him, only freeing him in return for several west-Hungarian counties. After this Béla travelled to Dalmatia where he sought shelter in the town of Trogir. He took care of the affairs of the southern provinces after Coloman's death, as several royal char-

---

9 *Thomae archidiaconi Spalatensis Historia Salonitanorum*, 272–75; *Master Roger*, 184–85. Cf. *Ioannis Dlugossii Annales seu Cronicae*, 4:28.

10 *Chronicon Posoniense*, chap. 69 (*Scriptores rerum Hungaricarum*, 2:42–43). *Thomae archidiaconi Spalatensis Historia Salonitanorum*, 288–89; *Continuatio Sancrucensis*, 2 (*Catalogus fontium historiae Hungaricae,,* no. 1782; *Monumenta Germaniae Historica. Scriptores (in folio)*, vol. 9, *Chronica et annales aevi Salici*, ed. G. H. Pertz (Hannover: Hahn, 1851), 640); Giovanni Villani, *Historie Florentine* (*Catalogus fontium historiae Hungaricae,,* no. 2541); *Codex diplomaticus Hungariae*, 4/2:354. *Ioannis Dlugossii Annales seu Cronicae*, 4:30. See Kanyó, "Kálmán herczeg," 441–42; Procházková, "Postavenie haličského kráľa," 74–75; Kádár, "Az Árpád-házi uralkodók," 94, 99–100; Goss, "Battle of Cathedrals," 152; Goss, "Bishop Stjepan II," 213, 220; Goss, "Slovak and Croatian Art in the Thirteenth Century," 267; Szabó, *A tatárjárás. A mongol hódítás*, 139; Cepetić and Goss, "A Note on the Rose Window in Čazma," 186; *Master Roger*, 185n3.

11 See Kürbisówna, "Żywot bł. Salomei," 145ff; Niezgoda, "Między historią, tradycją i legendą," 235–36, 240–45; Hollý, "Princess Salomea and Hungarian–Polish Relations," 33–34.

ters from this time prove. Béla gave grants to several men later because of their services after the Mongols left, and also because they provided support for the duke and later for the king in their time of need.[12]

Béla IV continued the duchy and its institutions as left by Coloman but appointed Denis, son of Denis from the Türje kindred, as the new *ban* and simultaneously duke of Slavonia. This practice of combining the banship with being ruler of the duchy reappeared many times before 1259, though there was an interlude between 1245 and 1257 where Béla's first-born son, Stephen, bore the ducal title, and later on the younger sibling, Béla, then became duke of whole Slavonia.[13]

---

[12] *Regesta regum stirpis Arpadianae*, nos. 709, 711, 715–16, 719, 721–22, 725, 728, 744, 1527, 1570. According to medieval Hungarian law, ducal grants were only legitimate after royal confirmations. See also Zsoldos, "Hercegek és hercegnők," 17.

[13] *Codex diplomaticus regni Croatiae*, 4:170; *Regesta regum stirpis Arpadianae*, no. 769. See Font, "Prince Rostislav in the Court of Béla IV." Cf. Kristó, *A feudális széttagolódás Magyarországon*, 48–49; Zsoldos, "Az ifjabb király országa," 235–36; Zsoldos, *Családi ügy*, 13; Zsoldos, *Magyarország világi archontológiája*, 44–45.

CONCLUSION: COLOMAN IN THE EYES OF POSTERITY

MÁRTA FONT and GÁBOR BARABÁS

SURPRISINGLY, TILL RECENTLY Coloman was of greater interest to Ukrainian, Slovak, and Croatian scholars than Hungarian historians. The main focus was on him as King of Galicia. His evaluation has been heavily dependent on his role in different national histories.

In Hungary, the first monograph dedicated to Prince Coloman was the Hungarian version of this same book, published only in 2017. A few studies concentrating on his life or his coronation had appeared in the late nineteenth and early twentieth century,[1] but thereafter he only appeared in specific contexts: his life in Halych and in the Scepus, or his role as duke of Slavonia. For instance, the famous Hungarian medievalist Gyula Kristó's university textbook also follows this approach: Coloman only appears in the context of Hungarian expansion in Galicia, or concerning the relations between King Andrew II and Prince Béla. Not surprisingly, Coloman received more attention in Kristó's monograph on the history of the Hungarian territorial reigns where he analyzed the nature of his rule, but nothing on his activities. Tibor Almási went further in his entry in the *Korai Magyar Történeti Lexikon* (*Lexicon of Early Hungarian History*), emphasizing that Coloman's policies were fairly independent of his father and emphasizing his peaceful relationship with his older brother, Béla.[2]

The extraordinary brotherly peace between Coloman and Béla became the subject of a fictional work in 1930. György Büky's short story "Prince Coloman" was published in *Napkelet*, a conservative post-first world war magazine. In this short story, Hungarian noblemen gathered in Buda (sic!) at the royal palace where Coloman was present, intending to complaint about the absent king, Béla, who had repeatedly wronged them in many ways. But Coloman refused to hear them out and emphasized his loyalty to his brother. We do not intend to rake through a fictional story for historical authenticity, nor its many inaccuracies, such as his one-year period in Galicia, but the good relation between Béla and Coloman became a literary inspiration and paradigm. Another quaint element to the tale is the statement that Coloman only married Salomea to help defend against the Mongol threat.[3] We see here an interplay between historical accuracy and fiction and reaching a wider public.

---

[1] Kanyó, "Kálmán herczeg,"; Kállay, "Mikor koronázták meg Kálmánt."

[2] Font, "II. András orosz politikája és hadjáratai," and see Font, *Geschichtsschreibung des 13. Jahrhunderts an der Grenze zweier Kulturen*; Kristó, *A feudális széttagolódás Magyarországon*, and Gyula Kristó, *Magyarország története 895–1301* [*History of Hungary 895–1301*] (Budapest: Osiris, 1998). See also *Korai magyar történeti*, 316 (entry by Tibor Almási)

[3] György Büky, "Kálmán herceg," *Napkelet* 8 (1930): 647–57.

Figure 10. Coloman's Equestrian Statue in Gödöllő
(with kind permission of Péter Terejánszky).

In Russian, Ukrainian, and Polish historiography every single author dealing with the history of Galicia–Volhynia[4] touches upon Coloman's role, but he is merely a minor character in their narratives. One stream of Polish historiography links him to the eastern policy of the prince of Kraków, Leszek the White, and evaluates his perceived success or failure in this regard. Other Polish historians see him from Salomea's point of view and focus on Coloman's wife's title as *regina* (queen). Salomea herself is presented as a remarkable, holy nun and a great benefactor.[5]

---

4 See further Hrushevsky, *Istorija Ukrainy–Rusi*; Крип'якевич, *Галицько-Волинське князівство*; Pashuto, *Ocherki po istorii*; Pashuto, *Vneshniaia politika*; Włodarski, *Polska i Ruś*; Котляр, *Формирование территории и возникновение городов Галицко-Волынской Руси*; Котляр, *Данило Галицький*; Майоров, *Галицко-Волынская Русь*; Головко, *Корона Данила Галицького*; Володимир Александрович and Леонтій Войтович, *Король Данило Романович* [King Danilo Romanovych] (Біла Церква: Пшонківський, 2013); Nagirnyj, *Polityka zagraniczna księstw tiem Halickiej i Wołyńskiej*; Bartnicki, *Polityka zagraniczna księgcia*; Dąbrowski, *Rodowód Romanowiczów*; Dąbrowski, *Daniel Romanowicz, biografia polityczna*; Dąbrowski, *Daniel Romanowicz Król Rusi. O ruskiej rodzine książęcej*; Jusupović, *Elity ziemi Halickiej i Wołyńskiej*; Chrzanowski, *Leszek Biały*; Волощук, *«Русь» в Угорському Королівстві*.

5 Włodarski, "Salomea królowa Halicka,"; Niezgoda, "Między historią, tradycją i legendą," and Kürbisówna, "Żywot bł. Salomei."

Ukrainian historiography—like the *GVC*—illustrates Coloman's short reign from the point of view of his opponent, Daniil. Coloma is presented essentially as a hindrance; while researchers mostly disregard Coloman's royal title and the role of customary law of the Rus'. In several cases they do not know the Hungarian background adequately; in other cases obsolete works from the late nineteenth and early twentieth century have led to unwarranted conclusions. For instance, Maiorov from Saint Petersburg thinks that the provisions of the Golden Bull of 1222 applied to the *boyars* of Galicia, and he similarly misinterpreted the naure of the so-called royal servants (*servientes regis*). Hungarian charters and recent Hungarian works are only really known by Myroslav Voloschuk in his study «*Русь*» *в Угорскому Королівстві*.

Among Slovak scholars Nataša Procházková has presented Coloman as an embodiment of the medieval ruler who tried to avoid conflicts while King of Galicia and Duke of Slavonia. Martin Homza has emphasized Coloman's exceptional relations to the Apostolic See, and his active supported for papal plans. He called Coloman one of the most significant members of the Árpádian dynasty in the thirteenth century in his study of the *Polish–Hungarian Chronicle*. Coloman's time in the Scepus was especially important for the region according to Homza, and he frequently called Coloman the duke of Scepus (*dux Scepusiae*, książę/wojewoda spiski/ Scepusský vojvoda),[6] as if the territory were an independent political unit, akin to a duchy. Procházková also dealt with the question of titles and believes that Béla and Coloman wanted to split up the Kingdom of Hungary, while in reality the decisions of Andrew II were never questioned, not even by Coloman, who himself bore a royal title.

Neither in all these countries, nor in Croatian and Bosnian historiography, has Coloman ever been the centre of research. Hungarians and Croats had a shared history in the shadow of the Ottoman threat and this common interest became the focus of attention. This prince from the thirteenth century was not a negative figure until the onset of so-called Illyrism, that is, the Illyrian movement of South Slavic intellectuals in 1835–48, a form of Croatian national revival against the Habsburg empire. Coloman simply was of no interest until the late nineteenth century, when reference works included him. Tadija Smičiklas was the first modern Croatian historian[7] at the end of the nineteenth century to illustrate Coloman and his brother, Béla IV, as positive figures, and Vjekoslav Klaić followed him in this manner. Certain schoolbooks from the Austrian–Hungarian Dualism era (1867–1918) mentioned Coloman's role in the battle of Muhi, yet the emphasis was placed on the involvement of his Croatian troops in the massacre. In short, Coloman was not presented poorly in early Croatian historiography, but he was relatively marginal.[8]

---

6 Procházková, "Postavenie haličského kráľa," 75; Homza, *Uhorsko polska kronika,* 40, 188, 192; Homza, "Včasnostredoveké dejiny Spiša," 1:148.

7 Tadija Smičiklas, *Poviest hrvatska,* 2 vols. (Zagreb, 1879–82).

8 See: Dénes Sokcsevits, *Magyar múlt horvát szemmel [The Hungarian Past in Croatian Eyes]* (Budapest: Kapu Könyvek, 2004), 9–164, 174–75, 181–82, 191; Emil Niederhauser, *A történetírás története Kelet-Európában [History of Historiography in Hungary]*, História könyvtár, Monográfiák 6 (Budapest: MTA TTI, 1995), 300–33.

By contrast, Coloman has become a focus of interest for Croatian and Bosnian historians in the last few decades regarding his activity in Bosnia and the so-called Bosnian heresy. His conflict with Ban Matej Ninoslav, his possible campaign(s) within Bosnia, and his connection to the bishopric of Bosnia have been the subject of several recent studies.[9] The duke appears in several recent works as a competent ruler and a great organizer who improved Slavonia and helped the urban development of the area. He is depicted as an energetic leader and a brave soldier. The plan to unite the archbishopric of Split (Spalato) and the bishopric of Zagreb is a favourite topic, and many theories have been propounded. Prof. Goss has even stated that Croats should remember Coloman as one of their greatest ever rulers.[10] This is perhaps rather exaggerated and might be seen as romanticism, but it is perhaps indicative of Coloman's legacy in Croatia.

Across this broad range of national traditions we can conclude that historiography depicts Coloman as an outstanding person of his era, and as an adult he is shown as having a distinct rule over Slavonia. Even as a child he had participated in national politics, but in Galicia he was an implement of his father's goals. The complex need to balance dynastic interests with contemporary political relations explains the attention that Coloman has received across Polish, Ukrainian, Slovak, and Croatian historiography. In Galicia, in today's western Ukraine, the institution of the kingdom was established through him being crowned its king, and his building in the Scepus contributed to the development of this and the wider region. In Slavonia it is rather the political organization of the territory for which he is credited. For Poles he was particularly relevant as husband of Blessed Salomea whose title as queen derives from Coloman, but who is best known as foundress of the Poor Clares in the Polish lands.

Assessing Coloman's Life

Coloman was a minor when he ruled Galicia, so he was in no position to shape the course of events. He suffered the effects of his father's policy and the circumstances there. In particular, the apparent cooperation between the King Andrew II of Hungary and Prince Leszek of Kraków was fraught with conflict, despite the Agreement of Scepus in 1214. There was no Polish–Hungarian coalition, it was a rivalry.[11] The competing rulers reached agreement several times, under various terms, and with various outcomes. Leszek the White might support at different times the claims of one or other princes of the Rus' (for instance, Vladimir Rurikovich, Roman Igorevich, or Daniil Romanovich). On

---

9 Mladen Ančić, "Bosanska banovina i njezino okruženje u prvoj polovici 13. stoljeća [The Bosnian Banate and its Environment in the First Half of the Thirteenth Century]," in *Fenomen "krstjani" u srednjovjekovnoj Bosni i Humu*, ed. Franjo Šanjek (Sarajevo and Zagreb: Institut za istoriju u Sarajevu Hrvatski / Institut za povijest, Zagreb), 11–25 at 23; Brković, "Bosansko-humski kršćani," 139, 144–45, 150, 160–61, 164–65; Margetić, "Neka pitanja abjuracije," 90, 95–102; Slišković, "Dominikanci i bosansko-humski krstjani," 487–92; Šuljak, "Bosansko-humski krstjani," 442–46; Rabić, "Im toten Winkel der Geschichte," 56–69; Majnarić, "Tending the Flock" 350–51.

10 Basić, "O pokušaju ujedinjenja,"; Goss, "Battle of Cathedrals," 152; Goss, "Bishop Stjepan II," 212, 220; Goss, "Slovak and Croatian Art in the Thirteenth Century," 261.

11 Pashuto, *Vneshniaia politika*, 241.

the other hand, Andrew II's sole purpose was to secure Hungarian supremacy, regardless of which son would be its representative: either Coloman as king, or the youngest sibling, Andrew, as prince.

Dissatisfaction from certain members of the Hungarian elite forced Andrew II to allow the coronation of his eldest son, Béla, in 1214, with the intention of spreading power in the realm. Lack of strong territorial power prevented this happening, even though a new court was established around the crown-prince, opening up new positions for the elite and thereby offering new ways to let them increase their influence. Events in Galicia had similar effects, and the same elite tried to benefit from Hungarian expansion there too. This situation had not changed much by the end of Coloman's reign, and the establishment of Prince Andrew's territorial rule and court in 1227 created a new locale for the elite to gain offices and grants. The Hungarian princes both contributed to King Andrew II's expansion, combined with the Christian mission to adjoining territories. Béla supported the conversion of the Cumans, Coloman focused on the struggle against the Bosnian heresy, and Andrew's rule was probably intended to facilitate the union of the local orthodox church with Rome, although the lack of support around him made this endeavour impossible, if there were indeed any practical attempts to do so at all.

In our opinion, Coloman's Galician kingdom established a model for how Hungary approached its north-eastern frontier. A few decades later, in 1253, and under different circumstances, Prince Daniil would be crowned with a diadem sent from the papal curia. The two cases, though not identical, bear common features since Daniil was raised in Hungary between 1206 and 1213, and he was probably well aware of the significance of the act of coronation. It was probably no coincidence that he sought alliances to the west after the Mongol invasion in 1241. To help resist the Mongols, he accepted the crown from Pope Innocent IV with the accompanying requirement for ecclesiastical union. The fact that Daniil desired the royal title can probably be traced back to Hungarian rule over the Principality of Galicia.[12]

Coloman and his wife, Salomea, were forced to leave Galicia around 1221. They moved to Hungary but settled in the Scepus, where he retained his royal title. At first Coloman took no part in the government of the region; at least, there are no documents from this period regarding measures for the territory, and those charters that do deal with affairs of Scepus were all issued at later dates. His seclusion ended in 1226 when his father placed him in charge of the provinces of Dalmatia, Croatia, and Slavonia, territories previously controlled by his brother, Prince Béla. In 1226 Coloman travelled to the coastal towns and presented himself as the new duke through several solemn entries. Only from 1229 onwards do the sources offer a detailed picture of his rule in the territory of whole Slavonia. Coloman handled a wide spectrum of issues. For instance, on several occasions he granted rights to *hospes* communities, that is, settlers (at Dubica, Samobor,

---

12 Font, *Árpád-házi királyok*, pp. 195–203; Dąbrowski, *Daniel Romanowicz król*, pp. 53–79; Márta Font, "Ungarn und Osteuropa zur Zeit des Königs Anderas II. (1205–1235)," in *Generalprobe Burzenland. Neue Forschungen zur Geschichte des Deutschen Ordens in Siebenbürgen und im Banat*, ed. Konrad Gündisch (Köln—Weimar—Wien: Böhlau, 2013), pp. 40–57. at pp. 42, 44–55; Font, "Daniil Romanovych," p. 104.

Varaždin and elsewhere), and actively helped Bishop Stephen of Zagreb, particularly in the planned union of his bishopric with the archbishopric of Split. He also supported his brother in the restitution of the royal benefactions of territory before and after 1235 (the death of their father). The duke of Slavonia also joined his family in the campaign against the Babenberg dynasty's Austrian provinces. Pope Gregory IX (1227–1241) entrusted him twice with the role of lay protector of widowed Polish duchesses.

Coloman occupied himself not only in the affairs of his duchy and his family, but also assumed the role of warlord. He probably invaded Bosnia and attacked its ruler (*ban*) Matej Ninoslav who had been accused of heresy. If he achieved a conquest it did not last long, however, as Béla IV had to lead a new campaign to Bosnia in 1247.[13] The duke's military skills were clear in the great courage he showed in the battle of Muhi in 1241, where he managed to repel the Mongol attack, dying just a few weeks later in Slavonia of the wounds he suffered on the battlefield.

Coloman's rule had a particular impact on the establishment of the concept of "whole Slavonia" and he assisted the urbanization of the area through the help he provided foreign settlers. As we have seen in a popular tale from a 1930 magazine publication, his relationship to his elder brother was paradigm of brotherly spirit and a unique phenomenon in the Árpádian dynasty. Not even Béla's accession to the throne at his expense cast a shadow on it.

Coloman, second son of Andrew II and brother of Béla IV, may not be the most famous member of the Árpáds, the first Hungarian dynasty, but he still deserves historical attention. His life is significant in many ways and has been interpreted variously not only in Hungarian histories, but also Ukrainian, Polish, Slovak, Croatian, and Bosnian historiography. He deserves to be known outside these countries and by a wider public. But scholarship has often misrepresented him, which is why the present authors have gone back to a close look at the sources, to trace the details and events, in order to give the life of such an extraordinary man the attention and coherent treatment he warrants.

---

[13] See Toru Senga, "IV. Béla külpolitikája és IV. Ince pápához intézett 'tatár-levele' [The Foreign Policy of Béla IV and his 'Tatar-Letter' to Innocent IV]," *Századok* 121 (1987): 584–612 at 605–7.

BIBLIOGRAPHY

Primary Sources

A tatárjárás emlékezete. Edited by Katona Tamás. Budapest: Magyar Helikon, 1981.
Catalogus fontium historiae Hungaricae. Edited by Albin F. Gombos. 3 vols. Budapestini: Academia Litterarum de Sancto Stephano Rege Nominata, 1937–38.
Chronica hungaro–polonica, pars I (textus cum varietate lectionum): ad codicum manu scriptorum fidem recensuit, praefatione notisque instruxi. Edited by Béla Karácsonyi. Acta Universitatis Szegediensis de Attila József nominatae. Acta Historica 26. Szeged: JATE Történettudományi Intézet, 1969.
Codex diplomaticus Arpadianus = Árpádkori új okmánytár – Codex diplomaticus Arpadianus continuatus. Edited by Gusztáv Wenzel. 12 vols. Pest–Budapest: MTA, 1860–74.
Codex diplomaticus regni Croatiae, Dalmatiae ac Sclavoniae. Edited by Tadija Smičiklas. 17 vols. Zagrabiae: Jugoslovenska Akademija Znanosti i Umetnosti, 1904–81.
Codex diplomaticus Hungariae ecclesiasticus ac civilis. Edited by Georgius Fejér. 11 vols. and multiple parts. Buda: Typographia Regiae Vniversitatis Vngaricae, 1829–44.
Codex diplomaticus et epistolaris Slovaciae. Edited by Richard Marsina. 2 vols. Bratislavae: Academia Scientiarum Slovaca, 1971–87.
DF = Magyar Nemzeti Levéltár Országos Levéltára, Mohács Előtti Gyűjtemény. Diplomatikai Fényképgyűjtemény [National Archive of Hungary. Photo Collection].
DL = Magyar Nemzeti Levéltár Országos Levéltára, Mohács Előtti Gyűjtemény. Diplomatikai Levéltár. [National Archive of Hungary. Diplomatic Collection]
Documenta Pontificum Romanorum historiam Ucrainae illustrantia. I (1075–1700). Romae: PPBasiliani, 1953.
Font, Márta. *Magyarok a Kijevi Évkönyvben*. Szegedi középkortörténeti könyvtár 11. Szeged: Szegedi Középkorász Műhely, 1996.
The Galician–Volhynian Chronicle. Annotated translation by George A. Perfecky. München: Fink, 1973.
Hodinka, Antal. *Az orosz évkönyvek magyar vonatkozásai*. Budapest: MTA, 1916.
Ioannis Dlugossii Annales seu Cronicae incliti Regni Poloniae. Libri XII (Cracoviae, 1873). 6 vols. Varsaviae: Wydawnictwo naukowe PWN, 1975. [Reprint includes Liber sextus (1174–1240), Liber septimus (1241–1294).]
Kronika halicko-wołyńska (Kronika Romanowiczów). Edited by Dariusz Dąbrowski and Adrian Jusupović in cooperation with Irina Juriewa, Aleksander Majorow, and Tatiana Wiłkuł. Monumenta Poloniae Historica, n.s. 16. Kraków: Avalon, 2017.
Magistri Vincentii Chronica Polonorum. Edited by Marian Plezia. Monumenta Poloniae Historica, n.s. 11. Kraków: Wydawnictwo Secesja, 1994.
Master Roger = Anonymus and Master Roger. Anonymus, Notary of King Béla: The Deeds of the Hungarians. Edited, translated, and annotated by Martyn Rady and László Veszprémy. *Master Roger's Epistle to the Sorrowful Lament upon the Destruction of the Kingdom of Hungary by the Tatars*. Translated and annotated by János M. Bak and Martyn Rady. Central European Medieval Texts 5. Budapest: CEU Press, 2010.
Monumenta Poloniae Historica. Edited by A. Bielowski and W. Kętrzyński. 6 vols. Lwów: Akademia Umiejętności, 1864–1893 (reprint: Warszawa: Państwowe Wydawnictwo Naukowe, 1960).
NPL = Новгородская первая летопись старшего и младшего изводов. Москва–Ленинград, 1950.
PSRL = Полное собрание русских летописей (ПСРЛ). Санкт-Петербург: Археографическая комиссия, 1843–1917; Ленинград: Археографическая комиссия, 1926-28; Москва–Ленинград: Академия наук, 1949-50; Москва: Языки славянской культуры, са. 1997.

PSRL, 1 (*Lavrentiev Chronicle*) = *Lavrent'evskaya Letopis* = Лаврентьевская летопись, ed. Борис М. Клосс. Москва: Языки славянской культуры, 2001². [Numbering in the footnotes is by the published columns.]

PSRL, 2 (*Ipatiev Chronicle*) = *Ipat'evskaya Letopis* = Ипатевская летопись, ed. Борис М. Клосс. Москва: Языки славянской культуры, 2001². [Numbering in the footnotes is by the published columns, except for Roman nnumbered pages in the introduction.]

PSRL, 7 (*Voskresensk Chronicle*) = *Voskresenskaya Letopis* = Летопись по Воскресенскому списку, ed. Борис М. Клосс. Москва: Языки славянской культуры, 2001². [Numbering in the footnotes is by the published columns.]

PSRL, 15 (*Tver' Chronicle*) = *Tverskoy Sbornik* = Тверской сборник, ed. Борис М. Клосс. Москва: Языки славянской культуры, 2000.

PSRL, 25 (*Muscovite Chronicle Compilations*) = *Moskovskiy Letopisnyj svod* = Московский летописный свод конца XV в, ed. Борис М. Клосс. Москва: Языки славянской культуры, 2004.

Regesta ducum, ducissarum = Az Árpád-házi hercegek, hercegnők és a királynék okleveleinek kritikai jegyzéke. – Regesta ducum, ducissarum stirpis Arpadianae necnon reginarum Hungariae critico-diplomatica. Edited by Attila Zsoldos. Budapest: MTA TTI, 2008.

Regesta Pontificum Romanorum inde ab anno post Christum Natum MCXCVIII ad annum MCCCIV. Edited by August Potthast. 2 vols. Berolini: Academia Litterarum Berolinensi, 1874.

Regesta regum stirpis Arpadianae critico-diplomatica—Az Árpád-házi királyok okleveleinek kritikai jegyzéke. Edited by Imre Szentpétery and Iván Borsa. Budapest: Academia Litterarum Hungarica, 1923–1943.

Regesti del Pontefice Onorii papae III. Dall' anno 1216 all' anno 1227. Edited by Petrus Pressutti. 2 vols. Roma: Befani, 1884.

Les Registres de Grégoire IX. Edited by Lucien Auvray. 4 vols. Paris: Ernest Thorin, 1890–1955.

Scriptores rerum Hungaricarum tempore ducum regumque stirpis Arpadianae gestarum / edendo operi praefuit Emericus Szentpétery, socii operis erant I. Balogh [et al.]. Edited by Kornél Szovák and László Veszprémy. Budapest: Nap, 1999.

Tatárjárás. Edited by Balázs Nagy. Budapest: Osiris, 2003.

Thomae archidiaconi Spalatensis Historia Salonitanorum atque Spalatinorum pontificum / Archdeacon Thomas of Split. History of the Bishops of Salona and Split. Edited by Olga Perić, et al. Central European Medieval Texts 4. Budapest: CEU Press, 2006.

Vetera monumenta historica Hungariam sacram illustrantia. Edited by Augustinus Theiner. 2 vols. Romae: Typis Vaticanis, 1859–60.

Selected Secondary Works

Almási, Tibor. "Egy ciszterci bíboros a pápai világhatalom szolgálatában. Pecorari Jakab magyarországi legációja [A Cistercian Cardinal in the Service of Papal Authority: Jacob of Pecoraria as Papal Legate in Hungary]." *Magyar Egyháztörténeti Vázlatok* 5 (1993): 129–41.

Bagi, Dániel. "Sclavonia a Magyar–lengyel krónikában [Sclavonia in the *Hungarian-Polish Chronicle*]." In *"Köztes-Európa" vonzásában. Ünnepi tanulmányok Font Márta 60. születésnapjára*. Edited by Dániel Bagi et al., 45–58. Pécs: Kronosz, 2012.

Balzer, Oskar. *Genealogia Piastów [Genealogy of the Piasts]*. Kraków: Avalon, 2005.

Barabás, Gábor. *Das Papsttum und Ungarn in der ersten Hälfte des 13. Jahrhunderts (ca. 1198–ca. 1241): Päpstliche Einflussnahme–Zusammenwirken–Interessengegensätze, Publikationen der ungarischen Geschichtsforschung in Wien, 6*. Wien: Institut für Ungarische Geschichtsforschung in Wien / Balassi Institut / Collegium Hungaricum Wien / Ungarische Archivdelegation beim Haus-, Hof- und Staatsarchiv, Wien, 2014.

——. "Prinz Koloman und Herzogin Viola von Oppeln. Beitrag zu einem historiographischen Disput." *Ungarn–Jahrbuch* 32 (2016): 1–24.

———. "The Titles of the Hungarian Royal Family in the Light of Hungarian and Papal Sources in the First Half of the Thirteenth Century." *Chronica: Annual of the Institute of History, University of Szeged* 13 (2017): 27–43.

Bárány, Attila. "II. András balkáni külpolitikája [Andrew II's Foreign Policy in the Balkans]." in *II. András és Székesfehérvár. King Andrerw II. and Székesfehérvár*. Edited by Terézia Kerny and András Smohay, 129–73. Székesfehérvár: Székesfehérvári Egyházmegyei Múzeum, 2012.

Bartnicki, Mariusz. *Polityka zagraniczna księcia Daniela Halickiego w latach 1217–1264 [The Foreign Policy of Prince Daniil of Galicia in the Years of 1217–1264]*. Lublin: Wydawnictwo Uniwersytetu Marii Curie-Skłodowskiej, 2005.

Basić, Ivan. "O pokušaju ujedinjenja zagrebačke i splitske crkve u XIII. stoljeću [Attempt at the Unification of the Churches of Zagreb and Split in the Thirteenth Century]." *Pro tempore* 3 (2006): 5–43.

Brković, Milko. "Bosansko-humski kršćani u križištu papinske i ugarske politike prema bosni i humu [The Christians of Bosnia and Hum at the Crossroads of Papal and Hungarian Politics Concerning Bosnia and Hum]." In *Fenomen "krstjani" u srednjovjekovnoj Bosni i Humu*. Edited by Franjo Šanjek, 129–78. Sarajevo and Zagreb: Institut za istoriju u Sarajevu Hrvatski / Institut za povijest, Zagreb, 2005.

Cepetić, Maja and Vladimir P. Goss. "A Note on the Rose Window in Čazma and on the Presence of the Royal Workshops in the Medieval Slavonia." *Starohrvatska prosvjeta* ser. 3, 37 (2010): 179–87.

Chrzanowski, Marek. *Leszek Biały. Książę krakowski i sandomierski. Princeps Poloniae (ok. 1184–23/24 listopada 1227) [Leszek the White, Duke of Kraków and Sandomierz, Princeps Poloniae (ca. 1184 to November 23/24, 1227)]*. Kraków: Avalon, 2013.

Csákó, Judit. "A Magyar–lengyel Krónika és a hazai elbeszélő hagyomány [The Hungarian-Polish Chronicle and the Domestic Narrative Tradition]." *Századok* 148 (2014): 289–334.

Dąbrowski, Dariusz. *Daniel Romanowicz król Rusi (ok. 1201–1264). Biografia polityczna [Daniil Romanowicz, King of Rus' (ca. 1201–1264). A Political Biography]*. Kraków: Avalon, 2012.

———. *Daniel Romanowicz Król Rusi. O ruskiej rodzinie książęcej, społeczeństwie i kulturze w XIII w [Daniil Romanowich, King of Rus'. On Rus'ian Princely Family, Society, and Culture in the Thirteenth Century]*. Kraków: Avalon, 2016.

———. *Genealogia Mścisławowiczów. Pierwsze pokolenia (do początku XIV wieku) [Genealogy of the Mścisławiczs: The First Generations (Prior to the Start of the Fourteenth Century)]*. Kraków: Avalon, 2008.

———. *Rodowód Romanowiczów książąt halicko-wołyńskich [Genealogy of the Romanowiczs in the Principalities of Galicia and Volhynia]*. Toruń: Wydawnictwo Historyczne, 2002.

———. "Slovak and Southern Slavic Threads in the Genealogy of the Piast and Rurikid Dynasties in the Thirteenth Century / Slovenské a južnoslovanské motívy v genealógiách Rurikovcov a Piastovcov v 13. storočí / Slovački i južnoslavenski motivi u genealogiji Rurikovića i Pjastovića u 13. Stoljeću." In *Slovakia and Croatia Vol I. Slovakia and Croatia Historical Parallels and Connections (until 1780) / Slowakei und Kroatien Historische Parallelen und Beziehungen (bis zum Jahre 1780)*. Edited by Veronika Kucharská et al., 110–19. Bratislava and Zagreb: Department of Slovak History, Faculty of Philosophy, Comenius University in Bratislava–Faculty of Humanities and Social Sciences of the University of Zagreb, 2013).

Dall'Aglio, Francesco. "Crusading in a Nearer East: the Balkan Politics of Honorius III and Gregory IX (1221–1241)." In *La Papauté et les croisades / The Papacy and the Crusades. Actes du VIIe Congrès de la Society for the Study of the Crusades and the Latin East / Proceedings of the VIIth Conference of the Society for the Study of the Crusades and the Latin East*. Edited by Michel Balard, 174–83. Crusades: Subsidia 3 (Farnham: Ashgate, 2011).

Dujmović, Danko and Vjekoslav Jukić. "The 'Koloman Renaissance' in North Western Croatia—An Unfinished Project." *Starohrvatska prosvjeta* ser. 3, 37 (2010): 171–82.

Feld, István. "Az erdőispánságok várai az Árpád-kori Magyarországon [Castles of the "Forest *comitati"* in Hungary in the Árpádian Era]." In *Arcana tabularii. Tanulmányok Solymosi László tiszteletére*. Edited by Attila Bárány, Gábor Dreska, and Kornél Szovák, 369–90. Budapest: MTA–DE–ELTE BTK–PPKE, 2014.

Fine, John V. A. *The Late Medieval Balkans: A Critical Survey from the Late Twelfth Century to the Ottoman Conquest*. Ann Arbor: The University of Michigan Press, 1987.

———. *When Ethnicity Did Not Matter in the Balkans: A Study of Identity in Pre-Nationalist Croatia, Dalmatia and Slavonia in the Medieval and Early-Modern Periods*. Ann Arbor: The University of Michigan Pres, 2006.

Font, Márta. "II. András orosz politikája és hadjáratai [Russian Foreign Policy and the Campaigns of Andrew II]," *Századok* 125 (1991): 107–44.

———. *Árpád-házi királyok és Rurikida fejedelmek [Árpádian Kings and Rurukid Princes]*. Szegedi Középkortörténeti Könyvtár 21. Szeged: Szegedi Középkorász Műhely, 2005.

———. "Даниил Романович «Галицкий» и Венгерское Королевство [Daniil Romanovych of 'Galicia' and the Kingdom of Hungary]." In *Письменность Галицко-Волыского княжества: историко-филологические исследования*. Edited by Jitka Komendová et al., 91–105. Olomouc: Univerzitá Palackého, 2016.

———. *Geschichtsschreibung des 13. Jahrhunderts an der Grenze zweier Kulturen. Das Königreich Ungarn und das Fürstentum Halitsch–Wolhynien*. Akademie der Wissenschaften und Literatur, Mainz. Mainz: Steiner, 2005.

———. *Koloman the Learned, King of Hungary*. Szeged: Szegedi Középkorász Műhely, 2001.

———. *Könyves Kálmán és kora [King Coloman the Learned and his Era]*. IPF kismonográfia sorozat 1. Szekszárd: Illyés Gyula Pedagógiai Főiskola, 1999.

———. "Prince Rostislav in the Court of Béla IV." *Russian History* 44 (2017): 486–504.

Fried, Johannes. *Der päpstliche Schutz für Laienfürsten. Die politische Geschichte des päpstlichen Schutzprivilegs für Laien (11.–13. Jahrhundert)*. Heidelberg: Winter, 1980.

Gál, Judit. "Az Árpád-házi királyok és hercegek ünnepélyes bevonulásai a dalmáciai városokba [Solemn Entries of the Árpádian Kings and Princes into the Cities of Dalmatia]." In *Micae Mediaevales IV. Fiatal történészek dolgozatai a középkori Magyarországról és Európáról*. Edited by Judit Gál et al., 59–76. Budapest: ELTE BTK Történelemtudományok Doktori Iskola, 2015.

———. "The Social Context of Hungarian Royal Grants to the Church in Dalmatia (1102–1301)." *Annual of Medieval Studies at CEU* 21 (2015): 47–63.

Goss, Vladimir P. "The Battle of Cathedrals: or How Zagreb almost Became an Archbishopric in the Thirteenth Century." In *Medioevo: l'Europa delle cattedrali; atti del convegno internazionale di studi, Parma, 19–23 settembre 2006*. Edited by Arturo Carlo Quintavalle, 146–54. Milano: Electa, 2007.

———. "Bishop Stjepan II and Herceg Koloman and the Beginnings of the Gothic in Croatia." *Hortus artium medievalium* 13 (2007): 211–24.

———. "Slovak and Croatian Art in the Thirteenth Century. Some Striking Analogies and Their Background / Umenie v Slavónsku a na Spiši v 13. storočí – niekoľko pozoruhodných analógiía ich pozadie / Umjetnost u Slavoniji i na Spišu u 13. stoljeću – neke upečatljive analogije i njihove pozadine." In *Slovakia and Croatia Vol I. Slovakia and Croatia Historical Parallels and Connections (until 1780)/Slowakei und Kroatien Historische Parallelen und Beziehungen (bis zum Jahre 1780)*. Edited by Veronika Kucharská et al., 260–68. Bratislava and Zagreb: Department of Slovak History, Faculty of Philosophy, Comenius University in Bratislava / Faculty of Humanities and Social Sciences of the University of Zagreb, 2013.

Gładysz, Mikołaj. *Zapomniani krzyżowcy: Polska wobec ruchu krucjatowego w XII–XIII wieku [Forgotten Crusaders: Poland and the Crusader Movement in the Twelfth and Thirteenth Centuries]* (Warszawa: DiG, 2004).

Györffy, György. "Szlavónia kialakulásának oklevélkritikai vizsgálata [A Critical Examination of the Charters on the Formation of Slavonia]." *Levéltári Közlemények* 41 (1970): 223–40.

Herbers, Klaus. *Geschichte des Papsttums im Mittelalter*. Darmstadt: Primus, 2012.
Hollý, Karol. "Princess Salomea and Hungarian–Polish Relations in the Period 1214–1241." *Historický Časopis* 55 Supplement (2007): 5–32.
Головко, Олександр Б. *Корона Данила Галицького. Волинь і Галичина в державно-політичному розвитку Центрально-Східной Європи та класичного середньовччя [The Crown of Daniil of Galicia: Volhynia and Galicia in the Political Development of East-Central Europe in the Classical Middle Ages]* (Київ: Стилос, 2006).
Homza, Martin. *Uhorsko polska kronika. Nedocenený prameň k dejinám strednej Európy [The Hungarian-Polish Chronicle. An Undervalued Source for the History of Central Europe]*. Bratislava: Libri historiae–Post Scriptum, 2009.
———. "Včasnostredoveké dejiny Spiša [Early History of Spiš]." In *Historia Scepusii*. Edited by Martin Homza and Stanisław A. Sroka, vol. 1, 126–327. Bratislava and Kraków: Avalon, 2009.
Hrushevsky, "Khronologia podij" = Грушевський, Михаил. "Хронологія подій Галицько-Волинской літописи Chronology of Events of the Galician–Volhynian Chronicle]." *Записи наукового Товариства ім Шевченка* 41 (1901): 1–72.
———, *Istorija Ukrainy–Rusi* = Грушевський, Михаил. *Історія України–Русі [The History of Ukraine-Rus]*. 3 vols. У Львови: Історично-філософична секція Наукового Товариства ім. Шевченка, 1905.
Janovská, Magdaléna. "Building Activities in Spiš in the Thirteenth Century in the Context of the Hungarian Kingdom / Stavebné aktivity na Spiši v 13. storočí v kontexte Uhorska / Aktivnost u Spiškoj regiji u 13. stoljeću u kontekstu Ugarske." In *Slovakia and Croatia: Historical Parallels and Connections (until 1780) / Slowakei und Kroatien: Historische Parallelen und Beziehungen (bis zum Jahre 1780)*. Edited by Veronika Kucharská et al., Slovakia and Croatia 1, 269–90. Bratislava and Zagreb: Department of Slovak History, Faculty of Philosophy, Comenius University in Bratislava / Faculty of Humanities and Social Sciences of the University of Zagreb, 2013.
Jusupović, Adrian. *Elity ziemi Halickiej i Wołyńskiej w czasach Romanowiczów (ok. 1205 – 1269) [The Elite of the Galician and Volhynian Lands in the Time of the Romanowiczs (ca. 1205–1269)]*. Pracowní badań nad dziejami Rusi Uniwersytetu Kazimierza Wielkiego w Bydgoszczy, Monografie 2. Kraków: Avalon, 2013.
Kádár, Tamás. "Az Árpád-házi uralkodók és az országlásuk idején hercegi címmel tartományi különhatalmat gyakorolt külhoni, fejedelmi származású előkelők, valamint azok családtagjainak elhalálozási és temetkezési adatai 997–1301 között [Information on the Deaths and Burials of the Rulers of the Árpádian Dynasty, the Dukes, and Their Family Members]." *Fons* 19 (2012): 57–108.
Kállay, Ubul. "Mikor koronázták meg Kálmánt, Halics felkent királyát a pápa által küldött koronával? [When Did the Coronation of Coloman, Anointed King of Galicia, Happen with the Papal Crown?]," *Századok* 37 (1903): 672–73.
Kanyó, Géza. "Kálmán herczeg 1208–1241 [Prince Coloman, 1208–1241]." *Katholikus Szemle* 9 (1895): 250–67, 414–45.
Kiss, Gergely. *Dél-Magyarországtól Itáliáig. Báncsa nembeli István (1205 k. – 1270) váci püspök, esztergomi érsek, az első magyarországi bíboros életpályája [From Southern Hungary to Italy: Biography of Stephen Báncsa (ca. 1205–1270), Bishop of Vác and Archbishop of Esztergom]*. Pécs: Kronosz, 2015.
———. *Királyi egyházak a középkori Magyarországon [Royal Churches in Medieval Hungary]*, Thesaurus historiae ecclesiasticae in Universitate Quinqueecclesiensi 3. Pécs: Pécsi Történettudományért Kulturális Egyesület, 2013.
Korai magyar történeti lexikon (9–14. század) [Lexicon of Early Hungarian History]. Edited by Gyula Kristó, and Pál Engel and Ferenc Makk. Budapest: Akadémiai Kiadó, 1994.
Körmendi, Tamás. "Szlavónia korai hovatartozása [Where did Slavonia Belong in the Tenth and Eleventh Centuries?]." *Századok* 146 (2012): 369–88.

Koszta, László. "Egy francia származású főpap Magyarországon. Bertalan pécsi püspök (1219–1251) [A Prelate of French Origin in Hungary: Bishop Bartholomew of Pécs (1219–1251)]." In László Koszta, *Írásbeliség és egyházszervezet. Fejezetek a középkori magyar egyház történetéből*. Capitulum 3, 23–44. Szeged: JATE Press, 2007.

Котляр, Микола Ф. *Данило Галицький [Daniil of Galicia]*. Киев: Альтернативи, 2002.

——. *Формирование территории и возникновение городов Галицко-Волынской Руси IX–XIII вв. [Creating Territory and the Birth of Towns in Galician–Volhynian Rus in the Ninth to Thirteenth Centuries]* (Киев: Наукова думка, 1985).

Kozłowski, Wojciech. "The Marriage of Bolesław of the Piasts and Kinga of the Árpáds in 1239 in the Shadow of the Mongol Menace." In *"In my Spirit and Thought I Remained a European of Hungarian Origin": Medieval Historical Studies in Memory of Zoltan J. Kosztolnyik*. Edited by István Petrovics, Sándor László Tóth, and Eleanor A. Congdon. Capitulum 6, 79–100. Szeged: JATE Press, 2010.

Крип'якевич, Іван П. *Галицько-Волинське князівство [The Galician–Volhynian Principality]*. Київ: Наукова думка, 1984.

Kristó, Gyula. *A feudális széttagolódás Magyarországon [Feudal Fragmentation in Hungary]*. Budapest: Akadémiai Kiadó, 1979.

Kürbisówna, Brygida. "Żywot bł. Salomei jako źródło historyczne [The Legend of Blessed Salomea as a Historical Source]." In *Studia historica w 35-lecie pracy naukowej Henryka Łowmiańskiego*. Edited by Aleksander Gieysztor et al., 145–54. Warszawa: Państwowe Wydawnictwo Naukowe, 1958.

Labanc, Peter. *Spišskí prepošti do roku 1405 [Provosts of Spiš Prior to 1405]*. Trnava: Filozofická Fakulta Trnavskej Univerzity v Trnave–Spolok Slovákov v Poľsku, 2011.

Lambert, Malcolm D. *The Cathars*. Oxford: Blackwell, 1998.

Lammich, Maria. *Fürstenbiographien des 13. Jahrhunderts in den Russischen Chroniken*. Köln: Kleikamp, 1973.

Lorenz, Manuel. "Bogomilen, Katharer und bosnische 'Christen': Der Transfer dualistischer Häresien zwischen schen Orient und Okzident (11. -13. Jh.)." In *Vermitteln—Übersetzen—Begegnen: Transferphänomene im europäischen Mittelalter und in der frühen Neuzeit; interdisziplinäre Annäherungen*. Edited by Balázs J. Nemes. Nova mediaevalia 9, 87–136. Göttingen: V&R Unipress, 2011.

Majnarić, Ivan. "Some Cases of Robbing the Papal Representatives along the Eastern Adriatic Coast in the Second Half of the Twelfth and during the Thirteenth Century." *Acta Histriae* 15 (2007): 493–506.

——.. "Tending the Flock: Clergy and a Discourse of War in the Wider Hinterland of the Eastern Adriatic during the Late Twelfth and Thirteenth Centuries." In *Between Sword and Prayer: Warfare and Medieval Clergy in Cultural Perspective*. Edited by Radosław Kotecki et al., 435–69. Explorations in Medieval Culture 3. Leiden: Brill, 2018.

Майоров, Александр В. *Галицко-Волынская Русь. Очерки социально-политических отношений в домонгольский период. Князь, бояре и городская община [Galician and Volhynian Rus': Studies on Social-Political Relations in Pre-Mongol Times. Prince, Boyars and Urban Society]*. Санкт-Петербург: Университетская книга, 2001.

Margetić, Lujo. "Neka pitanja abjuracije iz 1203. godine [Some Questions on the Oath of 1203]." In *Fenomen "krstjani" u srednjovjekovnoj Bosni i Humu*. Edited by Franjo Šanjek, 27–103. Sarajevo and Zagreb: Institut za istoriju u Sarajevu Hrvatski / Institut za povijest, Zagreb.

Marosi, Ernő. *A romanika Magyarországon [The Romanesque in Hungary]*. Budapest: Corvina, 2013.

——. *Die Anfänge der Gotik in Ungarn. Esztergom in der Kunst des 12.–13. Jahrhunderts*. Budapest: Akadémiai Kiadó, 1984.

Nagirnyj, Witalij. *Polityka zagraniczna księstw ziem Halickiej i Wołyńskiej w latach 1198 (1199)–1264 [The Foreign Policy of the Principalities of Galicia and Volhynia, 1198 (1199) to 1264]*. Prace Komisji Wschodnioeuropejskiej 12. Kraków: Polska Akademia Umiejętności, 2011.

Niezgoda, Cecylian. "Między historią, tradycją i legendą o bł. Salomei Piastównie (1211–1268) [Between History, Tradition, and the Legend of Blessed Salomea from the Piast Family]." *Studia Franciszkańce* 8 (1997): 233–47.

Pashuto, *Ocherki po istorii* = Пашуто, Владимир Т. *Очерки по истории Галицко-Волынской Руси [Studies on the History of Galician-Volhynian Rus]*. Москва: Академия наук СССР, 1950.

———, *Vneshniaia politika* = Пашуто, Владимир Т. *Внешняя политика Древней Руси [Foreign Politics of Old Rus']*. Москва: Академия наук СССР, 1968.

Pauler, Gyula. *A magyar nemzet története az Árpádházi királyok alatt [History of the Hungarian Nation under the Árpádian Kings]*. 2 vols. Budapest: Atheneum, 1899².

Procházková, Nataša. "Koloman Haličský na Spiši pred rokom 1241 [Coloman of Galicia in Spiš before 1241]." In *Terra Scepusiensis. Stan badań nad dziejami Spiszu*. Edited by Ryszard Gładkiewicz and Martin Homza, 243–49. Levoča and Wrocław: Slovensko-Poľska Komisia Humanitných Vied, 2003.

———. "Postavenie haličského kráľa a slavónskeho kniežaťa Kolomana z rodu Arpádovcov v uhorskej vnútornej a zahraničnej politike v prvej polovici 13. storočia [King of Galicia and Duke of Slavonia: Coloman of the Árpádian Dynasty, in the First Half of the Thirteenth Century]." *Medea* 2 (1998): 64–75.

———. "Some Notes on the Titles of Coloman of Galicia / K intulatúre Kolomana Haličského / O titulama Kolomana Haličkoga." In *Slovakia and Croatia, Vol I. Slovakia and Croatia Historical Parallels and Connections (until 1780) / Slowakei und Kroatien Historische Parallelen und Beziehungen (bis zum Jahre 1780)*. Edited by Veronika Kucharská et al., 104–9. Bratislava and Zagreb: Department of Slovak History, Faculty of Philosophy, Comenius University in Bratislava / Faculty of Humanities and Social Sciences of the University of Zagreb, 2013.

Rabić, Nedim. "Im toten Winkel der Geschichte: Johannes von Wildeshausen als Bischof von Bosnien 1233/34–1237." In *Die deutschen Dominikaner und Dominikanerinnen im Mittelalter*. Edited by Sabine von Heusinger et al., 53–69. Berlin: De Gruyter, 2016.

Rapov, *Kniazheskie vladeniia* = Рапов, Олег М. *Княжеские владения на Руси в X–первой половине XIII вв. [Possessions of Princes in Kievan Rus' in the Tenth to the First Half of the Thirteenth Centuries]*. Москва: Московский университет, 1977.

Rhode, Gotthold. *Ostgrenze Polens: politische Entwicklung, kulturelle Bedeutung und geistliche Auswirkung*. Ostmitteleuropa in der Vergangenheit und Gegenwart 2. Köln: Böhlau, 1955.

Romhányi, *Kolostorok és társaskáptalanok* = Romhányi, Beatrix F. *Kolostorok és társaskáptalanok a középkori Magyarországon [Monastic and Collegial Charters in Medieval Hungary]*. Budapest: Arcanum, 2008. CD-ROM

Runciman, Steven. *The Medieval Manichee: A Study of the Christian Dualist Heresy*. Cambridge: Cambridge University Press, 1947.

Senga, Toru. "Béla királyfi bolgár, halicsi és osztrák hadjárataihoz [On the Campaigns of Prince Béla to Bulgaria, Galicia, and Austria]." *Századok* 122 (1988): 36–51.

Slišković, Slavko. "Dominikanci i bosansko-humski krstjani [The Dominicans and the Christians of Bosnia and Hum]." In *Fenomen "krstjani" u srednjovjekovnoj Bosni i Humu*. Edited by Franjo Šanjek, 479–98. Sarajevo and Zagreb: Institut za istoriju u Sarajevu Hrvatski / Institut za povijest, Zagreb, 2005.

Sokcsevits, Dénes. *Horvátország a 7. századtól napjainkig [Croatia from the Seventh Century to the Present Day]*. Budapest: Mundus Novus, 2011.

Šuljak, Andrija. "Bosansko-humski krstjani i prijenos rezidencije bosanskih biskupa u Đakovo [The Christians of Bosnia and Hum and the Transfer of the Bosnian See to Đakovo]." In *Fenomen "krstjani" u srednjovjekovnoj Bosni i Humu*. Edited by Franjo Šanjek, 441–54. Sarajevo and Zagreb: Institut za istoriju u Sarajevu Hrvatski / Institut za povijest, Zagreb, 2005.

Szabó, János B. *A tatárjárás. A mongol hódítás és Magyarország [The Tartar Invasion. Mongol Expansion and Hungary]*. Budapest: Corvina, 2007.

Szczur, Stanisław. *Historia Polski. Średniowiecze [History of Poland: The Middle Ages]*. Kraków: Wydawnictwo Literackie, 2002.

Vida, Beáta. "A ciszterci rend kezdeteinek vitatott kérdései a Szepességben [Disputed Questions Regarding the Beginnings of the Cistercian Order in Spiš]." In *Fons, skepsis, lex. Ünnepi tanulmányok a 70 esztendős Makk Ferenc tiszteletére*. Edited by Tibor Almási et al., 461–67. Szeged: SZTE Történeti Segédtudományok Tanszék–Szegedi Középkorász Műhely, 2010.

Волощук, Мирослав. *«Русь» в Угорському Королівстві (XI–друга половина XIV ст.): суспільно-політична роль, майнови стосунки, міграції ["Rus" in the Hungarian Kingdom (From the Eleventh to the Second Half of the Fourteenth Centuries): Socio-political Roles, Potential Conflicts, Migration]*. Івано-Франківськ: Лілея НВ, 2014.

Weisz, Boglárka and Attila Zsoldos. "A báni joghatóság Szlavóniában és a Dráván túl [The Ban's Jurusidiction in Slavonia and Beyond the River Drava]." In *Fons, skepsis, lex. Ünnepi tanulmányok a 70 esztendős Makk Ferenc tiszteletére*. Edited by Tibor Almási et al., 469–82. Szeged: SZTE Történeti Segédtudományok Tanszék–Szegedi Középkorász Műhely, 2010.

Wertner, Mór. *Az Árpádok családi története [The Family History of the Árpáds]*. Történeti- nép- és földrajzi Tár LI. Nagy-Becskerek: Pleitz, 1892.

Włodarski, Bronisław, *Polska i Rus 1194–1340 [Poland and the Rus', 1194–1340]* (Warszawa: Wydawnictwo Naukowe PWN, 1966).

——. "Salomea królowa Halicka [Queen Salomea of Galicia]." *Nasza przeszłość* 17 (1957): 61–81.

Zientara, Benedykt. *Heinrich der Bärtige und seine Zeit: Politik und Gesellschaft im mittelalterlichen Schlesien*. München: Oldenbourg, 2002.

Zsoldos, Attila. "II. András Aranybullája [The Golden Bull of Andrew II]." *Történelmi Szemle* 53 (2011): 1–38.

——. "Az ifjabb király országa [The Land of the Younger King]." *Századok* 139 (2005): 231–60.

——. *Családi ügy. IV. Béla és István ifjabb király viszálya az 1260-as években [Family Affair. The Conflict of Béla IV and Stephen, the Younger King, in the 1260s]*. Budapest: MTA TTI, 2007.

——. "Hercegek és hercegnők az Árpád-kori Magyarországon [Princes and Princesses in Árpádian Hungary]." In *Hercegek és hercegségek a középkori Magyarországon*. Edited by Attila Zsoldos, 9–24. Székesfehérvár: Városi Levéltár és Kutatóintézet, 2016.

——. *Magyarország világi archontológiája. 1000–1301 [Secular Office-Holders (Archonotology) of Hungary. 1000–1301]*. Budapest: MTA TTI, 2011.

——. "Szepes megye kialakulása [The Formation of Spiš (Szepes) County]." *Történelmi szemle* 43 (2001): 19–31.

INDEX

Place Names

Belz: 15–16, 19, 36
Berestie: 15–16
Bosnia: 57, 61, 77, 81, 84–85, 97, 102–3, 109, 115–20
Bug, river: 19, 21, 36, 58
Čazma: 6, 19, 70, 93, 95, 96, 98, 102, 124
Chernigov: 12, 13, 16, 28, 48, 59
Cherven': 15
Đakovo: 102, 119
Dalmatia: 61, 64, 69–72, 75–76, 78–81, 86–87, 89, 91, 96–99, 112, 115–16, 118, 123–24
Dniester: 12, 21, 36, 59
Drava, river: 76–77, 81
Dubica, county: 100, 103, 131
Esztergom: 23, 31, 32, 33, 38, 50, 93, 94, 95, 106, 118, 123
Galicia, principality: 1, 3, 4, 6, 9, 11–19, 21–23, 26–29, 31–41, 43–59, 61, 63, 64, 70, 72, 73, 78, 80–82, 88, 97, 105, 107, 108, 109, 115, 123, 127–31
Gorodok: 53
Gömör, county: 23, 25–26, 64
Halych city: 1, 11–12, 15, 17, 31, 33, 36–39, 43–44, 51–55, 57–58, 61, 63, 79, 94, 127
Holm: 13, 15
Iaroslavl: 15, 36, 44
Jasov: 67, 102
Kalocsa: 31, 91, 96–97, 103, 106, 116, 123
Kecerlipóc: 69
Kraków: 1, 4–6, 11, 12, 15, 16, 18, 19, 21, 33–35, 39, 51, 58, 68, 111, 112, 113, 126, 130
Limnica: 36, 38
Liubachev: 21, 36, 51
Liubech: 28
Lutsk: 15, 16, 19.
Lukva: 36–38
Lvov: 15
Macsó: 57
Mazovia: 12, 15, 18–19, 111
Našice: 92, 101

Novgorod: 3, 12, 18, 28, 33, 51–52, 107
Novgorod Severskii: 19, 28
Nyitra: 23, 45, 75, 123
Opole: 109, 111–12
Pest: 122, 124
Pécs: 38, 76, 82, 87, 91–92, 101–2, 118–19
Pécsvárad: 91
Pereiaslavl, 47
Petrinja: 100
Ponizhie: 59
Poprád: 27
Peremyshl: 32, 33, 36, 50, 51, 53, 57–58, 107
Požega: 77–78, 102
Rogozhino: 53
Rovišće: 100–101, 108
Samobor: 131–32
San, river: 21, 36
Sandomierz: 34, 36, 49, 51, 98, 105, 109, 111
Sanok: 36
Sáros, county: 23, 64
Scepus, district: 1, 6, 19, 21–27, 31–36, 47, 51, 57, 61, 63–67, 69–70, 72, 80–82, 85, 88–89, 96, 102, 107–9, 129–31
Segesd: 87, 102, 124
Senj: 72
Skała: 34, 124
Slavonia: 1, 5, 6, 43, 57, 63–65, 67, 69–70, 72–78, 79–90, 91–97, 99–100, 102–3, 105–11, 129–23
Spiš castle: 64–65, 69, 94
Split: 70–73, 80–81, 84–85, 87, 91, 93, 96–99, 116, 130, 132
Székesfehérvár: 32, 103
Trepol': 51
Topusko: 94, 99
Torchesk: 51, 58–59
Trogir: 102, 124
Terebovl': 15
Transylvania: 23, 46, 57, 69, 73–75, 81, 94, 116, 123
Várad: 2, 121
Varaždin: 100, 132

Virovitica: 78, 99, 102
Vistula, river: 21, 36
Vladimir-Suzdal', principality: 11, 28, 47
Vladimir Volynsky: 12, 15-16, 19, 33, 51
Volhynia: 3, 11-19, 22, 28, 33-34, 36-37, 43-44, 50-55, 128
Vukovar: 99
Wieprz: 19, 58

Wrocław: 111
Zadar: 72, 100, 116
Zagreb: 1, 61, 65-66, 70, 80-87, 91-94, 96-97, 103, 118, 130, 132
Zawichost: 12, 124

Personal Names

Adolf, provost of Scepus: 27, 88
Andrew II, king of Hungary: 1-2, 6, 9, 11-12, 15-19, 21-23, 29, 31-34, 43-44, 47-48, 51, 53, 55-56, 57-58, 61, 63-64, 69, 71-74, 78, 79-81, 84-86, 92-95, 101-2, 105-9, 116, 118-20, 127, 129-32
Andrew, Hungarian prince: 36, 44, 48, 56-59, 63, 74, 76, 88, 100, 105, 107, 109, 131
Anna (?), widow of Roman Mstislavich: 12-13
Anna Châtillon, Queen of Hungary: 13
Bartholomew, bishop of Pécs: 82, 92
Béla III, King of Hungary: 11, 23, 26, 75, 76, 94-95
Béla IV, King of Hungary: 1, 6, 26, 34, 36, 43, 57, 61, 63-67, 69, 71-76, 78-81, 83-90, 94-95, 99-103, 105-9, 113, 115-16, 118-25, 127, 131-32
Benedict, son of Korlat: 45-47
Benedict, the „Antichrist": 45-47, 52
Benedict, the Bald: 45-47
Benedict, voivode of Transsylvania: 45-47
Berthold, archbishop of Kalocsa, patriarch of Aquileia: 63, 102, 106-7
Boguchwał, chronicler: 4
Bolesław III, prince of Poland: 4, 18
Bolesław IV, prince of Poland: 18
Bolesław V, prince of Sandomierz and Kraków: 34, 36, 88, 113
Boris, prince, son of Coloman the Learned: 2, 4
Calan, bishop of Pécs: 76, 84, 102
Casimir II the Just, prince of Kraków: 11, 15, 18
Casimir, prince of Opole: 55, 111-12
Coloman the Learned, king of Hungary: 1-2, 4, 89
Conrad II, prince of Znojmo: 18
Conrad, prince of Mazovia: 12, 15-16, 18-19, 52, 58, 111

Constance of Antiochia: 13
Daniil Romanovich: 4, 12-19, 21-22, 27, 33, 48, 51-54, 56-59, 105, 108, 113, 129-31
Demeter, of the Aba kindred: 31-32, 43, 47, 101
Denis, of the Türje kindred: 86, 125
Denis, son of Ampud: 23, 25, 26, 64, 66
Długosz, Jan, chronicler: 4-5, 19, 33, 35, 38, 44, 47, 52, 55, 112
Dmitr: 43, 53
Domald, former count of Split: 72, 116
Elizabeth, queen of Hungary: 63, 65
Euphrosyne Mstislavna, queen of Hungary: 11
File provost of Zagreb, ducal chancellor: 70, 87, 96, 101
File, Hungarian leader in Galicia: 23, 43-44, 49, 53-54
Friedrich II, duke of Austria: 109, 124
Friedrich II, emperor, 98: 106-7
Gertude, queen of Hungary, mother of Coloman: 2, 12, 31, 45, 63, 65, 71,
Géza II, king of Hungary: 11
Godysław Pasko/Baszko, chronicler: 4, 84, 121
Gregory IX, pope: 35, 82, 84, 91-93, 97-98, 103, 106-7, 109, 112, 117-21, 132, 136
Grzymisława of Sandomierz, mother of Queen Salomea: 19, 34-35, 82, 105, 109, 111-13
Hartvik, Hungarian bishop: 5
Henry II the Pious, duke of Silesia: 55, 113
Henry the Bearded, duke of Silesia: 111-12
Honorius III, pope: 31, 56, 63, 71, 74, 92, 116, 120
Iaropolk Kormilichich: 48
Iarosh: 55
Iaroslav (Osmomysl), prince of Galicia: 28, 37
Iaroslav Vsevolodich: 47
Iavolod Kormilichich: 48

Igorevichs (Roman, Rostislav, Sviatoslav, Vladimir): 16, 19, 21, 28, 48, 130
Ingvar, prince of Lutsk: 16, 19
Innocent III, pope: 1, 31–32, 51, 79, 115–16
Iury Dolgoruky: 18, 28
Iwan, Odrowąż, bishop of Kraków: 18, 51
Jacob Pecorari, cardinal-legate: 85, 103, 117, 121
John, archbishop of Esztergom: 23, 31–33, 50
Kinga (Kunigunda), daughter of Béla IV, wife of Bolesław V: 34–36, 88–89, 113
Kormilichich: 16, 48–50
Kötöny (Kotian), leader of the Cumans: 59
Lazar Domazhirec: 48
Leszek the White, prince of Kraków: 1, 4, 12, 15–19, 21–22, 31–36, 44, 49, 51–54, 56, 58, 105, 111, 128, 130.
Mieszko II, prince of Opole: 111
Mieszko III (Stary): 18
Mikhail Vsevolodich, prince of Chernigov: 12, 13, 58
Mstislav "the Mute": 16–17
Mstislav Iziaslavich: 18
Mstislav Mstislavich (Udaloy, Udatny), prince of Novgorod and Galicia: 3, 44, 48–49, 51–56, 57–59, 63, 107–8
Mstislav Romanovich: 3
Niketas Choniates, chronicler: 13
Odrowąż, kindred: 51
Oleg Sviatoslavich: 28
Pakosław Awdaniec: 18, 21, 23, 51
Peter, son of Töre: 45
Poth (Pot), Hungarian palatine: 45–46
Rambald de Carumb: 90, 92, 123
Roger of Apulia alias Rogerius: 2, 121–24
Roman Mstislavich: 11–14, 18, 22, 27–28, 33, 37, 48, 51, 58
Rostislav Mstislavich, grand prince of Kiev: 18
Rostislav Mikhailovich 12
Rurik Rostislavich: 12
Salomea, wife of Coloman: 1, 4–6, 21–22, 27, 33–35, 44, 51, 63–64, 67, 87–89, 103, 105, 107, 111, 113, 124, 127–28, 130–31
Solomon, of the Atyusz kindred: 23
Stephen I, king of Hungary: 5, 61, 76, 88
Stephen V, king of Hungary: 6, 65, 73–74, 99–100, 125
Stephen, bishop of Zagreb: 61, 70, 83, 87, 91–98, 103, 132
Sudislav, boyar: 36, 48–50, 58–59
Sudisław, castellanus: 16
Sviatopolk, grand prince of Kiev: 18
Thomas of Split, chronicler: 70, 84, 93, 97–98, 122–24
Ugrin, archbishop of Kalocsa: 91, 98, 103, 116–17, 122–23
Vasilko Romanovich: 12, 14, 16–17, 19, 21–22, 33, 48
Verhuslava, daughter of Vsevolod Mstislavich: 18
Viacheslav Tolstoy: 48
Viola, princess of Opole: 82, 109, 111–13
Vladimir Iaroslavich: 11, 15, 26, 28
Vladimir Monomakh: 28
Vladimirko Volodarevich: 28, 37
Vladislav Vitovich: 48
Volodislav Kormilichich: 16–17, 23, 48–50
Vsevolod Mstislavich, prince of Novgorod: 18
Vsevolod Iurievich, prince of Vladimir-Szuzda:l 47
Wincenty Kadłubek: 4, 33
Władysław Laskonogi: 51–52, 111
Władysław Odonic: 51–52, 55